BY THE GHOST LIGHT

ALSO BY R. H. THOMSON

The Lost Boys: Letters from the Sons in Two Acts, 1914–1923

BY THE GHOST LIGHT

WARS, MEMORY, AND FAMILIES

R. H. THOMSON

ALFRED A. KNOPF CANADA

PUBLISHED BY ALFRED A. KNOPF CANADA

Copyright © 2023 R. H. Thomson

www.penguinrandomhouse.ca

Knopf Canada and colophon are registered trademarks.

Library and Archives Canada Cataloguing in Publication

Title: By the ghost light : wars, memory, and families / R. H. Thomson.
Names: Thomson, R. H., author.
Identifiers: Canadiana (print) 20230162126 | Canadiana (ebook) 20230184340 | ISBN 9781039008380 (hardcover) | ISBN 9781039008397 (EPUB)
Subjects: LCSH: World War, 1914–1918—Personal narratives, Canadian. | LCSH: Thomson, R. H.—Family. | LCSH: Thomson family—Correspondence.
Classification: LCC D640.A2 T46 2023 | DDC 940.4/8171—dc23

Book design: Kelly Hill
Image credits: Destroyed German transport towards Serre, World War I. Royal New Zealand Returned and Services' Association; New Zealand official negatives, World War 1914–1918. Ref: 1/2-013487-G. Alexander Turnbull Library, Wellington, New Zealand. /records/23209973. This image has been cropped and colourized; (texture) dmitrıch / Adobe Stock; (clouds) eshma / Adobe Stock; Comedy and tragedy masks: Scott Freiheit – creator of *An Undiscovered Musicals* website / Wikimedia Commons

Printed in Canada

10 9 8 7 6 5 4 3 2 1

To all those who our wars lost, and then forgot.

"There were a great number of young men who had never been in a war and were consequently far from unwilling to join this one."

Thucydides, 5th century BCE

CONTENTS

A CHILDHOOD SUITCASE OF WARRIORS, VICTORIES AND HEROES

You who are reading this should know that *your* family stories are probably more interesting than the ones I will tell here. Mine have been rolling through my family for over a century. They are not of the . . . *do you remember the time that Great-Uncle Art* . . . variety; rather, they are stories that disturb me when I burrow down into the world in which they occurred. Many of yours are most likely amazing. Perhaps you think that your family doesn't have great stories? But whether you have lived in Canada for two or twenty-two thousand years, you have only to dig into the memories of your family or yourself to find them. A family's strength—and occasionally its curse—is the stories it remembers, stories that create a map by which to navigate the years ahead. They provide an architecture of purpose and meaning. The writer Thomas King went further by suggesting, "the truth about stories, is that that's all we are."

My childhood in a 1950s Ontario town was filled with tales about two global conflicts—the First and Second World Wars. We won both of them, or, more accurately, Canada had been on the winning side. My father fought in World War II and returned home. His five uncles fought in World War I; two of them *didn't* return home and two died afterwards from lung problems brought on by the war.

On my mother's side of the family, three great-uncles had lost their lives. Of the five on my father's side, only one grew old, and I have fond memories of him. Great-Uncle Art's dentures clicked when he spoke, and it was said that he kept a palm-sized piece of sourdough starter in a pouch beneath his shirt, a habit from his postwar years of prospecting in northern Ontario. And when Art came south to visit at Christmas, he'd teach us about snake eyes and boxcars as we rolled the dice for the horse-racing board game we played in our basement. My family's many warriors were all casualties of Canada's fight for democracy and freedom—and I've come to see the rhetoric rather than the reality in that statement.

Memory owns no real estate, yet it holds a powerful place in our lives. It is like an empty theatre that comes to life only when someone walks onstage and begins to speak. Entering your memories, fragile as they may be at times, animates the past. In the chapters that follow, my relatives enter and exit as if characters from a play who have been waiting their turn in the shadows of the theatre's wings.

There seems to be no limit as to how old "theatres" can be in which the past waits to be called. The Chauvet Cave in France, discovered in the 1990s, has wall paintings of animals that came to life when the first visitors brought burning torches into the cavern thirty thousand years ago, and more recently when explorers first crawled in with their flashlights. Released from the still darkness by the light passing over them, the horses and bears appear to move. On the departure of both visitors and lamps, the darkness and stillness return, and once again time disappears. Without motion there is no time and that is just a fact.

The theatres I've worked in banish complete darkness primarily for reasons of safety, but also from superstition. After each performance, before the cast and crew depart, a single lamp, called the ghost light, is placed onstage and left to burn all night. On my way home after a show, I've often lingered by the ghost light, the theatre now a dim cavern that an hour before was filled with life. I try to hear the echoes of the character's lives that were played out that evening.

My memories are such a light by which I look at my family's First World War history. As a teenager I read a few of the hundreds of great-uncles' and distant cousins' letters that had been sent back from the fighting in Europe—before setting them aside, since I didn't appreciate the world in which they were written. Now that I am older, great-uncles and grandmothers stand ready along the backstage walls, letters in hand. Cluttered about them like props for a play are swords, German army belt buckles, photo albums, war medals, a Steyr 1916 revolver and other family memorabilia. I want to bring my great-grandmother Mary Elizabeth and her sons into the light to hear how they navigated a war that brought needless destruction to millions.

Among war's casualties are the civilizations that fight them—unless you can convince yourself that there is a civilized way to kill fellow humans. The wounding of civilization is why, in a war's aftermath, countries begin the process of cleaning up. The postwar construction of monuments, remembrance rituals and rhetoric is an opportunity for nations to present an acceptable accounting for the death and devastation that has just taken place. Presumably that was the reason a German First World War trench mortar was installed at the cenotaph in front of my grade school in Richmond Hill, in whose classrooms I presumably learned everything I needed to know before becoming a teenager and moving on to high school.

Because the Second World War, in which my father served, had a clearer moral purpose than the *Great* War (as the First World War was called), it has been easier to clean up after. The task of justifying World War II's forty-five million deaths and massive public expenditures was more straightforward, since in 1939 Nazi Germany was obviously toxic and *had* to be defeated. But my great-uncles' war of 1914–1918, which killed an estimated nine and a half million soldiers, as well as the West's recent adventures fighting in Vietnam, Iraq and Afghanistan, didn't, for a lot of people, have much moral justification. That has meant that tidying up to successfully pack away their moral mess has been more difficult.

One aspect of the cleaning-up process is to forget the nightmarish realities of the conflict. Sadly, many of our remembrance rituals at city halls and cenotaphs, however honourably conducted in the *name* of remembering, have instead contributed to the forgetting. They ritualize memories of the wars in order to contain what is, in essence, *un*containable—namely, incredible pain and unimaginable loss. But we have now entered the disputed territory called the "politics of remembrance," and there will be more of that in this book.

I've been encouraged by what historian Jonathan F. Vance said to me when I asked his assistance in building an alternative form of war commemoration called *The World Remembers*:

> "We must never lose sight of the fact that history is not the history of nations or ideologies but of people."

I propose that it's the people who fought the wars, and it is those individuals whom we primarily forget, partly because *millions* died, and also because remembering so many unsettles us. Yes, collectives such as armies, nations and battalions also "fought" the wars, but really they were only people. That is why I began taking time off from my acting career to create *The World Remembers*, which would attempt to name *every* soldier who lost their life in the Great War— and I mean every Canadian, every Frenchman, every German, every Britisher, every Italian, every Austrian, every Russian and so on— from the more than thirty nations involved in the war. My proposal was completely crazed, since there was little possibility that I could ever find all their names. Not only would I have to navigate politicized histories as I appealed to nations about joining the project, but the accessibility and intactness of a previous century's war records, many from collapsed empires, were seriously in question. And, most importantly, I proposed that since *each* of those nine and a half million dead had had a mother who had wept, the names of both victors and vanquished would appear *together*. Even though my great-grandmother Mary Elizabeth was only one of millions of women who lost children, I knew of no war memorials that depicted mothers holding dead sons. In whatever form *The World Remembers* was going to create for the names to appear, we would make no distinctions based on rank, race, religion, gender or the army in which they had fought. Was it appropriate to include former enemies? I may have to call some of my great-uncles onstage and ask them.

I wanted a remembrance that included every nation because I know that *your* family stories are compelling since, in a manner of speaking, I heard them told night after night by visitors to my dressing room. I had written a play called *The Lost Boys*, based on the seven hundred letters that my great-uncles had sent home from the First World War battlefields. Since theatres rarely have much money, I wrote the script as a one-man show that I could perform. What sticks in my memory isn't what happened onstage; rather, it is what I heard in my dressing room afterwards.

For more than a hundred performances of *The Lost Boys* in Ottawa, Winnipeg and Toronto, I leapt about, acted up a storm, mused about the history revealed through the letters, mused further about the German revolvers and other macabre battle souvenirs that Great-Uncle Jack had sent home, and then lamented the lives that were lost. The show ran more than two hours, and after my bows, I sank down in my dressing-room chair to recover.

Almost always there would come a knock on the door and someone looking in to say "good show" or "interesting show"—which is code for *I didn't really care for it but I thought I'd say hello anyway.* Yet, regardless of what they'd felt about the piece, as I removed my makeup the visitors would begin telling me their family's war stories. Never once did I have to ask. What was being said was undeniably important to them. Their stories were always engaging and sometimes stunned me with their significance—both for the teller and for me, the listener, since many of them are still lodged in my memory.

Why had those stories tumbled out? Because people want to be heard. Because generations afterwards, their families still carried the after-shocks from past wars. Each tale revealed something about the teller, seeming somehow part of their identity. If this book were longer I would include a few of them. In a way, war had catastrophized their families, and perhaps *The Lost Boys* had reopened the door to those memories.

So, as a visitor to *your* dressing room, I will tell you stories about my family. It is pointless for me to try to convey the catastrophe of the Great War, first because I wasn't there and, second, because many of those who were have already done so. But I can tell you that in its constellation of horrors the number of dead from the French army who were unidentifiable, is a fearsome star. The historian Jay Winter expressed it this way:

> "For fully half the men who were killed in the war, nothing was left but their names."

After a war, along with the bodies and bits of bodies, most everything else *also* gets buried. It appears that nations normally prefer only items such as cenotaphs, memorials and cemetery head-stones to be left above ground. These are the tidied-up bits, the pieces of our nation's war stories that we are *encouraged* to know, usually involving heroes, sacrifices and victories. Then there are the parts preferably kept out of view. Most of war's "difficult" data gets buried; for example, never ask how many German prisoners were murdered by Canadian soldiers. Tragically, the mental wreckage of the combatants themselves also gets "disappeared" along with war's other detritus.[1]

There are records of what bomb damage inflicted on cities but there are no records of what was inflicted on the minds of citizens who lived in them. There are iconic photos of the 1943 firebomb-ing of Hamburg, the 2016 devastation of Aleppo, the destruction

---

1   An exception is the new Cathedral of the Russian Armed Forces, built outside Moscow in 2020. The lavish building's metal floor was constructed from the melted steel of captured German tanks.

of Mariupol in 2022 and the August 1945 nuclear decimation of Hiroshima, but there are no photos of the shredded mental states of the survivors. No one knows how many First World War veterans committed suicide in the decades after the fighting. But they did. If the suicide rate of Canadian soldiers returning from Afghanistan in the early 2000s or the British who fought the Argentinians in the 1982 Falklands War is any guide, it was in the thousands. After Afghanistan, we found out about troops who took their own lives because the media—not Veterans Affairs—decided to publish their names. But no one knows the names of the thousands of Canadian suicides from the First World War. They have not been included on any roll of honour or chiselled into a memorial stone. Governments ask soldiers to serve yet are inconvenienced when they return with mental wounds. Thankfully, in contrast with the treatment of veterans after the 1914–1918 and 1939–1945 wars, Canada has made progress in recognizing and assisting those with PTSD. Yet even today some former warriors sleep on cardboard along with the thousands of other homeless on our streets.

But what gets buried deepest, and for good reason, is the reality of the fighting. Since war *is* fighting, what gets buried is the reality of war. It has been said that the experience of combat cannot be conveyed to civilians. It is also something that many veterans will not speak of. And why would they? Why summon the shock and trauma in which we asked them to engage? But by burying the reality—or worse, by going further and spinning (or lying about) it—do we not help create the conditions that can lead to more wars?

In my childhood, stories about the wars were pervasive. My awkward teenage years in the 1960s were spent meticulously painting models of fighter aircraft from the Battle of Britain and re-enacting aerial dogfights in my bedroom. The fact that Canada's wars (or at least the sort that we chose to recognize as "wars") had been truly epic affairs from which we emerged victorious was woven into our culture. After Germany and Japan were defeated in 1945, our stories became filled with grit, glory, heroes and sacrifice, even though our side had detonated the world's first atomic bombs over Japan, and the possibility loomed that the next war would be nuclear and would be with Russia.

Stories become part of our mind's architecture, and none more so than those about war. Stories told *after* a war are part of the cleaning-up process. Those told *before* a war prime us for the fight—which is when the warmongers get busy with their tales. But in the cycling of "before-and-after" war stories, those that come *afterwards* are the most important. How and why they are told can indicate whether we learned anything from what we have just experienced, and if we will play the instrument of war again. The cycling of war stories will probably cease after a nuclear confrontation, since there will likely be no storytellers left to tell them.

As an actor in the narrative arts, I think the film and television industry shoulders some responsibility. I went to war movies when I was young because my father had fought in the navy. The films, made mostly in the 1950s (*Reach for the Sky* being my favourite, since it told the story of a British Spitfire pilot who, despite having artificial legs, continued to fly missions against the Germans), were usually self-congratulatory tales of battles that we had won. And why wouldn't they be? The Second World War had been a deadly struggle and victory had never seemed certain. Movies such as *The Battle of the River Plate*—which fired my imagination because of my dad's time at sea—were filmed using some of the same warships, men and aircraft that had actually *been* in the war, and therefore had some actual relationship to the violence that was depicted. Computer-generated imagery (CGI) had not yet been invented, so the onscreen violence had to come from actual explosives and not from a film company's explosion-filled digital fantasies.

My art, or more precisely my industry, now produces stories about conflict that assume little responsibility for the telling. And, let's be honest, the corporations make them to banquet on the profits. The entertainment violence of action movies has abandoned any relationship to real violence. Call it what you will—war-porn or action-candy—the creators are in the business of audience gathering. Yes, there have been some exceptional films that, with eyes wide open, have explored the murky morality of telling stories about war, but many producers have purchased their yachts by spinning fantasy-lies about violence. I don't begrudge them their yachts, but I do begrudge them for profiting from messaging that says violence is the best option for achieving justice, security and peace. They are warmongers by proxy.

Wars run on the violent deaths of our fellow beings. Yet seldom, if ever, do we tell the complete story of their deaths. Have you ever sat through a movie that spent hours showing the agony of a soldier burned over almost their entire body? No, you haven't. The young man who comes to mind was a World War I flyer who in 1916 took almost an entire anguished day to die. That is one of my family's stories. War stories will speak of the circumstances of a death but never the complete experience of dying. They give us the reasons, but not the dying. They provide the adverbs—bravely, painfully, violently, willingly, instantly, peacefully—but never the actual journey of the death. Only if the movie or book witnessed the minutes, hours or days that it took *each* soldier to die, only *then* would we be truly telling of their deaths. If the camera never strayed from the young pilot's face, *then* we would have told of my great-uncle Warren Pemberton's dying. Only if we never turned away would we have witnessed the deaths.

But we do turn away. We render the death of soldiers into the service of patriotism, politics or the profits that the action movie will make to buy a berth in the Bahamas for the producer's yacht. We have never been witnesses to the end, and I challenge you to name a movie or a history that ever has.

As much as I question wars and how we often dispose of their reality afterwards through the narratives within which we encase them, my respect for those who do the fighting remains. Our warriors do *our* bidding and assume risks that few of us would take.

Throughout history, the record of respect for those who have fought has fallen short. I am not referring to the heroes and generals who have been celebrated with statues, songs, stained glass, stone columns, paintings and books, but I am talking about ordinary soldiers—the young Scottish man in the British Army who in 1759 climbed a fifty-metre cliff to fight on the Plains of Abraham the next morning, or the Punjabi man who in 1916 climbed aboard a troopship to sail to Europe to fight for the British in France. Traditionally, the foot soldier was the property of the king—or whoever was in power—and, as property, when they no longer served a purpose, they were discharged and discarded. A few of our feudal attitudes have yet to vanish completely, and the idea of soldiers' lives being at the discretion of the king or the country is one of them. Soldiers have been buried nameless and anonymous. Their bones have been collected from former battlefields, ground up and sold for fertilizer. Their bodies have been forgotten, lost or, in the case of the Plains of Abraham, the location of their burial found only when watermain work was done 250 years later. We have made some progress in respecting the rank and file of our former fighters, but not nearly enough.

As I've said, many men from my childhood were warriors. My father and three uncles had been in the Second World War, and my grandfather and a legion of great-uncles from both sides of my family had fought in the First World War. My dad told of storms at sea, U-boat attacks and standing watch on his corvette's bridge as it crossed and recrossed the North Atlantic, escorting freighters with food and war materials for Britain. His stories ended well, since we won, he survived, my parents had me, and I loved my father, who made snow sculptures of bears on our lawn. When I was a child, stories with happy endings were *what* stories *were*. Some tales were frightening, but Hansel and Gretel survived the witch who had wanted to cook and eat them, and they lived happily ever after.

I ask your indulgence as I sort through the stories, since it has been a challenge to try to empty my memory suitcase of childhood assumptions. Do we ever truly *un*learn what was set down in our past?

I have been guided by what I read in a display at the Bundeswehr Museum of Military History in Dresden, Germany:

> "What people remember, and how, changes with time. Like in a huge archive, memories are stored, retrieved, embellished and even deleted in the collective and individual memories. For a long time war myths were used to justify claims to privileges and property as well as new wars. These myths fueled prejudices, hatred, and the desire for revenge."

Because my perspectives on soldiering, victory and defeat were a function of my growing up in a country that had always been on the winning side, before approaching nations about participating in *The World Remembers*, I had to appreciate the First World War through their eyes. To have credibility with German Foreign Affairs in Berlin or the Serb Ministry of Defence in Belgrade, I had to be aware of what informed the views that emerged from my mouth, as well as from theirs. There were men in my family who might have fought the grandfathers or great-grandfathers of those with whom I was meeting. In contrast with Canada's (seemingly) straightforward past, I began to appreciate the convolutions of the history of most First World War nations. And how, afterwards, people from Europe's three collapsing empires struggled to establish their own nations, and how Russia's brutal revolution and the Bolsheviks' communist ideals set out to disrupt governments around the world, how tyrannies arose in Germany and Italy in the 1930s, and then how the Cold War started after 1945. This history is a landscape you could get lost in.

In my memory suitcase, I have *a lot* of family, so at times the stage may get crowded. A few photos will appear as theatrical tableaux. But as with any performance, as the chapters roll by should you need reminding of *which* great-uncle was *whose* brother, a Dramatis Personae has been included at the end of this book. Parents and grandparents, uncles and aunts, great-uncles and great-aunts and cousins of all kinds will come and go. Some may seem shy, some may be loud, most will be heard through their letters but several will speak from dialogue imagined from my memories of them. And some will remain silent.

CHAPTER 1

WARRIORS WHEN I WAS YOUNG

my father

T he foundations of our imaginations are set in place when we are young, or so it was with me. We age, rebuild, expand and repaint, yet that first structure remains beneath our feet. The question is, are we bound by the stories that originally built our imaginative universe?

My father's navy jacket

My father's accounts of the Battle of the North Atlantic in World War II were part of my growing up. A photo of his ship, HMCS *Lunenburg*, hung in his study beside the ceremonial key to the town in Nova Scotia after which it was named. The solid brass

twenty-five-centimetre-long key had been presented to him by
Lunenburg's mayor when, after the war, the corvette was decommis-
sioned to be sold off for scrap. He had served as its commanding officer, and a small brass plaque from HMCS *Lunenburg* saying "C.O.'s
Cabin" was tacked to his study door. I would sit with him there, my
short legs dangling over the edge of a chair, amidst the smell of the
sweet tobacco that he packed into his pipe.

My father's stories embedded themselves in me. His time at sea
was adventure and parental heroism. I would not experience the
darker side of his war, but my brother, who was older by six years, had
felt its force when he was growing up—but that is my brother's tale to
tell. I would wear my dad's navy jacket as I piloted my orange-crate
Spitfire off the lawn and into the skies to fight the German Luftwaffe.
To me, wars were adventures with happy endings; I was certain that
the Third World War would come and I would be flying fighters.
At grade school, when our town's air-raid siren was tested, I thought
of the war movies I'd seen and wondered about Russian bombers and
if my mum had made jam sandwiches for lunch.

When Lief Larsen, known simply as "the Chief," having been
Lunenburg's chief engineer officer, visited, we would hear how he
had rolled up his sleeve and, reaching down into a steel drum of
bunker oil meant for the corvette's engines, discovered iron filings at
the bottom. *Lunenburg* had been refuelling in the Azores and the oil
had been stored on the jetty. They'd *suspected* sabotage, and the small
shreds of metal in the Chief's oily hand had proved it. Then my father
and Lief would nap after lunch. The rule for stories was, whatever
the danger, they always ended well.

When my great-uncle Art visited, the pipe smoke grew thick as
he and my father puffed and sucked while lighting up. Art was one of
my father's five uncles who had written letters home from the fighting
in Belgium, Egypt, Portuguese East Africa and France. I heard about
Art's brothers Jack and Harold and how the war had damaged their
lungs, so that in the 1920s they were often patients in a sanatorium.
Their stories had turned out well, even though, having survived the war,

they didn't live long enough to become old men. Art's other brothers, George and Joe, had been killed in 1917 and 1918, but to my young mind that was so deep in the past that their deaths held little meaning. Yet, as I got older and the past became more present, I began to see similarities between me and George. Looking at his photos now, I wonder if something of myself isn't gazing back. We were both tall, we studied the same subjects in high school (apart from the Greek that only George took) and we both earned a science degree at the University of Toronto—although with fifty years between us.

In my child's mind, the First World War was a musty place compared to my father's sea battles on the Atlantic. His officer's hat had his smell and even a stain of salt spray from his ship's corkscrewing through the winter storms. My six-year-old self wondered about the Great War veterans I saw sitting on park benches, who paraded to the cenotaph once a year or sat too still in nursing homes and smelt of body fluids and floor wax. My grade school principal had been a World War I army mule driver, but he wasn't musty. Mr. Scott punished students with a strap he kept up the sleeve of his jacket. I lived in fear of the strap, though I never received its fury. Except for Art, most veterans of the First World War were like the trench mortar at the war memorial in front of our school: the moving parts of our enemy's former instrument of death had long been frozen by layers of grey paint. That squat piece of German steel testified to our victory and after class I often climbed on it, waiting for a teacher's shout to GET DOWN. The barrel of our town's Great War trophy was full of candy wrappers and other midnight leftovers that I was still too young to recognize.

What passing bells for those who die as cattle?
Only the monstrous anger of the guns.

Wilfred Owen, the British soldier-poet, had been killed near the end of the war that also killed Joe, George, Warren and my other great-uncles. I didn't read Owen's poem "Anthem for Doomed Youth" until my twenties, and when I did, I began to think about what lay beneath the war stories of my childhood. In the candy house in the forest, the witch fattens up Hansel for better eating, but his sister Gretel outwits the woman who cannibalizes children, pushes her into an oven and burns her to death so that she and her brother can return home to their father. There are horrors in the German fairy tale "Hansel and Gretel," but its happily-ever-after ending kept them safely behind a closed door. Most likely there were also horrors and even "monstrous anger" beneath the stories that my father and Great-Uncle Art told, but they kept that darkness from me. Since our side won wars, stories ended well—except for the unfortunate deaths of our brave soldiers, and particularly the great-uncles that I never knew.

In the reassurance of our victories

In the 1950s Canada where I grew up, I felt secure. We were the big pink country at the top of the world map, a proud member of the British Empire, which then became the British Commonwealth. True, some Canadians weren't enthralled by being embraced by so much Britishness, but usually their skins weren't white, which meant we didn't think too much about them.

Russia was a threat. It was another big country at the top of the map on the classroom wall (as was Greenland, which I noticed wasn't green), but the Russians didn't count because they were communists. Every morning at school, we stood and sang "God Save the Queen" to Her Majesty, whose portrait was on the wall behind the teacher's desk. All was well with the world. My inability to appreciate peril applied as much to the danger of slipping off the barrel of the German trench mortar and smacking my head on the cement as to the possibility of nuclear incineration that our town's siren rehearsed warning us about. I am not sure that I grasped what *real* peril was, but I suspected that children in many other nations did.

It seems that most of us are slow to waken to alarms, be they military, political or the oncoming climate catastrophe. Living within stories of reassuring victories implied that the world was safe, even though all about me were signals to the contrary. In Grade Four, from my desk by the window, I could see Mr. Neal emerge from his car dealership across the road, rush up the front walk, hurry up three flights of stairs to the school roof and ring the bell that was rung *only* when there was a fire in town. Then our class heard him hurry down and cross back over to his automobile showroom to wait for the volunteer firefighters. That was a *real* alarm. For fire drills we also hurried down the stairs, whose wooden steps had been worn into gentle waves by generations of pupils' shoes, and then chattered in the playground, excited that class had been interrupted. We didn't drill for nuclear war.

One morning in Grade Four, Elizabeth Hutchison appeared in tears because she had dreamt that the Russians had invaded. But Elizabeth's fear seemed silly, not because I had a crush on her but because wars were things *we* won. I'd heard about our Cold War with the communists, but I was never sure what *cold* war was. From our house in Richmond Hill we could see Toronto, nineteen kilometres away. My father had built up the ground in front of our basement wall. The earth berm was probably four metres thick and would become the lawn where he carved the snow bears one winter. Only later did I realize that he also intended it to protect the basement from an atomic blast, should the Russians drop a nuclear bomb on Toronto. But neither our fortified basement nor the town's air-raid siren disturbed my peace. All my life I had lived with the assumption, undisturbed at the bottom of my memory suitcase, that history was safe. Well, it isn't.

Soldiering and enemies

The men in my family fought Germans in two wars. Soldiering was in almost every aspect of my growing up: games, stories, movies, toys and even LP records of military pipe bands. The Thomsons had emigrated from Scotland a century before, and one of my father's record albums showed a Scottish bagpiper looking mighty in his kilt and large black hat made from the fur of a bear. In step to the roll and click of the drums, I marched around the house to the tribal music of my ancestors. My dad also had records of the Don Cossack Choir, whose album covers showed the Russian singers wearing small woollen hats and baggy trousers. They sang with deep bass and high tenor voices. The Cossack soldiers had been defeated in Russia's revolution and civil war and had formed their choir while exiled in internment camps. Their voices, soaring in bursts of emotion, seemed to me like cries, and I wondered if it was because, having lost their war and become prisoners, they were *actually* crying. The Cossack music was my first inkling that war might bring pain and sorrow.

The Germans were, of course, *the* enemy, but I was uncertain where Germany was on the map. I'd heard that teenaged boys had been in the Hitler Youth movement and near the end of World War II were made to fight. I looked with disdain at pictures of six-year-old Germans playing at soldiers while wearing uniforms made of cardboard. Yet I saw only adventure in donning my father's navy jacket, shooting down Luftwaffe Messerschmitts with old fireworks that I'd nailed to the wooden wing of my backyard Spitfire, then deftly landing before running out of fuel. Innocence was mine and treachery theirs, because the stories told me so. Decades later, while working on *The World Remembers* in Berlin, the complex winds of history would tear away any remaining naïveté that I had.

My innocence continued on visits to my grandmother's house in Toronto, where, as a six-year-old my favourite game was war—even though my grandmother Helen had lost four brothers because of one. She was Art's oldest sister and often wore white gloves. From the basement, Helen would bring up boxes of toy soldiers that had once been my dad's. Enchanted by the heroics of battle, I freed them from their tissue-paper wrappings and prepared for war on her living room carpet. The lead soldiers had survived many battles, but my grandmother's younger brothers, George, Joe, Jack and Harold, had not. My mother had once said that Helen lived a retiring life because her face had *fallen* and, like a war that could be *cold*, the possibility that a face might fall baffled me.

Fighting my carpet wars, there was no question that Germans were the enemy, but I was unsure about the Indians in the box labelled "Cowboys and Indians." Otherwise, I had Scottish soldiers in kilts and Arab warriors in flowing robes, but the majority were red-coated British Grenadiers. My lead Indians invariably joined the enemy side, since their bare chests and feathered headdresses meant they weren't proper soldiers. Most of the British dragoons had matchsticks for necks, since their heads had broken off while riding their horses in previous battles. The Arabs marched in robes of blue and yellow and the dragoons galloped gallantly despite their goose-like necks since the matches were too long. But the bright red Grenadiers were my *best* soldiers since they were British, and in pictures in magazines I'd seen them guarding the Queen. I knew about soldiering.

War women and wedding dreams

I was in love with my toy army nurses in their long lead dresses who stood calmly beside the Boer War ambulance wagon. They were romantic because in war movies I'd seen nurses kissing soldiers. I was sure that one day *I* would marry an English nurse. It didn't occur to me that films such as *Reach for the Sky* never told of women who were mechanics or pilots. My godmother, Margaret Killmaster, who I sometimes saw at my grandmother's house, was said to have been a First World War operating-room nurse, but she was old, so I never considered that she might once have had romances. Movies didn't portray ladies as soldiers, since fighting wars was man's work.

The wounded lead men lay on their stretchers on the battlefield carpet and did not cry out in pain but were content. The nurses' mouths, a point of red paint, were pretty and I wondered about kissing them, but their mouths were smaller than Elizabeth Hutchison's, and that meant dreaming of smaller kisses. The wounded had bandages with red splashes for blood, but there was no such thing as invisible mental wounds. Having done their bit in the South African War, they were watched over by beautiful nurses. It didn't occur to me that the other old ladies who appeared at my grandmother's Christmas

parties and wore too much face powder had also been caregivers who
had married my great-uncles Jack and Harold when they were in their
dying years at the sanitarium. Again, their sagging dresses and wrin-
kled stockings banished any thought of romance.

The Boer War was another war that Canada helped Britain win.
I wanted to be a soldier loved by beautiful women, as lovely as my
lead nurses and as beautiful as my mother, who had loved my father,
kissed him and married him in his naval uniform, knowing he would
fight at sea and perhaps die.

The darkness in my suitcase of memories

Of course I knew that war *could* bring darkness, and there were
other fears besides the mule-driver's strap. My brother John told
me wolves lived in our basement. The bedroom we shared was at
the top of the cellar stairs, and at night I would shut the door tight
against their emerging from the darkness below. But the possibility that in war families had been murdered and burned in ovens,
just as Gretel had killed and burned the witch, seldom lingered
since, unlike the wolves and Elizabeth Hutchison's Russians, those
possibilities were banished by Canada's victories and by being part
of the bright glory of the British Empire. There *were* deep shadows in my childhood suitcase—including an ancestor's horrific act
of public cruelty that I would discover only years later—but our
stories of victory *inoculated* me against the nightmares that wars
had brought to hundreds of millions of people. Certainly, while
building *The World Remembers* and searching out the names of the
First World War dead, history's bleak corners informed my conversations in European capitals and the shadows of my childhood
became catalysts for learning. My own innocence—or, indeed, any
innocence—was, sadly, primarily an illusion.

Canada's good fortune was that war had never really come
to our country. Battle and bloodshed happened elsewhere in the
world—or at least, that was another hidden suitcase assumption.
Buried deepest perhaps were the aggression and destruction that

had been used against Canada's Indigenous peoples. Wars *had* taken place on our soil, but they had been categorized by colonists' minds as "settlement."

Her Majesty, British heroes and the prototype for a global commemoration

Growing up under the sun of the British Empire, I was unaware that it was setting. My family had always fought to support the motherland. My father's corvette was named His Majesty's Canadian Ship *Lunenburg*. English heroes populated my imagination, none shinier than the pilots who had heroically fought the Battle of Britain—hence my model painting and flying my orange-crate Spitfire. I never had German heroes, because enemies *didn't* have heroes—at least none that the stories mentioned.

Later in life I would have to appeal to our "mother" country to take part in *The World Remembers*, since I needed the British government to provide the British names, contribute some funding and agree to present a public display in London of all nine million names of those killed in the war. My appeal meant multitudes of meetings. But fortunately, five years earlier, in 2008, I had shared a podium with Her Majesty the Queen at the inauguration of a smaller, simpler version of the proposed display in London. The prototype had been created with the assistance of the Canadian High Commission and my lighting-designer friend Martin Conboy. The 68,000 names of *only* the Canadians who were lost in the First World War were projected over seven nights in Trafalgar Square—including George, Joe and, from my mother's side of the family, Warren, Fred and Wildy. Since no German names were included, the authorities had granted permission to stage the commemoration in London's famous square. And there, standing beside me, was the woman to whom I had sung every morning in school. The Queen was eighty-two at the time and had accepted the invitation to inaugurate the event because she believed that the people who fought wars should be remembered.

Having delivered our speeches inside the Canadian High Commission, Her Majesty, Prince Philip, myself, the High Commissioner
and his wife proceeded outdoors at twilight to watch the names
begin to be projected on the east wall of Canada House, facing
Trafalgar Square. Walking respectfully behind the woman who
represented more than a thousand years of British history, I hoped
that my hair was tidy and my tie was straight. The assembled crowd
gathered around her just as, six hundred years before, yeomen might
have gathered around King Henry the Fifth before the Battle of
Agincourt. One of my earliest memories was of cutting photos of her
coronation from magazines and pasting them in my first scrapbook.
Surely the government of her self-centric kingdom would be willing
to support my proposal to name *everyone* lost in the Great War.

It wasn't. Apparently, a remembrance for all nations, both victorious and vanquished, would not be enough about the United
Kingdom to warrant participation. However, as my quest continued
to recruit countries, no matter if a meeting was in Brussels, Moscow
or Berlin, when I produced photos of myself and Her Majesty on the
podium, it usually caught their attention.

The only off-script moment had come when I stepped up onto
the small red-carpeted dais and found myself *alone* with the monarch—definitely not as choreographed by the Palace's event-blocking
chart. Five of us were to be standing in the spotlights at the centre of
the Square: the Canadian High Commissioner Jim Wright, whose
determination had made the Trafalgar Square event actually happen; the Queen; her husband, the aging Prince Philip; Donna, the
High Commissioner's wife; and me. The Prince had muddled our
order by lagging behind on our procession to the podium to chat with
Donna. With an authority that came from decades of marriage and
centuries of her family being monarchs, Her Majesty whispered across
me with a force that she knew her husband would hear, "Philip, you
are supposed to be standing closer to me." History *is* personal, and
here was a private person who had led an endlessly public life in the
name of her tribe.

The stories that had tumbled out from my dressing-room visitors during *The Lost Boys* were what had, in effect, taken me to that famous square. I felt a responsibility that *all* the Canadian families' names must be seen—and hopefully, if all went well in the years ahead, the names from *every* part of the world would be similarly witnessed. An early November wind swept through as the band played "God Save the Queen." The thousand people attending saw the maple-leaf flag on the roof of Canada House flying fiercely. I had ensured that it was brightly lit, since I was determined that Britain would witness the names of the Canadians who had fought for them but never returned. Out of the growing darkness, the projected names began to appear on the stone wall of Canada House, high above us. I knew that my father would have been proud. A silence came over everyone present. In that moment I understood that the act of naming seems to summon the life of the person named.

Major Chris McKenna, one of three Canadian veterans recently returned from Afghanistan who had been invited as guests, spoke with Her Majesty about his great-great-uncle who had been killed in the 1914–1918 war. He said it meant a lot to be there and watch for the appearance of his ancestor, Adrian McKenna.

Other heroes besides British heroes

Wars invariably have many heroes. Comic books and television shows provided my childhood with even more. With plastic pistols or rifles in hand, I could be Roy Rogers or Davy Crockett, even though both were Americans. Crockett was the lesser of the two, since his coonskin cap wasn't a proper helmet and he had fought Mexicans at Fort Alamo; besides being brown, they were neither as mysterious as the Cossacks nor as important as the Germans. The Americans had fought on our side but they weren't *really* important, since they had been late joining both world wars.

Comic book characters with enormous muscles, square jaws and Halloween costumes were no match for the understated bravery of my British heroes and my father. In Grade Four—the year I first learned about refugees, when a Hungarian boy named Tomas joined our class—the teacher had us memorize the poem "High Flight," written by a World War II Spitfire pilot who was later killed.

> *Oh, I have slipped the surly bonds of Earth*
> *And danced the skies on laughter-silvered wings;*
> *Sunward I've climbed, and joined the tumbling mirth*
> *Of sun-split clouds,—and done a hundred things*
> *You have not dreamed of.*

Even in war John Gillespie Magee had been thoughtful, and his poem made him even *more* heroic. Struggling to learn it, I pondered his thoughtfulness, which I also associated with my father as a lieutenant in the navy. My mother had said that in the midst of battles with submarines that might continue for days, when he was not on the corvette's bridge, in order to fall asleep in his cabin my father had read books on philosophy.

Cries from the darkness at the end

My cousin Martin Holmes was the only hero I knew who was close to my age. I can still feel his paddle powering the canoe forward while I sat at its bottom, an exhilarated five-year-old rocked back by each of his strokes. I recall the speed but have no recollection of the lake we were on. Watching the water fly by on the other side of the gunwale, I hadn't known it was possible to go so fast in a canoe. Martin's strength and skill were typical of heroes. A year later, about the time I was pasting pictures in my scrapbook of the Queen's coronation, Martin was sixteen and drowned in an underwater swimming race. The news was kept from the children, but we knew something serious had happened when his father unexpectedly arrived at our cottage, where his young brothers were visiting. I observed Martin's dad slowly walk his next-oldest son up the road and into the woods for a quiet talk. There was a sudden cry from the forest at the breaking of the news, a sound so strange I was unsure if it was human. I had never heard of that kind of cry in any story I'd been told.

The sounds that break from us at moments of hard loss, or in the hours of a mother's labour at a child's birth, linger in memory. I don't know if my mother cried out in the struggle of my birth, but such a sound broke from her years later when I turned from my conversation with the police about my father's car crash to tell her that her husband was dead. That was how my father ended. No story can shield me from the darkness of Martin's drowning or my mother's cry in the instant of our loss.

The silenced stories in my suitcase

Besides fighting Mexicans at the Alamo and Germans in the skies, I also fought Indians in running battles with six-shooters. According to our rules, Indians never had guns, cowboys always won and if you *played* an Indian, you had to be unpredictable and whoop and jump about. I'd heard stories of Indians being cruel to settlers but never of settlers being cruel to Indians. I had been told a family story about long ago in Virginia: Indians had killed a white man and captured his wife and daughters, and a *terrible* fate awaited them. But with the help of a *kind* Indian, the woman, who was my very distant relative, escaped and went on to marry a Mr. Stacey, who was a carpenter in Upper Canada.

But in the wars on my grandmother's carpet, because of the cruelty of the movie-Indians I'd seen, they were the enemy who performed unspeakable acts with their tomahawks. I had yet to consider the "monstrous anger" of *our* guns.

I was confused when I found out that Tecumseh, a Shawnee chief, had fought on *our* side along with Sir Isaac (British) Brock against the Americans in the War of 1812. Yet even Tecumseh's warriors had painted their faces and taken scalps. There were no Indians in my grade school, but I read *Rolf in the Woods*, by Ernest Thompson Seton, and learned about a man named Quonab. Rolf was a white boy like me and the book described Quonab teaching him the ways of the forest. Every dawn the Indian would stand and sing to the rising sun, a ritual that I could not comprehend, even though I sang to the Queen each morning.

In Grade Four a new principal arrived at our school who was kinder than the mule driver and didn't give the strap. He brought a strange boy into our class and asked us to welcome Tomas, whose family had recently escaped from a revolution in Hungary. Russian tanks had invaded Tomas's city and killed people. He was tall, spoke no English, sat two rows over and I didn't know how to reach across to his Hungarian silence. So instead I thought about how he had lost his home because of the Soviet tanks, how he was a stranger in our land and therefore we *had* to be considerate. Indigenous boys my age whose families were the first inhabitants of this land were more distant in my imagination than that boy who had fled Budapest.

Years later, I learned that one of my great-great-great-great-grandmothers was "possibly" a Caughnawaga Mohawk. On the family tree, she is identified as Jane French. In 1779 Jane married my great-great-great-great-grandfather, who was a doctor and a British Indian Department official in Upper Canada. So now I know that while I was learning about wars, heroes and being safe, while I was watching Mr. Neal hurry to ring the fire bell or wondering about the revolution that Tomas had fled, I probably had distant cousins sitting at school desks like mine, whose family stories had *not* kept them safe. Taken from their families, their fears were not only of the strap but of losing who they *were*. In my possible-cousins' residential schools, the principal's job was not to ask students to be considerate of those who had had their home taken from them; it would be to deny my cousins their language, their homes and their culture. I had a little knowledge of where on the map Tomas's Hungarian pain came from, but the pain of my possible Indigenous relatives was more distant to me than the moon.

The suitcase

That, briefly, is my suitcase of first memories, assumptions and toy soldiers. Because my country had always been victorious, I grew up with a particular view of history. Invariably the enemy was from elsewhere. Of course, we all grow beyond our childhood—but then again, perhaps we don't.

I needed to be mindful of my simpler views of history lest they hinder me when proposing *The World Remembers* in Belgrade, Budapest or Bratislava. My advantage was that Canada *is* a land with few big-booted myths, be they founding, imperialist, expansionist, exceptionalist, defeatist or otherwise. Fewer myths—whether toxic or triumphant—therefore cluttered up my suitcase and my conversations. And perhaps possible partners would be more ready to listen because I was unburdened with an agenda other than building a commemoration to recognize *every* man and woman lost in the 1914–1918 war. But then again, having been raised in a nation with what I had assumed had been a simple history, I might not have the negotiating skills to reach agreements with countries bound by impossibly complex histories.

And here you have just witnessed my overthinking of the task of finding common ground for a remembrance among nations with divergent histories. As I said to myself then, "Just open your eyes and jump." Yet however great the risk of failure, I felt I could always learn from the stories that I was sure to hear.

CHAPTER 2

BELGRADE AND MY FATHER

In the Balkans . . . you are always on the losing side.
—overheard at a dinner in Belgrade

A lifeboat sits low in the water, laden down as it reaches shore
from a hospital ship. In the distance are moored two battleships. At first glance the lifeboat's cargo is a mound of old
coats, until you see hands and feet hanging out over the gunwales.
Some feet with boots and some without. There is little activity. It is a
listless, windless day, the smoke rising straight up from the funnel of
the distant battleship. Two corpses look blankly at the sky. Everything

is still except for the Serb sailor with his oar prodding his cargo to the wharf. A second Serb at the stern, fists on hips, stares down the photographer. Although the picture is grainy, there is much happening in the brain behind his eyes.

The banality of this hospital transport is crushing. I wanted the names of those piled there included in *The World Remembers*, which is why I went to Serbia on my odyssey to approach every nation that had fought in the First World War.

I was at a dinner in Belgrade with historians, archivists and foreign affairs officials to ask that on the centenary of the 1914–1918 conflict, *every* soldier killed, including every Serb, be acknowledged. Naming the dead would be our first act of remembering, and then the political memories could follow. I appreciated how naïve this might seem to those around the table, since their country had only recently emerged from the 1990s Balkans war, an ethically nasty conflict for which some of their former leaders had been tried for war crimes.

Where the idea of a global commemoration came from, I am not entirely sure. Yes, it was the visitors' stories in my dressing room and my great-uncles' war letters, but somehow my father also lay inside the idea. I was requesting that every nation that had fought in the First World War display, over the five centenary years of 2014 to 2018, the nine and a half million names on a public building in their capital city. To say that the politics, logistics, research and financing were daunting is an understatement, yet it was worth the attempt. Today's remembrance rituals are honourable but repetitive, and they perpetuate the previous century's world view. However respectful our Canadian memorials, they are embedded in a view from the past. As much as we assume they represent everyone, in fact they exclude many since Canada is now a nation of almost every people on Earth. On November 11, do we only address the (mainly) white descendants of those who fought the war? What about the Ukrainian Canadians, Chinese Canadians, German Canadians, Italian Canadians, Moroccan Canadians and all the others? Our country cannot continue to remember itself as we were in 1914, a century ago.

Wars don't stop when the bullets do. They reverberate down through generations. PTSD in soldiers and civilians, as well as the veteran suicides, affected families for decades afterwards. Twelve years after the Great War, my great-uncle Jack died of pneumonia, drowning in the ocean that finally filled his embattled lungs. He'd said in his war letters how his repeated exposure to the poison gas hadn't really bothered him, but it had got him in the end. My father was twenty-one at the time, and his uncle Jack's early death made him determined to fight the next war when it came.

The thousands of memorials built in response to the Great War are uncannily quiet about the aftermath of what happened—deaths by dismemberment, the grief of mothers, generals with questionable leadership skills, a multitude of needless deaths, a conscription crisis that drove apart English and French Canada, and tragically tenuous reasons why more than thirty nations went to war in 1914 and 1915. Since how we think of past wars influences how history is framed and social choices are made, surely conflicts must be remembered in their entirety. Think of the American debacle in Vietnam and, more recently, in Iraq. A dark positive of Vietnam is that the name of every dead American soldier was inscribed on a memorial in Washington. The negative in that dark positive is that the Vietnamese names are absent.

What has been written about the First World War could fill a library, but what has never been assembled or published are, for me, the truly important facts—the names of the millions who lost their lives. Yes, there are *partial* lists of the dead from some nations, and *almost complete* lists from others. But in several countries the records were destroyed in revolutions or by bombing in subsequent wars, and in others the names have never escaped the archival boxes to which they were consigned more than a hundred years ago. At the dinner in Belgrade I was told that Serbia "had no culture of remembrance until the Ministry of Labour and Social Policy introduced the idea. This year is the first we have a holiday for that day. A lot of work must be done for the education of remembrance."

I also realized that no ministry had yet assembled the names of Serbia's First World War dead. Not that I have any special skill in scheduling meetings, but mid-November 2012 was an opportune moment to be in Belgrade since the government was about to stage its *first* ever commemoration event for the wars the country had fought. Strange but true.

The day after the dinner, representatives of Russia, Britain, Hungary, the United States, France, Germany and other nations were to attend Serbia's inaugural November 11 ceremony. I would be surprised at what was included. Roman Waschuk, the Canadian ambassador at the time, had organized the dinner and sent out the invitations to key Serbian representatives. I was discovering that officials liked to see the Government of Canada sitting beside the actor guy making the pitch.

How Serbia approached the Great War's centenary was complicated by the fact that a (Bosnian) Serb political fanatic had kicked it all off in 1914. His bullets had killed the heir to Austria's throne and triggered the chain of events that killed many in *my* family, and perhaps in as many as fifteen million other families—that is, if we count civilian as well as military deaths. But, drugged up on political ideology, the Serb nationalist could never have imagined that. More bits of conversation caught in my memory: "Robert, we wear the guilty clothes of World War I."

The director of the National Archives had given me a reproduction of the July 28, 1914, telegram from Vienna stating Austria-Hungary's declaration of war. Its message in French—then the language of international diplomacy—was handwritten in pencil by a Belgrade telegraph clerk.

" . . . LE GOUVERNEMENT IMPÉRIAL ET ROYAL SE TROUVE DANS LA NÉCESSITÉ DE POURVOIR LUI-MÊME À LA SAUVEGARDE DE SES DROITS ET INTÉRÊTS ET DE RECOURIR À CET EFFECT À LA FORCE DES ARMES.   L'AUTRICHE-HONGRIE SE CONSIDÈRE DONC DE CE MOMENT EN ÉTAT DE GUERRE AVEC LA SERBIE."

We worked our way through what may have been an excellent main course. Being jet-lagged, I had only enough functioning brain cells to keep up with the discussion and take notes. Serbia's past looked at me from every side of the table. History is central to a country's national identity. It can selectively record the successes *or* the failures. It can be a story of aspiration *or* a catalogue of grievances. History can be poured like concrete into the building blocks of a nation's myths: books, buildings, websites, flags, statuary, anthems, street names, laws, songs, stories, stained-glass windows, paintings, movies, tapestries, military headdresses. Whose version of history will become part of the national story is argued about and sometimes fought over. In 2017, on the 150th anniversary of Confederation, Canadians wrestled with what exactly we were commemorating. By 2021 some statues of Sir John A. Macdonald and the educator Egerton Ryerson had been splashed with red paint or pulled from their pedestals over the controversy about their roles in creating the "Indian" residential schools.

Serbia's memory seemed as landlocked as its borders. Though the conversation was primarily in Serbian with translation, I appreciated the wry cynicism, especially from the history professor on my left, who commented to me in English, "And we intellectuals, well, all empires of power hate you. Professional cynicism is a place to find stability."

I wondered how much of Canada's memory was likewise locked in place by belief systems. Reading my great-uncles' letters, I had to grimace my way past their pro-British bravado and casual racism. Shining with pride about Canada's place in the British Empire framed their attitudes towards other countries and peoples—Americans, in particular, came out badly. The frame around my school's photo of Her Majesty was both literal and figurative. Framing brings a veneer of permanence. The stronger the frame, the longer the content may last. The more impressive the frame, the more impressed we want others to feel about what's inside it.

Apart from the quip about cynicism offering a haven for stability, I saw no friction between the military and political views at the table, and there was an undercurrent that Serbia's battered international reputation was undeserved. Just twelve years before, during their war in Kosovo, NATO had launched air strikes on Belgrade. Who in Canada remembers that? Serbian resentment lingers for the bombing, which had killed a number of civilians. The cruise missiles that hit the Ministry of Defence and other buildings—including, by mistake, the Chinese embassy—were not launched from Canadian ships or aircraft, but Ambassador Waschuk and I were undoubtedly *from* a NATO nation.

Twelve years later, the Ministry of Defence building at 5 Birčaninova Street was still infamous and unrepaired, a monument to the destruction that NATO had brought upon Serbia. History can be embedded in statues and memorials, or it can linger in rebar twisted apart by missiles. How long a grievance is sustained depends on how much history you wish to wring from it. Yet, according to some, leaving the damaged building standing was a procedural matter; an official told me that the ministry was waiting to sell the land for development.

The remembrance ceremonies the next day took place first at the Commonwealth War Graves Commission cemetery, then at the Russian cemetery, and finally at a Serbian one, all of which were close to the centre of Belgrade. The air was brisk but the sun was warm. At each cemetery, wreaths were laid by the attending ambassadors. There were few civilians and fewer children. An array of uniformed military attachés was on hand, as well as security details with their earpieces. Only the American detail wore business suits, while the Serbs and Russians preferred windbreakers, jeans and dark glasses. On the periphery stood a group of grey-haired, ponytailed men in black leather jackets.

Ambassador Waschuk, who officiated at the Commonwealth ceremony, had encouraged me to attend to get a sense of how the Serbs would shape their war remembrances in the years ahead. The dinner

the previous night had ended on a positive note and follow-up meetings had been arranged at the National Library and the Ministry of
Defence to explore the details of my proposal. As I did not have any
function at the cemeteries, my thoughts were free to wander.

I was surprised by the panache and bright colours of some of
the uniforms, especially the French soldiers, whose ceremonial dress
included red pants, deep-blue jackets and red and white plumes
on their headgear. In 1914, France's generals had been slow to grasp
that conspicuous dress was not a good match for modern weaponry
and had insisted their troops wear red pants into battle. Uniforms
with eye-catching colours and big hats (larger still when you added
fur, feathers or spikes) were to show prowess and cow the enemy.
Colourful eighteenth-century army uniforms were also helpful for
distinguishing who was who on battlefields often obscured by clouds
of black-powder smoke from the discharging flintlocks. But no longer.
With modern weapons, they became bullet-catchers.

Fifty years before 1914, the American Civil War had been the
midwife of industrialized warfare, delivering better artillery, repeating guns and widespread use of the rifled barrel, which made gunfire
more accurate. When weaponry was inaccurate, as it largely was until
the mid-nineteenth century, it didn't matter *what* soldiers wore, since
being hit was mainly a matter of chance. All this changed when more
precise armaments made bright uniforms good targets. Yet in 1914 the
French generals felt there was little to be learned from the Americans,
but as the fighting ramped up and the bodies stacked up, the French
gave up on gallantry and retired the red pants. Better to have a drab
live soldier than a stylishly dressed dead one.

Many of the nations I was approaching for *The World Remembers*
had delegations at the ceremonies. A Serbian military band played as
each ambassador proceeded forward to lay their wreath. The turnout
from the international embassies in Belgrade was impressive. But why
was everything repeated at three cemeteries?

An official with an order sheet gave each group the nod when
their turn came to pick up their wreath while the music played and

move forward to place it with the others. The musical selection was short and solemn and the bandmaster had no choice but to keep playing it. When the ceremony at the first location was complete, we moved to the Russian cemetery. Everything was repeated, the music recycled, the parties advanced and more wreaths were laid.

Had my father been beside me in his naval uniform amongst former friends and foes, what would he have felt? Russia had been close to his heart—not the Soviet Union's communists but the soulful pre-Revolution nation that he knew through its choirs and read about in its novels. "Here, have a look at this," he would say, passing me Fyodor Dostoyevsky's *Crime and Punishment*, whereupon I'd disappear into the world of Raskolnikov, the book's tortured student-hero. My dad was never so pleased as when, at theatre school, I consumed a thick biography of Tolstoy. As a student in Toronto in the 1920s, he'd liked spending time at the homes of Russian émigrés who had fled the Revolution. It was in their houses that his heart was first captured by their singing, and perhaps by a woman as well.

Into the second hour, at the third cemetery, I was sympathizing with the horn players since the November air had taken a toll on their lips and they were spelling each other off. Playing the same solemn music over and over might have been comical if the occasion hadn't been so serious. Remembrance was a learning curve.

I assumed that the triple-cemetery event was meant to address three Serbian constituencies: the European Union (EU), with whom they hoped to join economically; Russia, its traditional ally; and third, the nation whose reputation it wished to bolster—namely, its own. Wandering through my thoughts were the figures 265,000, the *estimated* number of Serbs killed in World War I, and 9,500,000, the *estimated* military deaths from all nations, two million of which were thought to be Russians. No numbers were ever acknowledged as the wreaths were being laid.

Apart from an unexpected display of emotion by the ponytailed men at the conclusion, by the third cemetery my attention had truly wandered, not from disrespect for the wreath-laying but because the ceremony was now, essentially, just signalling Serbia's respect for the EU, for Moscow and for the homeland. The height of the military headgear around me began to draw my attention. The higher the crown, the steeper the slope from the back of the hat to its peak. The Russian officers' hats had taken the lead. Theirs positively swooped up. How much taller *could* headgear go? The extremity certainly didn't detract from the gravity of the officer's face below. Were ever-higher hats pure bravura? Might army uniform designers ever have discarded their drafts, saying, *we simply cannot structure the swoop any closer to vertical.* Yet occasionally military headdresses *had* gone vertical. The eighteenth-century British Grenadiers' mitre caps, adorned with brass front-plates, *had* gone straight up. Was there a Russian army regulation stating that the height of the hat must *not* exceed the height of the wearer's face? Apparently not.

I was witnessing the return of military finery. For thousands of years size signalled power and tall hats had alighted on soldiers' heads. The plumage on the French helmets was remarkable. For what other purpose would a warrior wear bear fur, eagle feathers or other plumage up top, other than to demonstrate that they possessed the spirit of powerful animals? Soldiering is an ancient game. But the Great War's industrialized killing methods quickly banished battle-field finery and batted aside any advantage that animal imagery brought to military uniforms. The Grenadier Guards in my child-hood carpet-wars wore bear's fur (glossy black paint) on their heads to convey power, nothing more. *We are as ferocious as great beasts,* said the hats, and if a bear has ever set its sights on you, you will know there is really no defence. Yet the fierceness of one of nature's most powerful predators (including the human kind) was swatted aside by the First World War's machinery for delivering death. Most wild animals fled the fields and forests of the battle areas in France and Belgium. Only the rats remained.

Battlefields have always been nasty, mean and dirty, and the uni-forms of the Great War began to match that reality. Most British army officers, in keeping with the privileges of being from the upper class, still retained a batman—basically a military butler who pressed the major's shirts and saw to his other non-military needs. But apart from ironed shirts, any visual gallantry was banished from what was no longer gallant and all too frequently lethal, no matter how soldiering was being sold to the public back home. The scale of destruction at the Somme, Verdun, Passchendaele, Dresden, Coventry, Nagasaki, Stalingrad and Hiroshima came from military imaginations that were the extreme opposite of gallant. But there it was creeping back in the cemeteries of Belgrade. The Russians appeared the most brazen, perhaps because their president was re-establishing his country's former imperial glory. Certainly Moscow's missiles have been hard at work recently, reclaiming the hegemony of the tsars. The war in Ukraine is why the city of Mariupol, and others, can be included in the list above.

I once appeared in *The Nutcracker* with the National Ballet of Canada in Toronto. Unbelievable yet true. I was a "Cannon Doll." Tchaikovsky's ballet, first performed in 1892, tells of toys coming to life at Christmas. Two Russian Petrushka-like dolls—of which I was one—come onstage, fire confetti into the audience from a toy cannon, fall down and then run off. No dancing was required and no one was hurt. I was given a quick rehearsal an hour before the performance, the costume was clown-like, and it was a thrill to be amongst such hugely talented dancers. In the ballet there are also toy bears, princes, the Sugar Plum Fairy and tin soldiers with brocaded blue jackets and headgear based on the nineteenth-century Imperial Russian Army.

Those *same* hats and jackets—but of a quality that no dance company could afford—have now reappeared in the Kremlin. On the television news we can watch President Putin proceeding to his public appearances through the former tsars' Moscow residence as very real nutcracker soldiers open the golden doors before him. As Putin passes, the soldiers' heads pivot, drilled to angle their chins high, necks proud and eyes choreographed to allow only an oblique view of their headman. Their military uniforms *are* magnificent. Their precision footwork and timing would make the National Ballet's dancers proud. The finery of soldiers was intended to display prowess on the battlefields, reflect the power and the glory of the emperor and dazzle the peasants back home. And so it is today.

It was mid-afternoon when I left the cemeteries. Amongst the range of military dress that I'd seen, I had been reassured by Canada's modesty. Berets sat quietly on Canadian Army heads, neither stoked with pride nor inflated to impress others. The soldiers whom I have spoken with over the years appear to be practical people—after all, fighting is a practical business. In some of the forces of the major powers, there is a sense of entitlement but rarely an attitude of strut. Being a middle power, our core of modesty seems to come honestly.

Is that because we don't carry the burden of power as America does, or the legacy of once having had an empire? Or is it that, unlike Russia, Canada doesn't hunger for a former national glory or, unlike Serbia, we don't have a legacy of feeling internationally misunderstood? Or is it that within our borders, wherever Canadians turn, the faces around us are from every part of the world? As we choose to be a country of *all* peoples—a plurality of minorities— might we shed the curse of seeing the Other only as alien? Is this our new strength?

The German army uniforms at the cemeteries were also modest and absent of pride, but that had sprung from a different root: from the responsibility for an era of Nazi horror and the murder of millions of innocents. As a former German soldier once remarked to me, "*Robert, we don't do parades anymore.*"

The figures 265,000 and 9,500,000 appear here with an authority they simply do not have. Salting sentences with large numbers might signal that you have a handle on history, but no one *really* knows the numbers. For many reasons this might seem odd, but it isn't. Any final number remains only an estimate, and sometimes, as I was told by an archivist in Moscow, casualty numbers were inflated for political gain. In the decade after the First World War some nations wished to (over)stress the enormity of their losses.

The question is, what value do countries give to those killed in their armies? By 2012, as I began to build *The World Remembers*, I came to realize that only a minority of nations had assembled the hard data that allowed them to count their World War I dead; Belgium, for example, had rigorously researched its war deaths. Canada, Australia and the other nations of the former British Empire had the cemetery lists that the Commonwealth War Graves Commission had dutifully assembled. But many other countries had never gotten round to it, or had not bothered. And through that indifference, perhaps a million names may have slipped into oblivion because of shifting politics, contested histories, negligence or the destruction of archives. You would think that if someone lost their life for their nation that the country might care to remember their name. Apparently not always. As I explored possible sources to find the lists of the dead, I began to see that, apart from those who may have disappeared from the records altogether, more had been left in the dust of archival basements or buried by the shovels of national amnesia.

There had been tears at the third and final wreath-laying. Among the Serbian graves, after all the official delegations had finished and, almost as an afterthought, a final group stepped forward. They were the grey-haired, ponytailed men I had seen earlier standing on the periphery. Resembling a biker gang with their black leather jackets, some of them had wept. They were Serb army veterans of the 1990s war in Kosovo, cast adrift by a history that no longer wanted them. Balkan ghosts. Who knows what residue of tainted blood from the fighting remained on their hands. As can happen with castoff armies, some veterans dealt drugs, some perhaps trafficked weapons or women, and some perhaps had moved on to fight for other causes. Those veterans seemed not to have been given an official place in the Serbian remembrance story. They wore no blue blazers displaying service medals and poppies; no government staff saw to their needs. But at the end they were allowed to place a wreath. Their remembrance was of yet another Balkan war of tragedy and ethnic cleansing that meant no one's past could be entirely clean. And yet they cried. Just as the dead from the hospital ship lay equal in the rowboat on its way to shore, so too does grief lie equal in the heart, no matter how troubled the past from which it came.

CHAPTER 3

TABLEAU ON THE STEPS
LOOKING BACK AT YOU

P hotos are windows in time. Should anyone *in* them be looking into the lens, they will forever be regarding us. By 1914,
so many families owned cameras that our visual record of
war was greatly expanded. Many of those pictures have become
personal treasures, such as this one has for me. The Stratfords—
my father's side of the family—produced albums of snapshots of
my great-uncles as well as their sisters, mothers, cousins, forgotten
friends and brothers too young for the army. Each photo is a scene
populated with characters. I animate them in my mind, wondering how each would wish to be presented here. Irrationally, I hope
some will break their silence and speak. In the summer of 1919, the

Stratfords presented themselves on the front steps of a rented cottage near Gravenhurst, Ontario, basically as a *tableau vivant*. Taken nine months after the fighting stopped, to me it is their visual epilogue of the Great War.

A forgotten theatre in Sweden was rediscovered more than a century after it had been abandoned. For 129 years King Gustav III's theatre on the outskirts of Stockholm had been used to store furniture. On exploring its deserted rooms, the beams of the discoverer's flashlight found scenic backdrops hanging above the eighteenth-century stage, machinery for changing sets, wind and wave machines for stagehands to crank, and the actors' scripts from the final performance in 1792 still in their dressing rooms. The entire Drottningholm Palace Theatre was a "still life" waiting to be reanimated.

The *tableau vivant* is an old stage device in which performers arrange themselves as if in a dramatic painting. It was used to conclude acts of plays or operas and went on to become part of the over-the-top melodramas of the late nineteenth century. Through vaudeville and burlesque, the device survived into the twentieth century. But then the *tableau vivant* died—or almost did. Film and television publicists today arrange their casts in similarly mannered positions. I have been in such promotional shoots for TV productions, where marketing directors have requested poses that would not have been out of place in King Gustav III's eighteenth-century theatre in Drottningholm.

In the 1919 tableau on the cottage steps, all eyes are on the camera. It is their gaze that draws me into their stories.

Photography was invented in the 1840s and became the "affordable portraiture" for the middle class. Early professional photographers fashioned their backdrops and customers' poses to resemble oil paintings of the royal and the rich, since having your portrait painted was a sign of your higher social status. But because of the crudeness of the new technology, photographers required their subjects to sit utterly still for minutes while the photographic plate was being exposed. Rendered motionless in a bright studio that often smelled of acrid chemicals, while holding a pleasant expression, was an experience that was compared to early dentistry. In that stillness, however, more than the silver coating on the photographic plate was exposed.

At King Gustav III's theatre, along with the abandoned backdrops and stage machinery used to animate the world of the play, I want to believe that the echoes of the final performance also hung in the air—if only the explorer peering into the darkness had had the wit to listen. Likewise in early photos, I imagine a residue of the sitters' thinking might also exist, while their head was held immobile by a concealed steel brace on the back of the photographer's chair. Their eyes might lead us to their thoughts. As the minutes ticked by, perhaps they ruminated about the new science in the camera before them, or the photographer counting off the exposure time, or maybe just a bothersome boil on their backside. The chemical used to summon the sitter's image on the copper plate was a poisonous mercury vapour. If photographers weren't careful, they could end up with what was known as "hatter's disease," essentially mercury poisoning, a symptom of which was shaking like the Mad Hatter in *Alice in Wonderland*, who took bites out of his teacups. What those copperplate portraits captured was as much the camera observing the sitter as the sitter observing the camera.

When I first acted on film, the director could see that I was apprehensive and had little idea how to work in front of a lens. The camera's gaze, through its lens that resembles a large, lidless eye, can be off-putting if you are not an exhibitionist, which most good actors aren't. And in contrast to the transitory life of a stage character, a performance on film can exist forever. To guide me, the director said that *the* most important relationship on a movie set is the one between the lenses—the one in the camera and the one in the actor's eye. Film's power relies on the strength of that bond. But it is an *unequal* relationship, because the real power rests in the actor's eye. Strange but true. The reason for the inequality is that the technology of the memory behind the camera's lens—whether copper-plates or digital memory cards—is no match for what lies behind the human eye. *Our* eye/brain connectivity is remarkable. Everything that we see, our brain references against a lifetime of patterns, associations and recollections. But the camera's eye leads only to the technical designer's cul-de-sac of zeros and ones that have been subjected to data-compression algorithms written by the data scientists, while *our* eye leads to a malleable inner universe forged by millions of years of evolutionary adaptation. Much of what lies behind our eyes remains unexplored, yet the seemingly limitless potential of our brainscape has never been disputed.

What is more, before the nineteenth-century invention of cameras and the discovery of electromagnetic waves and photons of light, there was speculation that light actually emerged *from* the subject's eye and travelled *to* the observer. This certainly seems true when you behold a child's eyes sparkling with joy, or if you have witnessed the light vanishing from the eyes of the dying. A hater's eyes glow with rage, while those of lovers and infants are pools of unconditional love. Whatever the physics, the eyes have it.

⟶

In the summer of 1919, my great-grandmother Mary Elizabeth Stratford and her family arranged themselves on the cottage steps. Someone wanted a photo. By that time camera exposures took only a fraction of a second, but even so, the eleven individuals gathered in an impromptu tableau. Judging by the shadows, it was close to midday, and from the bare legs of the children, it was probably hot. The Great War had ended months before, and my great-grandmother (in the small hat and chequered dress) sits on the top step with fewer children than before the fighting began. Their tableau appears peaceful, yet lingering in their gazes are echoes of the violence of the preceding years.

Eyes can be windows to our very distant past, to the time when the *concept* of individuals as entities separate from the world somehow evolved. How we came to regard ourselves as being separate from our environment, and from others, is one of the mysteries of evolution. We weren't "made" that way, rather we "became" that way, and in unguarded moments it is possible to stumble on glimpses of that journey. Catching my face in the mirror in the morning, I usually try to avoid my eyes. *Just finish your shaving, Robert, and get your porridge on the stove.* Yet if I do look, I see *someone* gazing back. Of course it is Robert, but as I consider it, who I *actually* am is not nearly as definitive as the name.

Two irises regard me through successive generations of my family's eyes. Travelling further back still, they gaze at me from millions of years of the eye's evolutionary voyage, to a time when our visual cortex existed *only* to observe in order to survive. Glimpsing this unsettling self in the mirror opens doors that apparently offer no answers, since they lead only to unknowable sources. Who *is* that? The moment in the mirror holds and my razor is stilled. Time suspends. The face hangs like a scenic backdrop in an abandoned theatre. Where is the stage manager who will animate it? *Is* there a stage manager? Thankfully, *someone* finally emerges from somewhere backstage to turn the crank. The script with the name "Robert" on it is retrieved from a dressing room, the stage is occupied once more, the performer is in place, the shaving resumes and I get on with the day. Boldness is needed in such moments if I am not to shrink back to bed.

⌒⌒⌒

Introductions are in order. I think my grandmother Helen was behind the camera, so it was probably her voice that said, *Everyone ready?* In the tableau, on my great-grandmother Mary Elizabeth Stratford's left is her son Harold, in the white short-sleeved shirt. Also on her left and one step below is her son Jack, in a darker shirt. Jack was then thirty-one and had been engaged in serious fighting in the final seventeen months of the war. Both sons have now left the army and are visiting from the sanatorium fifty kilometres away in

Gravenhurst. With their scarred lungs they would be in and out of the institution for the rest of their shortened lives.

Mary Elizabeth's daughter Mayden sits in the middle, with her brother Harold behind her right shoulder and her brother Jack on her immediate left. She is twenty and truly deserves to be the centre of this picture, since in the troubled years ahead I think Mayden became the emotional core of the family. She is missing her other brothers, George and Joe, who were killed in the twenty-one months before the camera clicked. I consider the empty places on the top step as belonging to them. Also absent is her fifth brother, Art, who was with the King's African Rifles in what is now Mozambique, then Portuguese East Africa. Art was still in Africa waiting out the Spanish flu pandemic that would end up killing more people than the war. He also survived the fighting and would return to Toronto the following Thanksgiving and make mischief.

Seated on the far right in the broad-brimmed hat is my great-grandmother's niece Margaret Killmaster. She was a military nurse who had spent three years in operating rooms in Britain and France helping repair men the war had tried to take apart. Margaret would go on to become my godmother, yet I have few memories of her. My great-grandmother Mary Elizabeth does not appear robust, either because she's had thirteen children or because she has just spent four years watching a war walk through the lives of five of her sons. Later, Mayden and Margaret would nurse my great-grandmother in the years after her stroke, until her death thirteen years after this photo was taken.

Everyone on the steps had been tossed about by the slipstream of the Great War. They were familiar with its turbulence. Some, like Jack, had been literally knocked off their feet, as he described in a letter home: "Fritz got really mad and opened up with everything he had . . . dropped a big one right back of me and blew me right out of the trench." Margaret had dealt with the conflict's consequences on her operating table. And others, like Mayden, worried when letters arrived and rejoiced when her brothers returned. In my imagination

I am standing behind the camera with my grandmother. I hear them looking at me. *Who are you, great-nephew? We've never heard of you, yet you are telling this story?*

The others in the tableau are a collection of cousins whom I won't name here. A domestic drama is being played out in the back row, between the man on the extreme right and the woman on the extreme left. The three girls in bare feet are the couple's children, and their father, chin in hand, leans away from the group. He wears a heavy army jacket on what is clearly a hot summer day. His wife is the woman in the white dress, sitting as far from him as the steps allow. I won't say more, since the family is reluctant to have the quarrel told, but the man has just spent three and a half years in a German prisoner-of-war camp. Husband and wife remained married for the rest of their lives but had separate bedrooms. It will be noted (but not explained) that Harold sits *between* the two. Enough said.

The pigeon-toed young man with the bow tie is a cousin who'd gone to a "proper" school in England. He is probably wondering if he can get his hands on the German semi-automatic pistol that Jack had brought back from Belgium. Despite the shadows cast by the sun, I see much of this in their eyes.

Not seen is my grandmother Helen, the older sister of Jack, Mayden, Harold, Art, George and Joe. I believe Helen took the picture, just as years later she would bring toy soldiers up from her basement for my carpet wars. Her husband, Robert, isn't present because he is at work in a bank in Toronto. I am sure my grandmother took the photo because the children are smiling, her brothers and her cousin Margaret look pensive, the man and wife have no particular baggage with the operator of the shutter, and Mayden's eyes share with the camera a rapport that only sisters could have. In this tableau my heart belongs to Mayden, so I feel that it's especially she who regards me across time and space. *So there you are great-nephew, who I will grow close to later in my life.* Also absent from the photo is my father. He was Helen and Robert's oldest son and had just turned nine. He was probably out fishing. It was my father who told me about Jack's German gun that emerged from its leather holster one early morning that summer.

My great-aunt Mayden never married and lived at times in a small apartment on the top floor of her sister Helen's house. When not playing war on my grandmother's carpet, I would climb the stairs to see her and marvel at the Zulu feathers and spears that Art had brought back from Africa. After years of caring for her incapacitated mother, she did volunteer work at hospitals in Toronto. It was she who collected and sorted through the hundreds of war letters from her five brothers, her mother, her aunt, her cousins, friends of the family and even strangers in France. She was old by the time she had finished typing them all out. It was Mayden who leapt to her feet and applauded when she saw me in my first film on her television, the one in which the director had taught me about the power of eyes.

That day in 1919 Mayden looks resigned. Two of her brothers have already been killed, and the laboured breathing of the war-damaged lungs of Jack and Harold on either side of her is evident. She'd read Jack's letters with their descriptions of battle from which he carried the scars. Mayden would never see the European graves of Joe and George, and Art, the brother who addressed her in his letters home as "My love, my rose of the world," was still six thousand miles away in Africa. There seems a lifetime of determination on her face. In Mayden's final years, she and I were driving by a church near where my grandmother had lived, when she remarked that she hadn't stepped in that building since 1916. Why? I asked. "Because that was where my brothers were blessed before they went to war."

Perhaps I'm taking liberties with my animations, but my family follows me like a dramatis personae who, having lived their lives, are ready to leave the theatre. All about them are their letters, photos and *my* memories of what they said and did. Is that enough to recreate a script? But then again, the texts actors use in theatres, apart from a few stage directions, contain only the speeches that must be committed to memory. To bring life to the characters, you must step into their shoes with your imagination.

Mayden's gift to the family was that she not only *collected* the letters but also assembled them in separate ring-binders; booklets for each of her five brothers. The originals were mostly in pencil and in delicate condition, so she typed them out to preserve them for the family. In each brother's booklet, she cross-referenced the letters to include another brother's comment about a visit or a death. She inserted as many photos as she could find. It took her years. Bundles of the 760 originals were in her spare room, tied up with ribbons. She complained of how weary she was of the task. In the ring-binders for George and Joe, who'd been killed outright, she inserted letters of condolence from strangers, friends and fellow soldiers. Those for Harold and Jack, who died after the war in the sanatorium, have no such additions. If Mayden had not done that, I would never have written *The Lost Boys*, nor attempted to create an international commemoration to name each man or woman killed in the First World War.

The letters have become monologues, since when a brother responds to a question from someone writing from Canada, the questions have disappeared. Everything sent east across the Atlantic to France and Belgium by mothers, sisters and friends has been lost. Except for a question asked by Jack's oldest sister Helen, that he repeats in his reply: "You ask me in your letter if I like the Hun, or rather do I hate the Hun. Well if you want a straight answer, when you get to Heaven you ask the Hun."

Only the words that travelled west have survived. They were written on troop trains and transport ships; in training camps, rest camps or hospital beds; in a comfortable chair in an aunt's house in England while on leave or on the dirt floor of a dugout in battle—and once from a graveside. Reading them, it's as if I'm deaf in one ear.

However trivial the content of their letters sometimes seems, a war always lies just on the other side of the sentences. The captured semi-automatic the young cousin was waiting to get his hands on that summer of 1919 might be a lark to a bow-tied adolescent, but it was Jack's memento of the deaths of his brothers and *his* own killing of Germans, to whom he refers as "the Boche," "Fritz," "the Hun" or simply "G."

Apologies are owed to the family, since I am now stage-managing them like actors in a play. A few relatives pace frustrated in the wings because I've decided to give them *no* stage time. I dread having demoted my great-great-aunt Isabel, who lived in England and whose house became a refuge for the five brothers when they were recovering from wounds or on leave. Isabel had a *lot* to say; her opinions were sharp and she herself had stage-managed the lives of many in the family. I hesitate to think what words she might have for me, her unknown great-great-nephew who is reluctant to allow her an entrance.

There *will* be a cameo by Isabel's son, the dapper young man on the bottom step, concerning his recklessness with a firearm and my nine-year-old father. As remembered by others, my great-uncle Jack was a gentle man who wheezed as he breathed and who had been a relentless collector from the battlefields. "Moth" is how the brothers referred to their mother.

"Everything going fine here. How is everything with you? Am enclosing four shoulder straps, souvenirs, please send them on to Moth after you have looked at them. There is a history connected with each one, someday I'll tell you the story."

—Jack to Isabel's daughter Margie, August 12, 1918

"Another note from Jack yesterday saying—it was the 7th he wrote— that he was going to have a good rest now. He has been through a pretty hot time apparently, and from the number of G. shoulder straps he has sent us, and other things, I should judge he'd been very busy with his bayonet."

—Isabel to her sister Mary Elizabeth, September 13, 1918

"Gentle" Jack sent home German regimental shoulder straps, uniform buttons, army belt buckles embossed with *Gott Mit Uns*

(God With Us), brass belt-holders stamped with the Prussian crown and a Steyr semi-automatic pistol complete with leather holster. He mentions picking up other guns from battlefields, most of which he threw away. He also traded mementos with the British, French, Belgian and Australian soldiers whom he met, but it is safe to say that his German collection was not assembled through trade, since each of the contributors was in some stage of surrender.

"Don't worry about how I got the shoulder straps I sent you. They are easy to get, both off the live ones and the others. One officer didn't want to give me his, but I used a little 'perswasion' and he took his knife out and cut them off for me. The 'perswasion' stuff comes from the ammunition dumps every day."

And again, to his sister Helen:

"You ask me in your letter if I like the Hun, or rather do I hate the Hun. Well if you want a straight answer, when you get to Heaven you ask the Hun. They are all labeled 'Gott Mit Uns' and every time I get a chance I send them on their way 'to Gott.' Well this will be all for now. Must get on with Mayd's letter. Love to all. Your loving bro."

Four German belt buckles, century-old metallic echoes, lie before me now. Each had Jack's hand on it, a foreign soldier's belly behind it, and apart from the four pieces of metal invoking God, all the rest has returned to dust. What patriotic fever infected Jack and those "Hun" soldiers that they would engage in a such a contest for conquest? Do I throw out the buckles as so much trash, or should they live on as reminders of a tragic relationship between Jack and his four adversaries? Do they remain in my desk drawer until I hand them down to my sons as a symbol of . . . what? Of the story of their great-great-uncles' war? We have been hurling missiles at each other for millennia.

Jack wrote about church parades on Sunday in military camps and taking Holy Communion at the front. But if God was engaged in the fighting, then the deity certainly worked both sides of the battle. After Jack collected the buckles, they probably remained for months at the bottom of his kit bag. If the four Germans had surrendered, they probably spent months as prisoners of war. Or if they were dead, they had been laid at the bottom of a grave and their mothers had grieved. If any of the four survived, by the summer of 1919 they too might be sitting on steps with their families, thinking about missing brothers and what the world might have in store.

By 1933 Jack had suffocated as a consequence of his exposures to the poison gas that, despite his mask, had entered his lungs. Neither you nor I will be subject to that kind of airborne demise—unless we were in Syria during their recent civil war, when President Bashar al-Assad attacked his own people with sarin gas. Dying from such an assault would essentially be by drowning in the bubbles of hydrochloric acid that would be filling your lungs. I will let Lieutenant Wilfred Owen, the British World War I soldier-poet, describe it:

> *Gas! GAS! Quick boys!—An ecstasy of fumbling*
> *Fitting the clumsy helmets just in time;*
> *But someone still was yelling out and stumbling*
> *And flound'ring like a man in fire or lime—*
> *Dim through the misty panes and thick green light,*
> *As under a green sea, I saw him drowning.*

By 1933, the Germans whose buckles were in Jack's possession might also have died from the British Army's gas, or perhaps their lungs worked a little longer and they witnessed the next war. Like the scenery in the forgotten theatre in Sweden, the *Gott Mit Uns* buckles remain suspended in time, and I keep listening for the echoes.

Canadian soldiers were known for their collections of war souvenirs, and why not? They were far from home on a continent considered to be the centre of the civilized world. They would probably never visit Europe again, because they probably wouldn't be able to afford it. My great-uncles mailed home as many postcards of French cathedrals as they did pieces of German uniforms. When on leave, soldiers from most of the armies could get back to their homes in Britain, Germany or France and see their families, but not the Canadians. So wives were not kissed, babies were not made and girlfriends were left unadored. What to do? As the number of men in the graveyards by the battlefields grew, the thrill of having joined up to fight in a foreign field shrank. Regardless, young men desire good food, good drink and a good shag. All three were on the market and business was brisk in the towns behind the battle lines.

Mary Elizabeth's sons wrote of the first two desires but seldom the third, because, well, how much do you want your mother to know? However, medical records are not shy and George's casualty record shows six weeks in hospital for "V.D.S." (syphilis) and "G.D.S." (gonorrhea). The date on a letter Jack wrote coincides with that of his brother's "treatment" and Jack mentions paying him a visit. George's letters home from the hospital to his mother explain that he was there because of foot and ear problems. And why not? Jack knew, but he didn't tell.

Syphilis and gonorrhea *were* a concern because the diseases kept men out of the fighting for up to six weeks. The Canadian Army, preferring soldiers lined up in battle rather than in beds, had wanted to issue condoms. The high rates of "khaki fever," as it was called, were driven even higher by the "Mrs. Grundys" of Canada—the name assigned to the self-styled moralists who would later became the booze-banners who cheered on prohibition in the 1920s. The Mrs. Grundys championed sexual abstinence and insisted that condoms should *never* be distributed to soldiers. So they weren't and the men did the deed anyway. The result was that in 1915, more than a fifth of the Canadian Army was in hospital for treatment of venereal disease, which could involve threading the penis with a tube and forcing an irrigation solution containing arsenic into the bladder—a procedure referred to as the "hot umbrella." George survived the treatment to be buried alive later at Passchendaele. Jack's records reveal no such

medical tale, so he was either lucky, careful or abstemious as he continued sending war trophies home.

Fighting and sex are full-on physical encounters: both require
partners, both at their core can put a life at stake, both can be conducted *with* feeling or without, and both can be a lust-filled engagement. Performed coldly, both activities are inhuman, whereas a
passionate intimacy brings joy to sex but a depravity to killing. In
both activities, partners usually prefer to keep their passions between
themselves, and so a soldier writing home about an encounter on the
battlefield can be like a man writing home about an encounter in
bed. If it is done at all it usually involves generalities—except for Jack.
Of all the letters the brothers wrote, his contain the fullest description
of battle and are remarkable in their candor. Since Jack often uses
army-talk terms and slang such as battn, gold braid, B. Co., H.E. and
jake, I've provided a glossary at the end of the book.

"Well here I am just back from up the line and am glad to get back.
I'll try and give you a little description of my doing since leaving
England, and no one need get excited if they see my name in the
casualty list, as I only got biffed hard enough to have to get my head
dressed, which entitles me to put up a gold braid . . . The initiation
was good, believe me.

Well we arrived at our Head Q. that afternoon about 5:30 and
found the battn. had gone up into supports. We stayed at the H.Q.
that night and went up to join the battn. the next day. They were in
the front line, or at least out about 300 yards in front of our front
line ready to go over in the morning and they marched us in and split
us up among the old men. Fritz was shelling to beat the band and
got quite a few of our boys on the way. We went in single file and
the fellow 3 ahead of me went down, and when I came up I stopped
to see how badly he was hit, he was unconscious, but alive, so I
stopped long enough to open up his clothes, take off his equipment,
put his overcoat over him, and when I looked up I was all alone,
in 'No Man's Land.' I grubbed around in the dark for a while, with

my head down, and after a little while ran into a bunch of men, who turned out to be B. Co so I went up with them and just as we were getting into the advanced trench, A. Co. came up, so I was jake.

It was then about 3:30 a.m. and we were to go over at 4:30 so believe me I did some tall thinking in that hour. It isn't the chances or excitement that gets your nerve, but it's the waiting. I got in between two old men a little later, and in a few minutes word was passed along to fix bayonets and put 5 rounds in the magazine. Well I shook a little but nevertheless I got the bayonet in and put 10 rounds in the magazine and 1 in the breach, and a few minutes later, at 4:30 sharp our artillery opened up a barrage for 7 minutes raising 100 yards after every 5 minutes. After the 7 minutes we got word to get up and go over, which we did, not according to my idea of a charge though, but in this manner. I thought we would strip down and go over with a dash and a shout, but we didn't. We were fully clothed, and equipped with 120 rounds of ammunition, rifles, bayonet, entrenching tool, pack, 5 sand bags, shovel, 48 hour rations and numerous sundries, and we got up with our rifles slung over our backs and walked across 1200 yards of hissing hell, dropping at intervals into shell holes to get our wind, and it just took us about 1 hour to make Fritz's front line. It seemed like a week to me. You don't want to imagine that Fritz didn't get busy as soon as we did, because he did, and he made it a hell hole for us to go through. I got over within about 30 yards of Fritz's front line when I spys a Fritz with a machine gun in a piece of trench that hadn't been cleared and about the same time he saw me, so I jumped for a shell hole and made it, the fellow coming up behind me jumped too, but not quick enough, and he came into the same hole stone dead shot right between the eyes. That Fritz with a few others who had been missed, in about 30 yards of trench, kept us in that shell hole for about 30 minutes, but eventually we bombed his soul to ---- and went on over. Within the next few hours we had taken 2 villages and gone over to about 100 yards behind Fritz's support trench, which we held. The hand to hand fighting is what I like, but I've been disappointed in one thing, I couldn't get satisfaction for

Aunt Isabel, Fritz won't face the bayonet, and I hadn't the heart to
stick it in when he had his hands up.

I myself in one village took eight, 2 officers and 6 men, searched
them and sent them back. One of them was an iron cross man, I took
the ribbon off him but have since lost it. I also had a couple of revolvers
etc. which I threw away before I came out, as I couldn't carry them.
I was all in, and glad enough to get out with a whole skin. Right now
I'd be satisfied to go home, as I think I've done my share of fighting and
got my share of Huns. We made our objective all right and swung our
front line out about 100 yards past it. We got no more than settled when
Fritz counter-attacked but it didn't come off, what we took we held.

May 3. Didn't have time to finish this last night, and to-day finds
me a few miles farther back of the line in a rest camp, where I hope we
stay for a few days.

Well Sunday morning the artillery started at it hammer and tongs
and we just sat where we were and shook, and Sunday afternoon Fritz
got really mad and opened up on with everything he had, and believe
me our trenches were sure a hot place. First he knocked the wind out
of me 3 or 4 times, concussion, then when I was moving down the
trench he rapped me on the elbow with a piece of shell casing, so I put
back to my hole, then he dropped a big one right back of me and blew
me right out of the trench, but I crawled back again and a few minutes
later I got a bump back of the ear, just under my tin roof, and thank
the lord it wasn't coming any faster than it was or I wouldn't be here
now. Right after this our artillery opened up and Fritz left us alone
and went after them. We were relieved about midnight and come out
smiling short about 50%. I never stopped shaking until last night. I was
steady enough going over, and while we were scrapping, as a matter of
fact I stopped on the way over and lit a cigarette and went on, but lying
in a hole and being shelled sure gets you, I couldn't have lit a cigarette
then to save my soul, I was shaking too badly.

We were only in 2 days and 2 nights but they seemed like two years
to me. One of the old 10th boys told me he had seen bigger scraps but
none with more snap than the one we were in, and he said he never did

see Fritz put up a bombardment like he did on Sunday afternoon. Take it from me it was a real line breaking in for tender feet. My rifle was shattered into about 700 pieces, and holes put through both my mess tin and water bottle, so you see it was pretty thick. One good thing is they will keep us out of the thick of it for a while now, and that suits me jake, but I wouldn't take the whole lot for the experience I've had, and I got decorated too—GOLD BRAID.

I am glad I didn't try to write this letter to you all or I'd be writing for the duration. Will drop you letters regularly. Don't worry about me, I'll be all right. I'm lucky, I can see that. With lots of love to all, and hoping you are alright and well—don't forget to write.

Lovingly, Jack"—May 2 1917

Another almost full-frontal description of combat was sent about two weeks before the end of the war, when Jack was writing from hospital in England. The Spanish flu was raging and quarantines were in place throughout much of the world. Jack caught the virus and survived.

"Dearest Mayden,
Here's a scribble for you, Moth, Aunt I., Nettie, Susan, Graham, Jum, Margie, Reg, as a matter of fact, the whole damn family.

Received both your letters, September 14th and 22nd with enclosed snaps. Thanks for both, letters and snaps both fine.

Well here I am still in hospital, but 'marked out', that seems I'm going out sometime inside the next two or three days. Feel a whole lot better for my rest, and the grub has been good and the sisters nice, so taking everything into consideration I've done pretty well. The quarantine is still on out there are rumours to the effect that it's to be lifted on Monday, so that seems that I'm away on leave as soon as I get back to the depot. Then I have my leave after I start the O.T.C. and after I finish that, back to France. That's if the war lasts long enough, and if it doesn't it won't hurt my feeling a bit, as I'm not looking for excitement.

Well Mayd here goes, I'll tell you a little about what I've been
doing since I went back off leave in July. Well the night I arrived back
about July 25th after a 4-day trip up from the base, I reported to our
transport lines, the Battn. was in the lines to the right of Arras, so I
went up with the rations and reported back to the Company about
1:30 a.m. and was greeted with 'Hello Stratford just the man we're
looking for, want one more man for a raid tomorrow night', so I says,
'that's me.' The two companies supplying the raiding party were in
supports and the other two companies were in the line. There was
'no man's land' on this part of our line about 1200 yards across, and
the raiders were going out the night before and lay just outside the
German wire all day until 9 p.m. the next night, when our barrage was
to go up. First a smoke screen and then H.E. and overhead, and our
being over in front of his wire we were under his S.O.S. line before it
started. Well the raiders had gone up so I had to go up on my own,
and believe me I had to travel to make it before daylight.

We laid there all day and it poured rain, and at 9 p.m. up she went
and over we go, nothing much more to tell about, we were back and
the all clear was up by 10 p.m. We got 30 odd prisoners and had only
1 casualty, slightly wounded. A pretty successful raid, but believe me
the waiting on zero hour, and the conditions under which we waited
weren't all they were cracked up to be. We couldn't move or smoke
nor speak nor sleep, nor anything until zero. Then everything went up
together, and we walked and smoked and talked and scrapped all at
one time. Well, we settled down then and held the line until about the
end of the month, and one night the Imperials come in, unannounced,
and relieved us, and then we go in buses and got back, then we'd have a
ride on the broad gauge, then a ride in buses, then another march, then
another march, always at night and all night. Well by August 7th we
were in the wilderness, but where we didn't know.

However it turned out that we were in front of Amiens, a few kilo-
meters from where Joe was buried. I tried to get over to see his grave
but I couldn't get away, as we were to go over the next day, August 8th.
We were shown airmen's photos of the ground we were to go over and

everything was explained, and we moved up to our assembly position
that night after midnight, and at zero hour away we went, infantry,
tanks, aeroplanes, cavalry, transport, artillery and everything. Oh,
Lordy, Oh Lordy! You never saw anything like it in your life, and I can't
tell you what it was like, nor no one else can. I'd go back and do it over
ten times though, just for the fun of it.

Well old dear the 1st Division made a record, and the 10th Battn
had the final objective to take and I was with the 1st platoon to gain
the objective so saw some things worth doing, and seeing. 8 miles
deep (the way the crow flies) in 8 hours, taking prisoners at the rate of
30 per minute. This record has not been equaled by our Allies or the
enemy since the war started, so you see we did two things that day.
The Division on our right was an hour and a half behind us, and the
one on our left was 6 hours later. That night we could see Fritz bringing up re-enforcements, and the F.G.H. came up and dismounted and
came into the line with us. I met lots of officers and men who knew
Joe and we had some great old chats. As we were in the country that
they and Joe scrapped in before.

The next day at noon the 2nd Division and cavalry went through
us, and relieved us. This picture I'll never forget, as we were in a position there we could see for miles, and the way the infantry and cavalry
went through, shells breaking, men and horses dropping, our men
going ahead and Fritz prisoners coming back, ambulances, artillery,
tank etc. moving up—by Jove it was some sight, and there'll never
be another like it. We moved out that afternoon and over to our left
flank and went over there three times in the next week. Went through
and relieved the P.P.C.L.I.'s once. Well we came back from there and
went back to Arras and in and over on September 2nd. This was a
tougher scrap than the 8th August and we killed lots more Germans
and captured more stuff, but it took us 3 days to go the same distance
we went in 8 hours down south, but we got there just the same. We
were in that trip 8 days and three time over the top, then we came out
and had two week's rest and back again into Cambrai. This was a hell
of a scrap, I was in for 7 days and over the top 3 times, and left the

Battn in supports, and very much under strength. Gee, I'm about the oldest man in the battn now, and when I left there was hardly a man outside the O.C. and a few of H.Q. officers that I knew, and I went all through the three scraps without a scratch. Pretty lucky or I miss my guess. I didn't bother much the first two scraps but that last Cambrai show I sure did think at times that my number was up, but here I am you see, all in one piece and going strong.

Your loving bro. Jack"

These monologues are from a man who played a minor part in a monster war and then returned to the quiet of Canada. Jack's affair with fighting lasted seventeen months. He had had many part-ners, most of whom he outlasted. There is no way of knowing if he remembered any of the men he'd fought, or even if their eyes had met as they struggled. The thirty-one-year-old on the cottage steps had been "busy with his bayonet." The collection of belt buck-les, shoulder straps, buttons and revolvers had been taken from his spent battle partners. Stored in his kit bag, those souvenirs were his scrapbook of the war and of his desire to get even for the loss of his brothers. From time to time lighter items were mailed back to the family, but whether they were offered as evidence or curiosities, I cannot tell.

"Am sending Margie some souvenirs . . . my score with the Bosh is just about even now old dear, and if I happen to get away one of these days to Blighty I'll be able to go with a pretty clear conscience."

His affairs were with partners, but some were not. If there was no partner, then the affair was with fate. He wondered what had determined the speed of a shell casing fragment that had flown at him during an artillery bombardment, and which could have killed him, since it hit the back of his head so perfectly in the gap beneath his helmet.

The "anger of the guns" also sent shells set to detonate *above* the ground, spraying fate in all directions through swarms of iron fragments, each of which could deliver a bump, a deformity or a grave. It was all a matter of odds. Jack's life thread had been repeatedly blown and twisted about in that murderous casino. He'd been tossed in the air, concussed, hit by shrapnel, his equipment had holes torn through it, his rifle had been shattered—yet he'd survived.

Nine months after leaving the battlefields, he sits pensive in the sun by his sister Mayden's side. Of the three former soldiers in the tableau, only Jack had fully lived out his consent to the "unlimited liability" that armies demand from their recruits—namely their agreement in advance to accept possible dismemberment or death. Jack's combat friends, if they were alive, had by then dispersed. The unhappy husband in the army jacket had been taken prisoner by the Germans in his *first* engagement, so it was unlikely that he knew the intensity and euphoria of Jack's war. Jack's brother Harold never even got to a battlefield, because he had been invalided back to Canada with lung disease, brought on by spending a British winter in army tents. Jack's experiences could hardly have been understood by those who had never been there.

This is some of what I hear in the 1919 photograph. Jack's letters speak of the sights and sounds of his war but never the *smell* of it. Words cannot capture that. Only those who have experienced it can know. It's much like what a former astronaut told me of the moment after the International Space Station's airlock door closed behind a crew member coming in from maintenance work on the outside of the ISS—the smell of space. Unknowable if you've not experienced it.

Jack's cousin Margaret—the woman in the broad-brimmed hat—leans towards him as if *she* understands his war. Margaret was a nurse and her monologues (there is a sixth booklet of her letters) are about the medical battles, the nineteen-hour days in the operating theatre and the thousands of wounded who were wheeled before her, some with injuries beyond imagining. As head operating-room nurse in military hospitals in England and France, she'd known the smell, both literally and figuratively. Her aprons marked with blood, she'd stood on the stone floor and watched the knives and skills of her surgeons trying to turn back the fates, the guns and the infections. She had most likely gagged at the smell of the gas gangrene, emitted by the bacteria that could breed in the deep wounds.

In the sun on the cottage steps, Margaret and Jack must have been aware that they were familiar with what the others weren't. Their "outside" war had ended on November 11, 1918, but their interior war lived on whenever the normality of civilian life was not noisy enough to block it out. None of us will know what dreams may have awoken them or what images nested in their minds to be set off by a sight, sound or smell. As with the intimacy of any affair, they probably never spoke of the nightmares. But Margaret had a camera that would deliver me a gift I would receive decades after her death.

The tyranny of the day-to-day living creates an almost impenetrable membrane against our apprehension of the intimacy of any supremely violent human activity. But unless we acknowledge it, we may keep repeating it.

Leaving aside the strained marriage of the unhappy husband, I wondered what beaux or female friends might be missing from the photo. Jack was of average height with thinning hair, and in his late twenties when he did most of his fighting. When he shipped to France, he had left behind neither wife nor girlfriend, and his letters never mention romantic attractions while he was away. Joe, his cavalry officer brother who sported a waxed mustache, wrote of the "Queens" (French, Belgian and British women) he had met and adored. He was delighted to encounter pretty ladies who couldn't speak English, since it meant sitting very close together while looking things up in his translation book. Seeing French women on beaches in skin-tight bathing suits was another ode to joy for Joe. But he had been killed the year before the shutter clicked.

Jack's younger brother Art wrote of an exchange in Africa with his corporal Chapuchapu about possibly sharing multiple wives, but then some of Art's letters engaged in mischief. Only once does Jack speak of wanting to find someone to marry. After the war, at the sanatorium in Gravenhurst, he met and married Florence Kelly, one of his caregivers. But the marriage was short since he died within three years. In 1917, at twenty-nine, he'd written his mother that his hair was going grey, and of how soon after George's death he had been able to travel up the line to see where his little brother's affair with fighting had ended. What words do you choose in order not to bring more grief to your mother?

"Have just returned from a visit to George's unit where I found out about poor old George . . . It seems pretty rotten luck, as Capt Little put it, that he should go so far and then get it where and when he did. They had been up in the line three days and been through one of the worst bombardments they had ever experienced and everything went fine and things were comparatively quiet, about an hour before they were to be relieved on their last trip in Belgium, George who was evidently in charge of the Company, was up on top arranging guides for the relief, when a whiz-bang came over and got him, and he was killed instantly, which is something to be thankful for, as I would hate to think he had been wounded and probably buried alive in the mud. The conditions were such that they were unable to bring his body out, so they buried him just back of the line. One of his brother officers has full particulars, location etc. of the grave and is forwarding same to Joe.

Everyone I spoke to had a good word to say for poor old Geordie, and it was quite easy to see that he was liked and respected by everyone that knew him.

These are just a few rough facts, Mother dear, and pretty crudely put together, but Joe will be able to give you more detail as he will go into things more thoroughly than I did—I was only speaking with the officers for a few minutes while the Battn was on the move, and there were things I forgot to ask I wanted to know.

Capt. Little asked me to come over and have dinner with him and the officers who were with Geordie the night that he was killed. But I don't think I'll go, it's bad enough over here as it is, and everybody is kept pretty busy thinking about themselves, so I don't think I'll bother these fellows. They are all strangers to me, so I guess I will keep away . . . Am enclosing Geordie's last letter to me, and pass, which I used this morning."

Captain Little probably didn't tell Jack the details that I would discover decades later, namely that his brother had been buried for ten minutes, dug out alive, then carried by a fellow soldier for at least another ten minutes to the medical dressing station, in a disused machine-gun emplacement called a pillbox, by which time the last light had disappeared from George's eyes. So the affair had not ended instantly.

There is a chance that Captain Little *did* tell Jack, who then chose *not* to tell his mother, but I can't really believe that. What would be the point? Quick deaths were desired by combatants and a compassionate fiction told to families at home. I know it took at least ten minutes to carry the dying George to see a medical officer in the concrete pillbox, because I timed it. On a trip to Belgium I located where the front line had been on November 17, 1917, just north of the town of Passchendaele. That was where my great-uncle had been buried by the "Minnie" fired from a German trench mortar, much like the one in front of my school. I found the pillbox's location with help from researchers at the local museum. So, with a friend draped over my shoulder, I struggled along the route. I felt it was the least I could do.

Three weeks later Jack wrote again to his mother.

"The mention of poor old Geordie in your letter makes the whole thing seem like a dream to me. I only wish it were, and I'll be glad when all the letters from Canada, written previous to your knowing the news, have been received. Mother dear, you don't know how thankful we should be that poor Geordie was spared any suffering. The stories from Belgium of the exposure and suffering would make your blood run cold, and in lots of cases where the wounded are unable to get out themselves, they lay in the mud and eventually die of exposure. Thank God that poor Geordie didn't get any of that, but that he was killed instantly.

It does seem tough luck that Geordie should get hit as he did when everything was quiet and just before they were relieved, and then again, considering everything we have been pretty lucky to get through this far without getting worse than we have. I only wish I could have got it instead of Geordie."

George was the first whose odds came up short, and Joe lost his luck five months later. The empty places on the top step in the photo belong to them.

"I only wish I could have got it instead of Geordie."

A sentence can sit on the surface of a letter like the tip of an iceberg, while the thought that drove the typist's fingers remains in the waters below. Little in Jack's letters unsettles me as much as this sentence, and I believe it also troubled Mayden. She had typed out hundreds of letters and made few mistakes, but her fingers slipped on this sentence. She stumbled on the words "got it." Mayden's typed pages of Jack's letters are the only versions that now exist because most of the originals have since been lost. Another tragedy. Yes, conducting forensics on your great-aunt's stenographic skills seems odd, but I am certain that Jack wrote "got it," but what Mayden *keyed* was "for ir."

"I only wish I could have for ir instead of Geordie."

Three times in five key strokes her fingers slipped to the left. Was it merely the speed of her typing or was that a moment of inattention as she reflected on the words "got it"—distracted by the thought of her tall brother George who'd been killed and her other brother Jack who wished *he* had been instead. Of those gathered in the 1919 tableau, Mayden and Jack sit the closest, their shoulders almost overlapping.

The monologues of the letters refer to fate but almost never to fear. Well, in addition to a hesitancy to describe sexual encounters, would *you* tell your mother your fears about fighting? No, especially while serving in armies that prided themselves as organizations that turned boys into men. But again Jack is an exception, describing how before his baptism in battle, he had been shaking so badly that he couldn't hold a match to light his cigarette. Fear, like the army's unlimited liability clause, was part of the job but never meant to be worn as part of the uniform. Fate was another matter, and soldiers had no reluctance referring to the casino of their odds. They even made up a marching song about it set to the tune of "Auld Lang Syne."

> *We're here because we're here because we're here because we're here,*
> *We're here because we're here because we're here because we're here.*

In the spring of the final year of the war, fate was on Jack's mind when writing Mary Elizabeth.

"The big feature is to forget. It's a great old war all right and sometimes it makes you wonder how you ever got through some of the places you've been in, and I'm commencing to think there's more than luck on your side when you do. But that is one of the worst things you can do out here is to think, the big feature is to forget.

A letter a couple of days ago from Aunt Isabel brought me the sad news about poor Joe. It is tough Mother dear and you and the dear ones at home will have all my sympathy and I hope that you won't fret or worry too much. Things like this must almost be expected. The main thing is that men who give their lives in scraps, like the one F.G.H. were in don't realize anything, but are just conscious of the roar and din of the battle, and when the end comes it is instantaneous.

I went to church parade Sunday [and] also took communion, and thought a lot about you, all day, knowing you would be going to early communion. The next day we went up the line and I did a lot of thinking that day too. I wish you could see the country, not the war, it's simply beautiful. Every shade of green that you can imagine and everything so fresh. Some change from the mud scenes we have been used to. We don't really see the best of it either, as we don't get far enough from the line, but even No Man's Land is green in spots."

And to his aunt Isabel Osbourne in England and her daughter, Margaret:

"Personally I'm satisfied with my lot, and I don't care what happens, so long as I push enough of the Boche over the divide ahead of me, at the same time there isn't a man in the whole army that wants to get through O.K. more than I do, and I'll make it too old dear, so don't worry. Don't worry about the German gas old dear, it is darn uncomfortable stuff to have to put up with, but our masks are good and we have very few casualties from it that aren't due to carelessness. I'm just afraid that you will worry about me, and it makes me hate the line.

Gee, but Fritz nearly got my measure last trip up Margie, he put a big boy right in beside me, but as luck would have it, it came from a long distance and I heard it just in time to leap. It pitched in some loose dirt not more than 15 feet from me, and went down so deep before it detonated that when it did go up, concussion, shrapnel and everything went straight up in the air, and all I got was a couple of bumps from falling chalk. I'll bet you would have laughed if you could have seen me. I had my tin lizzie strapped on my shoulder and I was trying to get it on before the lumps came down, I darn near strangled myself, but I didn't get Lizzie where I wanted her, but no lumps fell on my accumulation of intelligence so it didn't matter. Old Fritz evidently got his eye on us and believe me, he almost wore my stomach out before we got under cover."

The armies that had been caught in the chokehold of the trench system's stalemate for almost four years finally broke free in 1918. Jack wrote of his battalion's advances in the war's last hundred days. It is a pleasure to hear him share his euphoria with his mother about beating the Germans, beating the odds and defying the army censors, who wouldn't allow information about battles to be included in letters home.

"Everything is going much as usual over here and we have been having some of the most glorious weather and scrapping you can imagine. Gee but we did tangle with the Hun a couple of times. One scrap we had not long ago our Battalion, about 700 strong, went in and in about 8 hours had our objective, killing over 600 Huns, taking over 700 prisoners, capturing over 200 machine guns and 22 field guns and other war arms and material which they didn't count. Our casualties were under 300 and 30 some odd killed. That's what I call hooking one on Fritz, what do you think? The censor may not like this, but it's the truth and it's too good to keep, so there you are, if I go to the clink for it.

I sometimes wish I could get sick and go to hospital for a rest, but I can't so there you are. I'm a healthy brute I am. Well Moth dear this will be all for now. Will write again in a day or two. Take good care of yourself and don't worry about me or anything."

And the day before his thirtieth birthday, just weeks before the war's end, Jack writes:

"Well here I am again, and still going strong. Tomorrow will be my birthday and I guess I'll have to celebrate it in hospital, but not in bed. I beat them to it and got up to-day and am up to stay. Had a go at that darn Spanish Flu and was pretty groggy for a few days, but am all O.K. again and will be out of here in a day or two and then I go on leave. The flu did me more good than harm I think, as I got a lot of gas and

stuff off my neck, lungs and stomach, and outside of being a little weak
I'm as fit as a fiddle again."

On the final day of the war he wrote to Mary Elizabeth. Jack
had survived, he'd recovered from the influenza and, like hundreds
of thousands of other soldiers, was waiting in a military camp in
England for transport to Canada. Ten weeks later he was home.

"Well Moth dear, this will be my last letter from this side. Don't worry
if you don't hear from me for some time as I can't say for sure when we
sail, and perhaps we'll get a good fast boat and perhaps not. Will try to
wire just as soon as we land . . . If I don't make it home by Christmas
Moth dear here's wishing you all, Aunt I., Marg., Nettie, Jumbo and
the family a Merry Christmas, and I'll see you shortly afterwards.

Your loving son, Jack"

CHAPTER 4

CLIMBING THE CLASS SYSTEM—BUT MADE EQUAL AT THE END

George (Geordie) Stratford, 1917

George fought first as a private, then a corporal and was promoted to lieutenant before being killed by a "Minnie." The
army had accepted my great-uncle's application for a commission in December 1916, and after a training course, Geordie moved
up the ladder to officer class—the territory of Britain's ruling elites,
who assumed that officers should be from the *upper* class, since being
of "better stock" meant they would be born leaders. Not true and
not good.

George's promotion *did* mean more pay, more responsibility, a new uniform and an opportunity to send a new photo to his mother. The Stratfords lived in Brantford, Ontario, and considered themselves upper middle class—at least, a photo of their 1910 Christmas dinner shows them in formal dress, with the men in starched shirt fronts. George, Jack and Harold had enlisted as privates while Art and Joe joined the army as officers. The Great War would become a watershed of sorts between the Old and New Worlds, between the entrenched powers of the privileged class and the growing appetite for more equality. The war would help bring about the collapse of empires and the fall of the royal houses of Germany, Russia, Austria and Turkey. Britain's monarchy survived, yet the faith of the common people in the leadership of the landed gentry suffered a social gassing from which it has never really recovered.

The crumbling of the old (mainly European) social order also influenced what we defined as wars and our attitude towards the dead that resulted from them. Most Canadians probably regard Canada's military past with respect—made easier by the fact that it seemed we always won. And indeed, we did make significant contributions to the twentieth century's two world wars. All well and good. But I know of no memorials for the roughly 130 Canadians killed while fighting with American forces in the war in Vietnam. Their history is not taught, nor is it mentioned on November 11; it is excluded from what we consider our military past. And where are the names of the perhaps seven hundred Canadians killed in the Spanish Civil War in the late 1930s, the first of Canada's citizens to face down the fascists?

The assumption that we have *always* commemorated those who died in battle is not really true. Our armies only began to acknowledge fallen foot soldiers as individuals just over a hundred years ago when my great-uncles were fighting in France and Belgium. Before that, officers were remembered and enlisted men basically were not. Before the First World War, framing and building our nation's war memories were activities of Canada's ruling class. Our hierarchy comes in part from having been governed for centuries by British monarchs and their representatives, governors general who came from the manor houses of Britain's landed aristocracy. Now, thankfully, the GGs *are* Canadian and their power is restricted to "asking" the leader of the party that receives the most votes in an election to form the government and to sign into law bills passed by our parliament.

Before 1914, class divisions continued even after death. Slain officers often received memorials in churches or monuments in cities, but the working-class rank-and-file soldiers were basically forgotten. General Wolfe's body was carried from the Plains of Abraham, packed in rum (some say salt) and then shipped back to Britain, where he got a monument in London's Westminster Abbey, a statue in a park in Greenwich, a stained-glass window in the English church where he was baptized, an island named after him in Ontario and a painting in our National Gallery in Ottawa. *No one* remembered the hundreds who were killed with him in that 1759 battle and were shovelled into mass graves. Two hundred and fifty years later, some of their bones were located by accident when Quebec City was doing water main work. Disposing of soldiers' bodies, as well as our memories of them, was a matter of class. British officers got their names and service records published each year in books called the *Army Lists* while the military registered rank-and-file soldiers primarily as numbers. Regiments began making lists of wounded or dead foot soldiers only because officers needed to know how many men were available for battle the next day.

But at the time of the Great War, social consciousness was growing. The sheer number of casualties challenged the customary disregard for the deaths of traditionally working-class troops. Remember that, centuries ago, the men who carried pikes and halberds were the property of the dukes in whose regiments they served. The legacy of the ownership of humans by other humans doesn't vanish overnight. It lingers even today. Social and democratic movements in Europe and North America began to break the class frame that had locked that legacy of ownership in place. The shift really began with the French Revolution, when France's *people's* army was composed of citizens of the new republic rather than foreign mercenaries and/or peasants from the estates of French aristocrats. But the idea of *equality* of the war dead really only came of age with the First World War.

My family and millions of others benefited because, no matter their rank, the bodies of our relatives were no longer lowered into mass graves, most of which would have been unmarked. In the Great War, each corpse (if they could find enough of it) was eventually given a plot of earth in a well-cared-for cemetery. By 1918, belief in the privileges of high birth was being worn thin by ideas about the inherent worth of every human life.

The privileged classes, which included the British Army's command staff, were suspicious of social forces that had not only lopped heads off monarchs in France but were also threatening entire power structures, such as in revolutionary Russia. When faced with cataloguing hundreds of thousands of scattered graves of British and Commonwealth soldiers, a British educator, Fabian Ware (he'd tried to join the army but at forty-four was considered too old to fight), proposed a new approach. As the dead were being located and reburied in organized cemeteries, Ware wanted them to lie side by side *as equals*, regardless of rank, race, social status, merit or religion. This proposal caused a fracas in Britain, since it meant doing away with a social frame that had been in place for more than a thousand years: that noble birth brought privileges even in death.

Fabian Ware had become the commander of the Red Cross's mobile ambulance unit that was locating and marking soldiers' graves, most of which were in hasty burial places close to the battlefields or in boneyards outside the back doors of field hospitals. Ware made his suggestion while the Great War was underway and the dead were piling up—close to 400,000 British Commonwealth soldiers had been killed by the end of 1916. Realizing that the ordinary soldier might again disappear from memory, he proposed that in death equality should rule: each body would be named; each would be given an identical headstone; each buried in the vicinity of where they had died, and officers and commoners would lie side by side. And no body would be repatriated home, no matter how wealthy, powerful or privileged the family.

Ware's idea was called "anti-Christian." It was debated in the British Parliament. Some traditionalists objected to history being reframed—or, rather, de-framed. His proposal was a revolution in the politics of war memory. Sir Fabian Ware—yes, he was later knighted for his work—prevailed, and soon grave robbers were at work in soldiers' cemeteries. But it was the desperate rather than the powerful who wanted to repatriate corpses. Thieves with shovels and flashlights were hired by families determined that a lost son or husband be dug up from a cemetery in Belgium or France and brought home.

Local constabularies caught most of the midnight adventurers, but not Canada's determined (some said obsessed) Mrs. Anna Durie of Toronto. On her second attempt in the darkness of a French night, *seven years* after the war, she herself supervised the partial opening of her son's grave and the scraping out of the coffin's contents. Anna Durie then sailed back home with his bits. The Imperial War Graves Commission's report on the exhumation noted that "the coffin was empty with the exception of a few small pieces of bones and some fragments of officer's clothing." So she didn't quite get everything, but the majority of the remains of her son, Captain William Arthur Durie, are now in Toronto's St. James Cemetery.

The historical frame that Sir Fabian did not remove, and which still remains, is that of the victor and the vanquished—you bury your bodies in your cemetery and we'll bury ours in ours. That was the frame I was trying to loosen by having *The World Remembers* display the names of dead soldiers together, no matter their army. Yet even now, more than a century after the fighting stopped and with no one still alive who had a first-hand connection to the war, that frame still retains its emotional steel. There are traditionalists who feel that we honour the fallen *only* by never forgetting who they fought against. To do less would lead to dishonour. Therefore, to recognize the dead of our former enemies (Germany mainly) just as we acknowledge our own would betray our soldiers who sacrificed their lives for _____, and here you can insert any number of nouns: justice, freedom, peace, democracy, security, patriotic duty, et cetera.

We can argue about what Canadians *did* die for in the 1914–1918 war, but it certainly wasn't democracy or the freedom of Canada or Britain. Traditionalists insist—and there is steel in their view—that we must *never* honour the enemy's dead. Ever. In a way they have a point: displaying the names of both victor and vanquished together is absolutely *un*tribal. But tradition can conceal prejudices and impede our progress. We must guard against social signals that perpetuate the divisions among us—including how we conduct ourselves on November 11—particularly if we embed the concepts of identity and dishonour in our framing of remembrance. The dead are dead. They are past caring. It is the living who feel that their beliefs are somehow threatened if we relinquish our differences. Building national identities based on difference has been our habit since the first spear was thrown.

In trying to find a consensus among nations about naming every lost World War I soldier, it was important to know how members of the military regarded the idea. I couldn't ask my father or my great-uncles for their opinions, since they were no more. But when I gave a talk about the possible global commemoration at the Canadian Forces College in Toronto, the audience of officers agreed that now was the time when *everyone* could be named. However, it was a former Italian soldier who put it best. Early in my odyssey to recruit World War I nations for *The World Remembers*, Gianluca Callipari was working the security checkpoint at the Canadian embassy in Rome. I was waiting for a taxi to take me to the technical unit of the Italian President's Council to explore the sources of Italian names. So I asked former Sergeant Callipari what he would think if a new commemoration displayed the names of both victors and vanquished from the First World War. This was his reply:

"When we soldiers are beneath the ground, we are equal. Only the serious people living above the ground make the differences. The dead are the children of the earth, whose parents have no nationality."

CHAPTER 5

POWER IN THE ROWBOAT

my father in 1919 on a Muskoka dock

The First World War was the landscape of my father's childhood. In the summer of 1919 his soldier-uncles were at the family's rented cottage along with his bow-tied cousin who, having got his hands on Jack's German gun, then rowed nine-year-old Woodburn Thomson out one morning to fire it before breakfast.

In Wood's (my dad's nickname) world, Germany was the villain, England stood at the centre of civilization, and Canada had
contributed to the glory of the British Empire by helping it win the
Great War. In 1918 the first wave of the Spanish flu pandemic arrived,
Wood's school was shut down and everyone wore masks. But by
November 11 of that year, the war was won, the masks were off, a holiday was declared, the family car was draped with the biggest Union
Jack possible, and Wood and his parents drove down King Street in
the greatest celebration in Toronto's history.

He'd been five when he stood with his mother and father in the
crowds at Toronto's Union Station to wave goodbye to his uncles
George, Joe and Harold and the other soldiers as they boarded trains
for Quebec City and Halifax, where ships would take them to Britain.
With his mother and his Aunt Mayden, Wood had knelt at Grace
Church on-the-Hill in Toronto, where his uncles were blessed before
they went to war. Victory Bond posters in the Thomson home portrayed valiant Canadian soldiers and dastardly Germans—it was the
Hun who had used *poison* gas. He saw his mother go quiet whenever
letters from Belgium and France arrived. His uncles, while in training
or transit, visited their house and were part of his life.

Joe was the cavalry officer with the waxed mustache and sword
who had enlisted with the Brant Dragoons and later transferred to
the Fort Garry Horse. My father, eager to swing his uncle's sword,
pursued his younger brother round the house, leaving nicks on doors
that the frightened Garth had slammed behind him.

His tall uncle George was studying at the University of Toronto
and came for home-cooked meals. Perched on the university student's
shoulders, Wood would have been well over seven feet, dangerous in
doorways, but his uncle's dipped knees at the last second saved the day
for excited nephews. Geordie was also part clown and would pretend
to be Charlie Chaplin, the silent-film funny man whom Wood had
seen at the cinema. At five, you recall impressions more than details.

My father wouldn't have known his uncles Jack and Art until
after the war. In 1910, the year Woodburn was born, Jack had moved

to Calgary to work as a bookkeeper and Art was a cadet at the Royal
Military College in Kingston. Art Stratford's blue and red RMC uniform was a boy's dream. Soon after war was declared, Art had shipped
directly to the fighting in Belgium, but his photo was on a table in the
front hall, showing his cadet's cap at a rakish angle. My father's uncles
were a spirited bunch, or so he told me.

Horseplay was a family habit and when the uncles appeared the
games began. Being the first of his generation, Wood received the bulk
of their attention, but pranks didn't end with nephews. My grandmother Helen, the uncles' big sister, had attended finishing school
in Switzerland and wanted a respectable life. She got that when she
married Robert Thomson, my grandfather, and became a banker's
wife. Art, on finally returning from war in October 1919 from his
posting in Tanganyika (then named German East Africa), had, as was
his habit, informed *no one* of his arrival. After disembarking from the
train at Union Station, he went into the men's washroom and took
off his army uniform. Unlike his older brother Jack, Art hadn't collected guns and bits of German uniforms, but instead brought back
the traditional warrior dress of the Black South African soldiers with
whom he had served.

Amongst the substantial sinks and urinals that resembled vertical
bathtubs in Protestant Toronto's railway station, Art stripped down,
painted his face and ribs and donned his Zulu warrior outfit. Armed
with a hide shield and his short stabbing assegai spear, he took the
streetcar up Spadina Avenue to his sister Helen's house. Again unannounced, he slipped in through the kitchen door just as the meal was
about to be served. In the confusion and alarm, Helen dropped the
dinner, or so the story was told.

I knew Art only as an elderly man in his final years as a gold pros-
pector and fishing guide near Missanabie, north of Sudbury. As he
grew frailer, he'd come south to Toronto for Christmas. The following
letter has been read many times in our family. Art had begun his war
in Belgium and wrote about the Christmas Day greetings and dares he
shared with the enemy after the first four months of fighting. He and

most of his men had climbed out of their trenches and met the German soldiers halfway. They'd spent the afternoon talking and singing.

"About noon on Christmas Day one of the Germans, they can nearly all speak English, shouted over 'Merry Christmas' and of course we shouted back, 'Merry Christmas.' 'Come over here.' one of them called. 'You come over here' we answered. 'We'll come half way if you come the other half,' replied the German. So a couple of our men stood up in the trench and the Germans did the same. Pretty soon we were scrambling towards one another, without rifles of course, and we met halfway.

Both sides were a little shy at first but we soon warmed up and shook hands and laughed and joked. Soon one of them said 'You sing us a song and we'll sing you one'. So we gave them 'Tipperary' which they liked very much. They sang us a couple of songs, I don't know what they were, but they sounded all right. It was rather an experience. The Germans told our men frankly that they didn't mind charging the French, but they charged our lines, 'with much less gusto'. The men had a huge time with the Germans and all were mighty sorry when dusk began to fall and we thought it time to get back to our lines. All this rather helped pass away the day out here. We had great fires in the trenches and spent the remainder of the evening singing. The Germans told us they were fed up with the war. I did get mournful a couple of times on Christmas. I just couldn't help it when I thought of how far I was from home and my loved ones. Oh mush."

At four years old, Woodburn probably didn't appreciate everything that Art's letter implied, but the Christmas truce in No Man's Land became part of the lore of his warrior uncles.

As I mentioned earlier, Wood's Uncle Jack had gone to Calgary to work as bookkeeper for the Metal Shingle and Siding Company. After he joined the army in Alberta, his troop train had routed through Ottawa on its way to Halifax for the voyage to Britain. Wood was not part of the family's trip to the nation's capital to bid his uncle farewell. But he did see the battle trophies as they began to arrive in the mail, and told tales at school about the German buttons that Jack was sending especially to him.

Wood watched the war through his child's eyes. His uncles' letters—at least the parts suitable for small boys—were read aloud by his parents. He helped his mother pack parcels of cake and heavy socks to mail to her brothers. He was seven when he saw her go quiet after the telegram arrived announcing the death of the Charlie Chaplin man, his tall Uncle George. He watched his mother raise money for the war effort through Victory Bond drives and helped carry the rolls of campaign posters that said "How Can I Serve Canada?" Soldiers in kilts stood grinning in fields of poppies, holding up four fingers and saying "*Doing My Bit – FOUR YEARS – Do Yours, BUY Victory Bonds.*" In another poster Germans in the conning tower of their submarine were firing at a drowning Canadian nurse held in the arms of a defiant soldier, while both of them drifted helpless in the sea. The nurse's hair had spread out on the water like a heroine from an Arthurian legend. My father would not have understood the poster's subtitle, "Kultur vs. Humanity."

Just before Wood's eighth birthday, the family home went silent a second time. The cavalry uncle with the waxed mustache had been killed. Later they learned that Joe been awarded the Military Cross. A newspaper reported "*CAPT. JOSEPH STRATFORD KILLED— Second of Five Sons of Mrs. Stratford to Pay Supreme Penalty.*" About that time Woodburn was probably given his first lead soldiers: Grenadier Guards with red coats, galloping dragoons and a Boer War ambulance set. There were wounded men on stretchers, hands casually behind their heads because nurses with small red mouths were watching over them. Wood played reckless games of war on the carpet and the dragoons' necks began to be broken.

Victory in 1918 sparked a fierce yet relieved patriotism in Canada. Buildings in Toronto were decorated with bunting and flags. In some parts of the city the German kaiser was burned in effigy. My father couldn't know that those victory celebrations would begin a memorializing (his future son would term it a "forgetting") that many would later call a catastrophe. But for the eight-year-old riding with his parents in the car on King Street that mid-November day, there was no greater pride than being part of the invincibility of the British Empire. Like the military marches played at home on a windup gramophone, the war had walked with Wood step by step as he was growing up. He cheered amidst the horns, church bells, noisemakers, joy-seekers and shouting. Maybe he remembered his uncles. And then everyone sang:

> *Rule Britannia! Britannia rule the waves*
> *Britons never, never, never shall be slaves.*

That victory became the backdrop for my father's future. War with lead soldiers continued being played on carpets, because no one expects eight-year-olds to grasp that it is our appetite for aggression that attracts many of us to the games we play. At thirteen, his mother's youngest brother Rick visited to tell them of his recent journey to Europe and his failure to find tall George's burial place in Belgium. To this day, George's body has *never* been found. And Rick then presented the family with photos he'd taken of meeting a strange woman in France who had become a second mother to Joe, who had been billeted in her house for nearly two months in 1916. Following Rick's visit to Madame Mialaret, the Frenchwoman had written Mary Elizabeth, Joe's *"vraie maman,"* saying that it was as if *he* had also been *her* son and that she could only weep for the loss of one who was indeed goodness itself. Her request was for Madame Stratford to send her a photograph of Joe, *"que je conserverai toujours."*

The next year, when he was fourteen, Wood attended the dedication of the Soldiers' Tower at the University of Toronto, a monument to students who had studied there and lost their lives, such as his Uncle George. By the base of the memorial's forty-four-metre tower was a verse from the English seventeenth-century poet Milton, suggesting how mourners should view the deaths.

Nothing is here for tears, nothing to wail
Or knock the breast, no weakness, no contempt,
Dispraise, or blame,—nothing but well and fair,
And what may quiet us in a death so noble.

George's name, together with 627 others, was carved into the stone beside Milton's words. The fact that the war may have been a costly mistake was not referenced in the Ontario lieutenant-governor's remarks at the dedication ceremony. The LG's choice of words, about possessing freedom by being ready to defend it, was part of the victory rhetoric intended to help the tidying up after the war.

"To the glorious memory of the students of this University who fell in the Great War 1914–1918. Take these men for your examples. Like them, remember that prosperity can only be free, that freedom is the sure possession of those alone who have the courage to defend it."

My father was seventeen when he attended the burial of his Uncle Harold, who had died in the sanitorium in Gravenhurst. Six years after that it was the funeral of Jack, who'd sent back the guns, German buttons and belt buckles. But by then it was 1933 and my father was studying at Cambridge University in Great Britain, where he and many others wondered when the next war with Germany might begin.

⸺⸺

The summer of 1919 was probably the first time Wood got to know Jack. Perhaps he was surprised that the uncle who had done so much fighting was in fact soft-spoken, not at all like the grinning soldier in the Victory Bonds poster. His mother had told him why Jack wheezed when he breathed. Wood knew some of the stories about his uncle's battles and the prisoners he had taken, since he had told them in school when he showed off the German army buttons that he'd been sent. He also knew that Jack and Harold were patients at the sanatorium in Gravenhurst.

Around the cottage dinner table that summer, the conversation was most likely about jobs, mosquitoes, the Bolshevik revolution in Russia and the Winnipeg General Strike. My father probably wanted to hear more about the buttons and battles, and when everyone was swimming, he looked for the scars from the wounds on Jack's elbow and the back of his head. Then there was the 9mm Steyr semi-automatic that his uncle had brought with him in his bag to the cottage.

Once out of its German army holster, it was three pounds of steel that smelled of gun oil. It lay beside a small box of bullets on the seat of the rowboat. The pigeon-toed cousin from the photo on the steps had decided that he and the nine-year-old Woodburn would do some shooting before breakfast. The others would still be in bed, and it was too early for anyone else to be out on the lake.

Holding your first gun was a way station on the road to manhood. Firing your first gun, usually a hunting rifle and usually in target practice, was a baptism for boys who wanted the power to make tin cans dance. But to grip a trophy taken from a surrendering German soldier in the Kaiser's army—who perhaps had fired at defenceless nurses in the sea—went far beyond playing war by lining up painted lead men on carpeted floors.

It took an adult's strength to slide back the mechanism that cocked the 1916 Steyr and allowed it to be loaded. The adolescent cousin pressed the bullets down into the magazine clip and put one in the breech. The heat of the day was not yet upon them and the lake was empty of swimmers. The clip held eight bullets. The cousin fired first, no doubt aiming at imaginary Huns lurking in the woods on the opposite shore. The shots echoed off the rocks and travelled back over the water. The rowboat rocked slightly. Firing in a bay meant that each squeeze of the trigger brought sequences of echoes as the concussion met rocks farther and farther away. Wood looked to see if any of the spent shell casings ejected after each shot had landed in the rowboat. *Souvenirs*. The cousin looked back to ensure no one was emerging from the cottage to stop them, and then cocked the Hun's gun and handed it to my dad.

That summer my godmother Margaret had already been busy with bandages, repairing the pigeon-toed cousin's foot. He might have stepped on a fish hook. Someone snapped a picture. The gauze Margaret wrapped it in was substantial enough to indicate that the cut was serious. The swimmers had gathered, intent on the injury being attended to by a *military* nurse. Perhaps he'd stepped on a nail? Perhaps the cousin was accident-prone?

The day you fire a gun, you make a mark on the world. The moment the bullet leaves the barrel, ambiguity vanishes and authority appears. Who has not hungered for certainty? The bullet travels at *your* will, whether striking a lake, a tin can behind a cottage, a deer in your first hunt or a German in your first war.

Wood needed both hands to handle the recoil. He fired and fired until the magazine was empty and figures appeared on the cottage porch. The gunshots, heard through the cabin's walls, had woken Jack, his grandmother, his mother, Mayden, Harold, Margaret Killmaster, the unhappy man from the photo and his wife and their three girls.

As the rowboat returned, Woodburn's grin was that of the kilted soldier in the Victory Bonds poster, intoxicated with having handled power. The Steyr had echoed across the water *and* through the hearts of the family. Boys were expected to be adventurous; bullet holes would be punched in tin cans and there would be hunting in the fall. But it was Jack who, after ensuring that the semi-automatic's chamber was empty and that his war was back in its holster, took Wood and his pigeon-toed cousin for a quiet talk away from all the others.

I remember the Steyr in its battered brown leather case in a bottom drawer in my father's study.

CHAPTER 6

AN ARCHIVE IN MOSCOW

Но кто мы такие, если мы равнодушны к нашему прошлому,
к конфликтам, которые потрясли мир в двадцатом веке?

[But if we are indifferent to the past and the conflicts of the
twentieth century that overwhelmed the world, who are we?]
—from my letter to President Putin

register of the killed, wounded and missing of the Special Unit
of the Izmailovsky Regiment, one of the oldest companies
in the Tsar's Imperial Army

Russian and Serb histories have long been entwined. A month
before proposing *The World Remembers* at the dinner in
Belgrade in 2012, I had spent five days in Moscow, where
I was looking for support to commemorate all the names of the
dead from the Great War. My impressions of Russia had come from

composers, novels and plays. I'd learned about the director Konstantin Stanislavski of the Moscow Art Theatre and had been trained in his acting technique, in which the performer was required to enter the imaginative world of the character. The tragicomedies of Anton Chekhov offered glimpses into the Russian view of life. My father had spent time in the 1920s with the Russian émigré community in Toronto, the "White" Russian families who, having supported the Tsar, had fled the Bolshevik revolution. At nineteen, captured by the emotion he'd felt in their homes, he became infatuated with a young woman—or so the story goes. My father would speak of the singing that took place at the young woman's home in the evenings. The émigré community's influence was undoubtedly why the Don Cossack Choir records were played in our home and perhaps that's why my father bought an accordion. I have a photo of him wearing a Russian wool hat, holding his accordion and sporting a big pretend Cossack mustache. The battered samovar in the background had been a prop in a play my mother had directed at the local community theatre. These memories accompanied me to Moscow.

Before buying my entry visa at the Russian consulate in Toronto (a process conducted like a Cold War leftover), I'd met Russia's ambassador in Ottawa. Georgiy Mamedov heard me out and then politely reminded me, "Robert, you have to understand that our history is complex, very complex." The ambassador told me that the Second World War was referred to as the "Great Patriotic War" and the First World War was a forgotten imperialist adventure that had resulted in revolution, a civil war and then almost seventy years of Communist totalitarianism. Both wars had brought extreme suffering to Russia, a fact rarely acknowledged by the West.

The country's First World War military deaths ranged between one and a half and almost two million. If you include civilians, you add millions more.

These are only estimates, because no one had *ever* counted. Why not? On that visit to Moscow, it appeared that the authorities lacked either the interest or the budget to research the remains of their

1914–1917 military records. The official view was that the war was a tragedy that had left nothing to celebrate. Before my visit I had asked Ambassador Mamedov about the names of their lost soldiers, and he replied that the records of the tsarist Imperial Army would be difficult to locate—*if* they existed at all.

The Russian embassy in Ottawa, like its American counterpart, resembles a fortress. Its heavy steel gate opened only after I had been questioned through intercom and video cameras. Embassy security is usually proportional to the aggressiveness of a nation's foreign policy. Sitting on a large sofa in a cavernous room, Ambassador Mamedov was voluble, while the young military attaché who sat opposite taking notes was not. I was enjoying our conversation about Russia's past, much as I had enjoyed climbing on the German trench mortar in front of my school—*What an enormous piece of utterly foreign yet intriguing history.* I mentioned that I'd been reading Solzhenitsyn's *The Red Wheel: March 1917*, a sprawling novel about the chaos of the revolution. But Mamedov was less enthused, suggesting that Solzhenitsyn's works were not to be trusted.

There had been soldiers in both our families. The ambassador's father and one of his grandfathers had been officers in the White Army, which supported the Tsar. Then the Reds (the Bolsheviks) won the civil war, consolidated their power and ushered in the Soviet Union's totalitarian decades. And what of the Cossacks? I asked. "They fought with the Whites, and so also on the losing side. And also, you should know, a small force of Canadian troops that had been sent to fight the Reds in Siberia." A generation later, before the 1941–1945 war, Mamedov's father had been the Soviet military attaché in Berlin, while his second grandfather was executed by the Soviets after the war. "A complex history," Mamedov continued, and by that he meant both his nation's and his family's. When set against my assumptions of Canada's lightweight past, the enormity of the events in Russia took my breath away. I drank the tea and munched the biscuits that were offered while I mulled over the improbability of my quest to locate the names from the Tsar's Imperial Army. I recalled what the director of

France's 1914–1918 Centenary Commission had told me months earlier: "Robert, you don't really have a project if you do not include Russia."

Georgiy Mamedov and I had reached the point of being personal. He said that I had a "Protestant" approach to the past. I bristled, but he was right, since in contrast to the convulsions of Russia's history, the frame through which I viewed the past had been small, uncluttered, uncontradictory and unambiguous. The ambassador offered that history is an ever-changing series of perspectives and nuances. But he *was* interested in the international commemoration and said he would help me secure meetings with military organizations in Moscow. No doubt he had both political and personal reasons for doing so.

And so I travelled to a country with which we had fought a Cold War for more than forty years. Its history was beyond anything I could imagine. Little wonder that Tolstoy's novel *War and Peace* clocks in at over a thousand pages, and no surprise that Shostakovich's radiant yet grotesque compositions of perseverance and despair are musical landscapes that can overwhelm any sense that individuals matter— much like the Soviet Union's political and security system, in which individual Russian lives had been mere specks.

Our embassy in Moscow connected me with Lomonosov University's history department, and there I pressed them about whether the 1914–1917 records still existed. "Difficult question" was the response. The Russian Red Cross had made lists of the dead, but those had been lost. In the totalitarian years of the Soviet Union, Stalin had ordered an entire World War I hospital cemetery in Moscow destroyed. Also, mass graves from 1914 of more than 160,000 Russian soldiers in East Prussia had also been *disappeared*. The ruling Communist Party had spun the violent chaos of the 1917 rebellion as a glorious workers' revolution. As they did so they were erasing the history of imperial Russia under the tsars, or as one professor put it, "Our national history was brutally interrupted by the Bolsheviks and the West is unconcerned about Russia's part in a forgotten war."

My trip seemed like a fool's errand until Margaret Watts, my contact at the Canadian embassy, located an adjunct of the State

Archive for Military History in a building that appeared to be out of a Tolstoy tale. What I had been told might *not* have survived appeared there. The rundown mansion had once belonged to a Russian aristocrat. In 1917 it had been overrun by revolutionaries, and ever since it had been used for military document storage. From the street it was just another building in need of repair. Margaret, the translator and I were dropped off at an entrance arch that had known better days. "Yes, this is the address," said the driver. A chained dog barked itself to attention—not an uncommon sight, since there are many guard dogs in Moscow. Finding our way through the archway, built to accommodate the nobleman's nineteenth-century horses and carriages, we stood in a deserted courtyard.

Upon ringing a bell, we were ushered into a dim, damp, high-ceilinged entrance hall by two men in blue coveralls. Introductions were made in Russian. Presuming the coveralled men were from maintenance, I nodded hello as my name was referenced, and then they led us up what had been the mansion's grand staircase. In fact, they were the archivists. Electrical wiring, looping along the hallway walls, followed us to their long, narrow and cold office. It was November and a small electric heater was trying hard. The five of us seemed to be the only people in the building.

I explained that we were looking for the names of dead First World War soldiers. Through our translator, the unlikely archivists, Evgeny and Valery, replied, "Yes, war cemeteries had been destroyed and military record-keeping had become chaotic after February 1917." I said that for me it was the people killed who mattered, more than the war's politics or patriotism. I said that those lost soldiers, ignored by history, might be buried a second time by our indifference—which was a bit of a stretch, but the decrepit state of the building was depressing me about the likelihood of ever of finding the names. I was ready to try anything. I proposed that the centenary of the Great War might be our only chance to publicly recognize *each* of those names, thereby briefly bringing them to life. That those soldiers from long ago mattered.

Looking across the language canyon between us, I saw a change
in the pair I'd mistaken for janitors. Comparing notes afterwards,
Margaret and I both noticed that Evgeny Machekin and Valery
Shabanov were no longer "officially" responding to "foreigners'" questions but had instead become personally involved. That Margaret and
I were Canadian meant they must have categorized us as *totally* foreign, a concept not easily grasped by those of us from the West.

The archivists applied no official gloss to the story they began
to tell. This is some of what I remember. "In 1917, because of the
workers' strikes and revolution, the Russian army had become dis-
organized . . . *yes*, historians could *not* agree on a final number of the
war dead . . . *yes*, the first historical books were produced in 1922, but
the revolutionaries used the number of dead as propaganda. . . . *yes*,
in 1922 at a conference in Vienna, the Soviets had exaggerated the
numbers of dead to receive more funding. Some provinces had prepared lists of the dead that were quite accurate . . . for 1917 and 1918
there were absolutely *no* lists of Russian soldiers in Ukraine, Latvia
or Germany, since the revolutionary chaos was at its peak. Military
deaths in Russian hospitals in 1917 had *not* been recorded at all."

Evgeny disappeared for a second and then reappeared with two
volumes from a collection of records from the Tsar's 1914 Imperial
Army. The title (translated) read:

"Register of the Members of the Special Unit of the Izmailovsky
Regiment, Wounded, Injured, Killed and Missing in Action for
the Period from August 20th to October 1st 1914."

They were handwritten and filled with names. The swirling pen-
manship was in Cyrillic. Evgeny told us that they had *perhaps* two
thousand such books, which could mean hundreds of thousands of
names. Turning the pages felt like opening graves. Evgeny continued:
"One in five of the books *might* be missing . . . *yes*, they were all handwritten . . . the existing regimental books that we have, cover only
the years 1914 to 1916, because few had survived the *catastrophe* that

followed . . . or some regiments, mostly from the Ukraine and the Baltic states, *probably all* the books were lost . . . only *common* soldiers' names were written and only because the Tsar's law *commanded* imperial officers to record the names of the injured, the missing and the dead . . . *this* collection of books *might* contain *one million* names."

The building, the archivists and the volumes seemed to be history that had been hibernating. Evgeny became passionate, and the mansion suddenly seemed crowded with ghosts.

Margaret had had the wit to bring a camera and began to take photos. I asked if any duplicate copies of the books existed? Despite his coveralls, Evgeny was a deputy director at the Russian State Archive for Military History. He shook his head saying, "*No*, there was no microfilm, no scans, no photocopies, no digital records." "Only what is here," offered Valery, who was head of the department. A large tiled woodstove that had warmed the nobleman's family in the nineteenth century still provided heat in the twenty-first. Accustomed to the white-gloved protocols of other nations' archives, I noticed Evgeny's un-gloved approach to the *Register of the Members of the Special Unit of the Izmailovsky Regiment*. There was not a standard storage box in sight.

On the wall by Valery's desk was a small painting of the aristocrat in whose house we sat. Beginning to appreciate what we were attempting, Evgeny went on: "In the winter of 1917, many books and other archive materials were *piled up* and used as firewood *in this building* because troops, mainly from Latvia, were billeted here and wanted to keep warm."

The tall tiled stove was just to my right. "After the revolution, pages were *torn out* by Red Army soldiers who wanted to *disappear* their imperial pasts to prevent reprisals against them. They hoped that, without an imperial past, they might be eligible for Soviet land grants." Not only had the Tsar and his family been executed by the revolutionaries, the history they represented had also been silenced.

Evgeny asked us not to use any of the *Soviet* lists presented in Geneva in the 1920s, because they were *propaganda* for extracting more war reparation money from Germany. Indeed, the Soviets had not been the only ones. After the war the French had been tallying up their destroyed barns and dead cows to extract compensation from the defeated Germans, but, as we had just heard, the Bolsheviks had been over-adding dead men. *Archival doping.*

Somewhere in my head the Don Cossacks were singing. Those regimental registers might hold the names of the fathers, brothers and friends of the men whom I'd heard in song in my home. Their choir was composed of men who'd survived both the Great War *and* the Russian civil war and had sung while in internment camps. Perhaps the records my father had played contained a little of the grief for those whose names were in the books before me.

Whatever the total number of lost Russian soldiers—and it was certainly more than one million—it is a number beyond emotional comprehension. We can "think" it with our brains but we cannot see it with our hearts. The number sits as an abstract rather than a reality in our minds, but in Russia's case, the source of this particular sequence of zeros was a sea of human pain. Our humanity may have failed us if we ever say the words "one million dead" without pause.

. . . pause . . .

I returned to my hotel on Moscow's magnificent metro system. The regimental books had excited yet disturbed me. Stalin started building the subways in the 1930s, and there is a grandeur to the design of the stations. However hard I try to wrap my mind around the millions murdered in the past, what of the billions who might perish in a nuclear confrontation of the future? Parts of the Metro's Arbatsko-Pokrovskaya line were constructed during the Cold War and dug seventy metres below the surface. Its designers had Armageddon in mind. How many missiles on how many launching platforms, on land or sea, were at that moment targeted on the city in which I was travelling? The Moscow Metro has stations that can be tightly sealed and serve as shelters.

The Cold War led scientists, including Albert Einstein, to create the Doomsday Clock, to signal their estimate of how close we are to our nuclear finale. In 2022 the Bulletin of the Atomic Scientists set the clock at ninety seconds to midnight, the closest we have *ever* come to the catastrophe. Yet we *don't* wonder. Is it that we just don't want to know? What mental sleight of hand deflects the possibility of such horror? Our military knows. One estimate is that ten to twenty nuclear warheads are targeted on Russia's capital, each with a destructive power twenty-five times that of what was dropped on Hiroshima.

It has been ten years since I met Evgeny and Valery, who, I have been told, are still working in the archives. Following our 2012 conversation at 2-ya Baumanskaya Ulitsa, I sent a letter to President Putin requesting Russia's participation in *The World Remembers*. It went unanswered. There must be a way in which Russia's tragic First World War history might be included in our global commemoration, but the very hot war in Ukraine has been making that impossible.

CHAPTER 7

WAR WOMEN—THE CHEERLEADERS AND NURSES

I s war just a man's game? No, it has never really been that; it's just that many people have chosen to see it that way. In an earlier chapter I hesitantly ushered my great-great-aunt Isabel off the stage, but her heavy heels have been pacing the wings, disapproving of her banishment and miffed that her great-great-nephew should be critical of her British Empire, let alone suspicious of most forms of patriotism. The stage manager has asked her several times to keep the noise down, but she *insists* on being heard. So I now summon her onstage. From the war letters, photos and other family memorabilia piled up backstage, I give you my great-grandmother's sister, Isabel Blanche Osbourne, the aunt of my five great-uncles. Her opening speech is worthy of a newly independent woman from a George Bernard Shaw play.

"Lady A. says there is a Belgian priest here who was bound & gagged while German soldiers brought out the nuns from a convent & outraged them before his eyes! & so on & on, each story worse than the last—do you think there is a God? And the U.S.A.! cowards and poltroons I think—signatories to the Hague convention[2]—and not a word of protest about the awful atrocities, murders and disregard of every law of warfare—Italy too—just as bad—each sitting on the fence, holding back thinking only of themselves and the almighty dollar."

—letter to her sister, winter of 1915

Americans were "cowards and poltroons" because, despite the tales in the press of German atrocities after the Kaiser's army swept through Belgium in the war's opening gambit, it would be another two years before the United States entered the war. Isabel's contempt for Italy, also late to join the fighting, was because that country was unsure whether it would support the British-French alliance or the Austrians and Germans.

Isabel and her family had moved to England a few years before the war began, because her husband's business interests in Britain were

---

2   The Hague Convention of 1899 and later 1907 was an international attempt to address the conduct of war and the protection of civilians and civilian property in wartime. Among the topics agreed to in the Convention were procedures for declaring war, prohibition of the discharge of projectiles or explosives from balloons, and "Use of Projectiles with the Sole Object to Spread Asphyxiating Poisonous Gases."

picking up. *Every* week she wrote to her sister, my great-grandmother Mary Elizabeth Stratford, in Brantford, Ontario. Isabel's teenaged son—the bow-tied boy on the cottage steps—was not yet old enough to follow the drums, but her sister's five sons had either joined or were about to join the army. I can't be sure if Isabel actually believed the rape stories coming out of Belgium or that German soldiers had cut the breasts off Belgian nuns. She probably did. Given the contagion of misinformation infecting our time, we cannot be shocked by theirs. Atrocity propaganda is used because it is effective, in spite of its questionable connection to the truth. Growing up, I'd heard that "Indians" had done unspeakably gruesome things to white settlers, which was why we were justified in conquering the First Nations. And when Iraq invaded Kuwait in 1990, Nayirah al-Sabah testified to the Congressional Human Rights Caucus:

"I saw Iraqi soldiers come into the hospital with guns. They took the babies out of the incubators, took the incubators and left the children to die on the cold floor. It was horrifying. I could not help but think of my nephew, who was born premature and might have died that day as well."

It was later revealed that fifteen-year-old Nayirah was the Kuwaiti ambassador's daughter. What she described, she had not seen. She had been used by an American public relations firm, Hill & Knowlton, to give false testimony to encourage US military intervention against the Iraqi regime. Just as tales of the rape of Belgian nuns helped vilify the German Kaiser, Nayirah's claim of murdered Kuwaiti babies gathered wide media attention and helped generate outrage against Iraq's Saddam Hussein. It is worth remembering that, thirteen years later, a seething American patriotism descended on Iraq.

Perhaps Isabel's friend Lady A. had been reading the just published *German Atrocities: A Record of Shameless Deeds* by William Le Queux, which referred to the Kaiser's army as "a vast gang of Jack-the-Rippers." Again I give you Isabel:

"The war is becoming more devilish every moment and the worst fighting hasn't begun! When we begin to press the swine dogs back, it will be terrible . . . I always get a lump in my throat when I see the dears marching along with their heavy packs on their backs—so hot and dusty—but cheerful and smiling—so few will return. It seems just wonderful to me to think that each one of them has volunteered of his own free will to die for his country."

—letter to her sister, spring of 1915

My great-great-aunt's patriotism marched in lockstep with the war fever of the time. Her hatred of Huns probably shielded her from any doubts about her faith in the Empire. And just as the new alternating current electricity lit the lamps in her house, so her cycling of loyalty-hatred-loyalty-hatred generated Isabel's energy to get through the war. As the fighting ground on for four years, moral certainty became the drug that could dull her despair at the ever-increasing number of deaths on the battlefields and the deprivations at home. I admire her hugely, but I *never* could have lived with her.

Isabel's house was in Bournemouth, on the south coast of England, where she lived with her two children and her servants. Along with the sea air coming in off the English Channel, the family could sometimes hear the faint sounds of heavy artillery from two hundred kilometres away in Belgium. Early in the war her husband died of a heart attack and her daughter, Margie, an asthmatic, never made it past thirty. Her boy Jack evolved into the adolescent who rowed out my nine-year-old father and the Steyr pistol one summer morning in 1919 to murder German ghosts. Isabel took no prisoners; her obsessions were her family and the British Empire's myths and wars. She might lower herself to her knees in church—perhaps only to put God on notice—but she probably never kneeled for anything else.

Unlike the women who served as army nurses in France and England, Isabel's war was at a distance and, like the sounds of the big guns from across the water in Belgium, only the reverberations arrived on her doorstep. The nurses, however, worked right on the shores of the fighting. Tides of wounded washed up after major battles, littering operating tables and filling wards. Arriving week after week, the soldiers usually recovered, and if their four limbs and five senses were in working order, they would be shipped back to the army. The wards would then be emptier until the next tide washed in.

My great-great-aunt opened her door and her bank account to my five great-uncles whenever they were on leave or convalescing from wounds. And for that, I thank her. Isabel's household staff cooked their meals and tended the gardens that grew their vegetables. The chauffeur met them at the train station in the "motor," and if my great-uncles had come directly from the front lines, they were told to take off their army clothes and leave them outside the back door—relatives were welcome but lice were not. Isabel's servants washed what was worth saving and threw the rest in the garbage.

My great-uncles loved staying with Isabel and sent her many of their German trophies. In her guest bedroom closets she kept clean clothes for her nephews, as well as the guns, buttons, shoulder straps and belt buckles they'd stripped from the uniforms of the "swine dogs." By the war's end, after Joe and George had become "landowners" in Europe, her closets held the remnants of both dead Canadians and dead Germans. Isabel had the privileges of wealth, the prudery of a Protestant and she was loyal.

"I think we are making preparations for a big push . . . A German prisoner told an officer whom M.K. [Margaret Killmaster] met here that they would rather fight anyone rather than the Canadians. Bless our boys, aren't they just the best ever."

—letter to her sister, summer of 1915

It gives me great pleasure to give Isabel the stage, since war stories usually restrict women to walk-ons or banish them from the theatre altogether. Even during my journey through capital cities for *The World Remembers*, at most meetings women played only supporting roles. At an international gathering in Paris, convened by France to consider joint World War I centenary commemoration projects, among the eighty or so delegates I counted fewer than ten women. The ministers from the thirty attending nations were *all* men. That conference in 2013 gave me a priceless opportunity to pitch the project.

We convened in the Salon Turenne of the historic Musée de l'Armée in Paris, where paintings of Louis XIV's Dutch conquests adorned the walls. Amongst the prancing horses and heroic men, women were nowhere to be seen. There were, however, bare-breasted ones by Louis's side as he declared war on Holland. In the painting at the end of Salon Turenne, a topless angel of victory (again a young woman) watched over France's acceptance of the Dutch surrender. No women could be seen in the framed prints of the burning and looting by Louis XIV's soldiers, since women were not doing the burning or looting. But, just out of sight in the seventeenth-century artist's etching of a massacre at a Dutch village, they were being raped.

Traditionally when patriarchy speaks of war, seven roles are assigned to women: (1) ministering angel, (2) nurturing mother, (3) distraught widow, (4) fragile innocent, (5) cheerleader, (6) rape victim or (7) prostitute. In each of these parts women are rarely protagonists.

Of my family's war women that I remember from when I was young—(Isabel was dead, God bless her)—my mother, grandmothers, great-grandmothers, aunts, great-aunts and great-great-aunts played all those roles except for the last two. Well, probably not the distraught widow either, since *distraught* was not part of my family's emotional vocabulary. So they were simply widows. At my grandmother's house in Toronto, looking up from the carpet while playing with my soldiers, I was respectful of them, I thought they smelled of face powder and old age, but I didn't *know* them. I loved my mother, who thankfully wasn't a war widow.

Their stories had all slipped into the silences between the "big" histories. Tales of war and historical chronicles of important lives were usually about men. I never really knew my relatives in the rustling old-fashioned dresses and high shoes. No, not quite true. I remember Margaret Killmaster, the nurse in the broad-brimmed hat in the cottage photo taken in 1919. Pausing in the battles with my lead men and looking up at the grownups, I knew only that my godmother Margaret *might* have been a war nurse. But *really* she was just another old person in a roomful of reserved women who preferred the crusts cut off their sandwiches. Yet she had spent almost three years in military hospitals with young men's blood on her aprons as the surgeons patched up what the war had been dismembering. I cannot imagine her world in which white buckets were filled with body parts that orderlies took out and buried in the grounds of the hospital. She had been the head operating-room nurse and, perhaps because of the lives that had been lost or won on the army surgeon's table before her, she had a voice that matched the ashtrays she filled with her cigarette butts.

Margaret hadn't married. She was one of eighteen family women whom I remember: seven had warrior husbands, three being widowed; six were spinsters; and five had civilian husbands. Isabel had written near the end of the war that Margaret had *intended* to marry, but no one recalls what became of the man. Clusters of elderly women lived in the houses to which we made family visits. My father's three spinster aunts lived in Hamilton, Ontario, and my mother's three aunts were in a white house in Victoria, BC. My beloved great-aunt Mayden—also believed to have had a World War I beau but never married—sometimes lived with Florence Stratford, Jack's widow, in a house in Toronto. These eighteen stories should not be confined to the wings because the stage is filled with men. Unlike the silent female professors at Lomonsov University in Moscow whose names I never noted, here are theirs: Margaret, Mayden, Florence, Catherine, Nell, Anne, Margaret, Helen, Mab, Armine, Suzie, Sophie, Mary, Joyce, Cicely, Kay, Philippa and Lona.

Wars, warriors and veterans had been part of the lives of all these women. Assault, sexual assault or rape were rarely referred to in polite company (at least, I heard nothing about it). How many of them might have been abused at some point in their life was a question discarded along with the crusts from their sandwiches. No, I'm not suggesting that all men or all returning soldiers are wife-beaters or rapists, but women *were* on the receiving end of the traumas that too often travelled back with the veterans. My family did *quietly* speak about Lona, who became a bride in 1923, but whose marriage of terror lasted only a week. Her abusive husband had come back from the World War I battlefields most likely with a head full of mental scars. It was Lona Holmes's sister-in-law, my grandmother Philippa, who stepped in and removed her from the nightmare. I say *quietly*, because, almost two decades later, Lona took her own life.

I also recall that a man might be referred to as NSIT—Not Safe in Taxis. Again, it is not that many of the women *were* assaulted or that all veterans had PTSD, but to assume otherwise gives in to a suffocating propriety that deprives the truth of oxygen. Each of the eighteen had known young men who had gone to fight and who on their return were never quite themselves again. Beside her front door Mayden kept a small defensive weapon, a gift from my godmother, Margaret Killmaster. It was called a cosh, and Mayden was not averse to showing us how she would use it. Margaret had it for personal protection when, just after the war, she was teaching nursing in Romania. Also referred to as a blackjack, it was a lump of lead the shape of an egg, fixed to a short handle made from a coiled spring. *Cooosshh* would be the sound it might make when swung by an elderly woman at an attacker's skull. Its braided black leather covering was so worn that my great-aunt had wrapped it in one of her old nylon stockings.

The battlefront of the Great War has been well documented, but not the sexual front. Isabel addressed it, though:

"Aren't there some awful women in the world? I hear all women are ordered out of Boulogne . . . the same rotten business in the South African war. I believe the immorality, wherever soldiers are billeted, is simply awful . . . Lady A. says that the Indians here at the Mount Dore have to be protected with barbed wire from the women. She exaggerates so fearfully I don't believe half she says. But it is true about the hundreds of Belgian women in this country who are going to have German babies—Somehow I can't get over this . . ."

—letter to her sister, 1915

The "awful women" Isabel refers to were playing role number 7. In my great-great-aunt's view, army camps attracted immorality and sex workers. "Indians" refers to the almost one million young men from imperial India who sailed to Europe to fight for the British, and who knows how many babies from how many romantic liaisons were left behind when they returned home. The "Belgian women going to have German babies" were pregnant refugees who arrived in Britain presumably having been raped by the swine-dog Germans. Little wonder then that, in her letters, Isabel often swings her umbrella at issues with such moral certainty. There were women's patrols that went even further, stationing themselves on the platforms at London's Victoria Station as troop trains arrived fresh from the fighting in France. Their intent was to deter any "disreputable" women who came looking for "assignations" with soldiers who had a few days' leave and were looking for female company.

Throughout history, patriarchies have been created, maintained and narrated by men. Women were to love them, feed them, breed with them, mother them, nurse them, champion them and obey them. Only gradually were they permitted to debate with them. However, women exerted power in other ways, and Canadian men did *finally* allow them to vote in 1918. But still the man's realm claimed the brains, brawn and balls, while women were consigned to compassion, sensuality and ovary functions.

Every gender interaction, however slight, usually involved a power equation. My tall grandmother Philippa, to prevent her husband looking shorter than her, would slightly bend her knees whenever photos of the couple were taken. I never realized this until a sharp-eyed cousin pointed it out. Every position a woman assumed—whether in mourning, in bed or in birth, tending the wounded, serving the vegetables, cheering the warriors or working the brothels—was meant to redirect power to the man. Are we surprised at the violence directed at the suffragettes who before the Great War wanted the *power* of the vote? No. Are we surprised that rape, the most ruthless calculus in the gender equation's arsenal, is also a weapon of war? No. The patriarchs have ceded territory, but the remaining inequalities hobble us all.

The cheerleaders

Women were not only victims of war; many were also cheerleaders for it. My great-great-aunt Isabel's vilification of the enemy and glorification of her team's warriors had her cheering from the sidelines. All well and good if it's a football game, but cheerleaders help drive wars.

"Oh the magnificent courage and steadfastness of our men. How flesh and blood can stand the strain, I don't know—Arthur will be among the bravest of them all of that I am sure."

—letter to her sister, November 1914

In the Great War's early years, for some there was an attitude that a battlefield is a version of a sports field. A British officer in 1916 led an attack on enemy lines by having his men kick two leather soccer balls in front of them as they advanced. The young captain's action was bleakly ironic—*not* because it was the first day of the Battle of the Somme, which would become a major slaughter, and *not* because some officers regarded war as a form of sport, but because sport *is* surrogate war. We will never know if twenty-one-year-old Captain Wilfred Nevill of the East Surrey Regiment appreciated the irony, since by the end of that day he and more than seventeen thousand other British Empire soldiers had been killed. London's *Daily Mail* newspaper glorified the incident in print, and the battle continued for twenty more weeks.

On through the hail of slaughter,
Where gallant comrades fall,
Where blood is poured like water,
They drive the trickling ball.
The fear of death before them,
Is but an empty name;
True to the land that bore them,
The SURREYS played the game.

Of course war is *not* a sport, but to some degree every sport *is* a war—albeit a metaphoric one. The sport/war metaphor may have become a cliché, but it survives because its truth lends it power. George Orwell said it best: "serious sport . . . is war minus the shooting," and that famous writer had been in both. All play *is* practice for one of the skills we need to live our lives, and every sport is about prevailing over your opponent.

Football is the most literal of our war-sports, with its small armies of athletes, much like eighteenth-century armies, lining up against each other on plastic grass. Chanting and dancing cheerleaders (usually women) are meant to inspire both warriors and spectators. Brawn battles brawn on the field while women, usually minimally clothed, perform high kicks and sometimes splits. The entertainment is both the battle of the men and the bodies of the women. The least literal of the battle-sports are cricket, golf and baseball, but even at their metaphoric remove, why would *anyone* care about the trajectory of a ball except that on its flight path depends the fate of the tribe. Of course, in a game's execution there can be inspiring displays of skill and even beauty. Nevertheless, the spectator's roar very easily becomes a battle cry. Should victory or defeat have to be decided by a penalty shot, the faces of fans reveal that winning means survival.

Sport gives us the opportunity to exercise our appetite for conflict safely. It is rules-based war with no deaths and minimal blood. Wars with rules were actually fought in Europe in the seventeenth and eighteenth centuries. There were no referees then, but there were conventions for battle, and honour demanded that they be observed. Oddly, those principles did not extend to the raping afterwards, since the victims were (mostly) women. Such are the limits of patriarchy's honour.

The excitement generated is the result of a special kind of storytelling. Wars generate three tiers of stories: those told before, those told during, and those told after. The tales told *during* a war are also the sweet spot of sports announcers. Consider the recent brutal war in Ukraine and the stories it has generated. Listening to the accounts of the battles and missile strikes *while* the destruction still rages is unnerving, since no one knows how many will suffer or how it will end. We follow the news and media feeds looking for "plays" or battlefield strategies that either side might use to end the uncertainty. Stories told during wars have an unsettling excitement that I hear in Isabel's anxious letters about the First World War that, until the final months of 1918, no one knew which side would win.

"I wish they [the British] would use [poison] gas, don't you? We've had it already laid on for ages but they haven't had permission to use it. I hear it is much worse than the German article and invisible, I hope this is true—it is now goodness knows for us to retaliate—we've been too humane and too polite."

—letter to her sister, summer of 1915

In our sport-wars, we get to enjoy safely what we ultimately fear—tribe-on-tribe conflict and death. In our seats safe in the stands, we know that, win or lose, everyone will live to play another day. But whether I were on a battlefield or a sports field, I would want Isabel leading the cheering.

"I tell you this war will make a difference and a far better world— how it has bound the Empire together—done away largely with extravagance and selfishness and brought out the best in everyone."

—letter to her sister, winter of 1914

"Some of Arthur's stories make me cry every time I think of them. A Tommy blinded by a shot at 4 o'clock in the morning, lying near him in the trenches all day until night when the wounded are taken away—with nothing to alleviate the agony but smokes—A. said he just fed him on cigarettes—this story came out when I told him a man had been around trying to get people to sign an anti-cigarette thing—against sending cigs to the front. Arthur couldn't get over his rage, and if he could have got hold of the man he would have torn him limb from limb."

—letter to her sister, spring of 1915

Apart from the high kicks and splits, I believe that my great-great-aunt Isabel was as much a cheerleader as those employed today by the National Football League. Cheerleading also took place in 1815 at a ball in Brussels before the Battle of Waterloo, where women danced as well as swooned. Not only was Waterloo one of the seminal battles of European history, but the Duchess of Richmond had arranged a ball beforehand. Unbelievably, my mother had a tenuous connection to that occasion. Described at the time as a brilliant affair, the ball was held on the evening before the fighting at Quatre Bras, the prologue to the main battle two days later between the armies of Napoleon and the Duke of Wellington. Hosted by the Duchess, it was attended by ladies, officers and even the Duke himself, who was about to be the author of the French emperor's defeat. We are told that just after midnight Wellington had supper but did not dance. "Quite a crowd" gathered to watch the reels of the Gordon Highlanders. If Henry O'Neill's painting *Before Waterloo* is anything to go by, the women admired, danced and finally swooned when the officers departed for battle—some without enough time to change out of their dress uniforms, and some whose bones might later be ground up for fertilizer by profiteering British merchants.

I knew about the ball from a story my mother told me. At twelve years old, Cicely had attended a dance in Victoria, where she grew up. Her mother—tall Philippa who bent her knees in photos—had told

Cicely that she *must* dance with an elderly man who had requested her for his partner. My mother said that she wasn't pleased to have to dance with an old man, but she did. Her duty fulfilled and back by Philippa's side, Cicely learned that she had just danced with a man who had danced with a woman who had danced at the ball on the eve of the Battle of Waterloo. That dance was in 1931. The old gentleman had probably been a teenager in the 1860s when he partnered an elderly woman, which implies that the woman was probably in her teens when she attended the ball in Belgium. O'Neill's painting of the Duchess's event on June 15, 1815, depicts elegant mothers with young daughters surrounded by a swirl of male military finery. The Duchess and the other women were more fully dressed than the cheerleaders on our sports fields, but they were cheerleaders just the same.

Dearest Isabel, you would have been beyond thrilled to join the Duchess of Richmond's championing of the men. A century later you did your own cheering for your warrior nephews. I admire you as an outspoken and generous tribal woman, but we part company when your patriotism vilifies those who choose *not* to fight. In the last year of the war it seems that your hatred of the Hun no longer sustained you. In one of your weekly letters to your sister, you admit that "the agony of the world is becoming intolerable." Yet you were still pleased whenever your nephew Jack had been "busy with his bayonet" and the collection of pieces of German uniform in your closets grew. I am sorry that as the war slogged on your despair grew, but I was relieved when you *finally* admitted to the wastage of young men's lives that no patriotism, however passionate, could explain away. Yet you were reluctant to express your misgivings. With your confidence cratering, you dreaded a postwar Britain with food and fuel shortages and millions of returning soldiers, men whom you had called "steadfast" but were now apprehensive of. When the tide finally turned against Germany, I understand your wanting to pack up and return to Canada. With your husband dead little kept you in England. But still, why abandon your nephews and nieces who were still in service?

"For a year or two after peace it is going to be awful here, everybody says—All those millions of men demobilized and let loose—There will be every sort of crime—Of course there are the usual different opinions about how long it [the war] is going to last—At Craighead the other day, I was in a small ward where there was only one Canadian and about ten British—They all declared loudly and agreed, we had Germany beaten now and that it would be over by Christmas—I left that ward bucked up and went into another where there were four Canadians who declared just as loudly that it was going on for five more years."

—letter to her sister, spring of 1918

Spiritualism had made a resurgence during the war, perhaps because millions had been killed away from their homes, mothers, wives and children. Many felt a connection with their departed ones. Isabel's neighbour Mrs. Turnbull, according to this letter three months before the Armistice, had been visited by the sobbing spirit of her dying soldier son.

"Spent a harrowing hour and a half with Mrs. Turnbull yesterday afternoon—she is in a terrible state—Insists that her Jack was not killed instantly and that he suffered agonies among strangers and enemies. Says she knows he didn't die until the night of July 10th, as he was with her all that night, crying and sobbing—And she won't believe anything else—poor soul—The question of her coming to us, she begged me to leave open as she cannot make up her mind what to do—she oughtn't to be alone for a moment—so I hope she will come, altho' it will be a strain—Poor thing—she is just heart-broken and will not be comforted— Dr. Muspratt has heard and his boy is dead too, since January—It seems to me that the agony of the world is becoming intolerable—Poor Dr. M looks just awful and is working harder than ever and driving more recklessly—One can see that his heart is broken."

—letter to her sister, summer of 1918

Did you ever wonder, Isabel, if the war may have been a betrayal of the people by their leaders? Probably not. Or what about the radical view that the young had been cheated by the old? Moral certainty is not moral courage. Certitude is a posture, not a strength. Despite your admirable outspokenness, I will never know what you thought about the jailing of the suffragettes who were demanding the vote, and of their hunger strikes while in prison. Being from privilege, you saw the world from the top down, were hesitant to question leaders or side with their challengers. You certainly abhorred the revolution in Russia, the execution of the Tsar; you wanted Lenin, champion of the workers, to be hung. You feared the millions of men at the bottom of the ladder, whom you felt might bring crime and chaos.

Yet Isabel, your turmoil led you to leave for Canada only a few weeks before the end of the war. When your nephew Arthur was in the trenches in 1914, there was another young man, Peter, also in uniform—albeit a German one—just a few kilometres away, whose mother *was* politically outspoken. You probably would have had no time for Peter's mother, Käthe Kollwitz, an artist who lived in Berlin and spoke out about the betrayal of the young by those in power. But I would like the two of you to meet.

CHAPTER 8

WAR WOMEN——MOTHERS

Käthe Kollwitz

My great-great-aunt Isabel Osbourne and Käthe Kollwitz were mothers of conviction yet separated by the English Channel and an ideological ocean. The one reluctantly expressed her regrets about war to her sister in Canada; the other, in Germany, wasn't shy about her despair at the decimation of the youth of Europe. Käthe's son Peter had volunteered for the Kaiser's army and she had wept. When he was killed in the first weeks of the war, she replied to a friend's condolence letter:

"Dear Frau Schroeder and dear Dora! Your pretty shawl will no longer be able to warm our boy. He lies dead under the earth. He fell at Dixmuiden, the first in his regiment. He did not suffer. At dawn the regiment buried him; his friends laid him in the grave. Then they went on with their terrible tasks. We thank God that he was so gently taken away before the carnage. Please do not come to see us yet. But thank you for the sorrow we know you feel."

Isabel, I want you to meet Käthe and hear her response to the war. She transformed her grief and dismay into etchings, engravings and sculpture. Again and again she returned to the subject of the death of a child. Before the war, Käthe's drawings and engravings had focused on the poor, the underprivileged, the sanctity of children and motherhood. After Peter was killed in Belgium, rather than close the curtains of her house and sit in mourning, she refuted the war, she wrote and searched for how to create a memorial to Peter that would also be a monument for *all* the lost sons. Here, she responds to a letter from a friend of her son:

"You are dear to me, Krems, because you loved Peter and he loved you. You have lost your friend. There is a wound in our lives that will never heal. Nor should it. To give birth to a child, to raise him, and after eighteen precious years to see his talents developing, to see what rich fruit the tree will bear—and then to have it cut short! I have in mind a sculpture in honour of Peter. That is one goal for living. You write that you will keep faith with Peter. You will, I know."

Arne Schrader, a former soldier who was commemorations director at the Volksbund Deutsche Kriegsgräberfürsorge (Germany's war graves commission), told me about Käthe Kollwitz when I spoke with him about *The World Remembers*. He and I first met in 2012 at a meeting with Germany's World War I centenary commissioner, and we have stayed in contact ever since. He said they had commissioned a copy of the Kollwitz statues called the *Grieving Parents* to be placed in a burial ground in Rzhev, Russia, that holds the remains of German soldiers from the Second World War. The original *Grieving Parents* can be seen in a First World War cemetery near Dixmuide in Belgium, where Käthe's son Peter lies in a mass grave.

In 1914, both Käthe Kollwitz and the German Republic were in their mid-forties. While her nation strutted its militarism, she couldn't fathom war's attraction for the young. Kaiser Wilhelm II had described her work as art from the gutter, a reference to Käthe's social conscience about Germany's underclass. Her husband, Karl, who was a physician in Berlin, used an early form of medical insurance to maintain a clinic for those with little means. The couple were middle class but, unlike Isabel, they viewed the world from the bottom up. Käthe considered herself a socialist and in 1919 was the first woman to be admitted to the Prussian Arts Academy. Propriety and discretion not being her strengths, when the fascists seized power in the 1930s, they labelled her work degenerate and she was expelled from the Academy. Through her letters and journals we can hear a little of how she mourned her son.

"Today I heard lovely music. Beethoven and Schumann and Reger at the Opera House.

A young, blinded soldier was there. He was led to his seat. There he sat very stiffly, without stirring, his hands resting on his knees. His head erect and tilted back somewhat. On his chest hung the Iron Cross. I had to keep looking at him—it cut me to the quick."

—letter to her son Hans, February 6, 1915

"Peter was 'seed for the planting that must not be ground.' If it had been possible for Father or me to die for him, so that he might live, oh how gladly we would have gone."

—letter to Hans, February 21, 1915

I have no idea how my great-grandmother Mary Elizabeth grieved for her sons Joe and George Stratford. Käthe's engravings and portraits are rich with intimacy and compassion for the sufferers. Their figures are all skin, bone and emotion. She wished her images to be "wholly felt," and at times they are intensely so. Before the war she drew *Mother with Dead Child,* for which she and Peter, who was seven at the time, served as models.

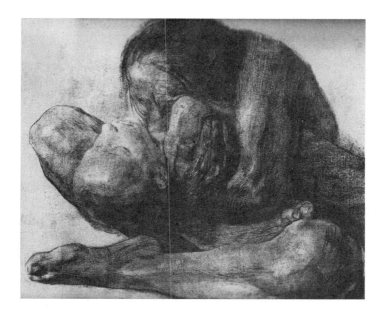

"I made sketches in the mirror of myself holding him in my arms. It was very exhausting and I let out a groan. Then his childish voice piped up to comfort me: 'Never mind, Mother, it will be beautiful'."

—letter to Arthur Bonus, undated

Unlike Isabel, Käthe avoided the hatred/loyalty trap that war sets for us. Her politics were not driven by loyalty to any political organization but rather fuelled by her social conscience. Like Isabel, she was capable of outrage, but unlike Isabel, she was intimate with melancholy. Käthe had two sons. The elder, Hans, had been drafted into the medical service at the beginning of the war and her youngest, Peter, was buried in Belgium. More than a year after his death she wrote:

"Where are my children now? What is left to their mother? One boy
to the right and one to the left, my right son and my left son, as they
called themselves. One dead and one so far away, and I cannot help him,
cannot give to him out of myself. All has changed forever. Changed, and
I am impoverished. My whole life as a mother is really behind me now.
I often have a terrible longing to have it back again—to have children,
my boys, one to the right and one to the left; to dance with them as
formerly when spring arrived and Peter came with flowers and we
danced a springtide dance."

—journal entry, January 17, 1916

Trying to see a war from the loser's point of view shifted my
assumptions about what it means to win. At times I wonder if losing might provide a clearer perspective on conflict. My father, who
fought the Nazis in World War II, became friends afterwards with a
former member of the German Luftwaffe, but their friendship concerned their mutual love of sailing. War has no winners; it is just that
one side loses less. This was the view shared by R. Stacey Laforme,
elected chief of the Mississaugas of the Credit First Nation, when
he spoke of the Ojibwe perspective on conflict. Stacey was another
acquaintance I had made through *The World Remembers*. Käthe might
have agreed that war has no winners, but she was bewildered about
why the young always seem willing to fight.

"Everything remains as obscure as ever for me. Why is that? It's not only
our youth who go willingly and joyfully into the war; it's the same in all
nations. People who would be friends under other conditions now hurl
themselves at one another as enemies. Are the young really without judg-
ment? Do they always rush into it as soon as they are called? Without
looking closer? Do they rush into war because they want to, because it is
in their blood so that they accept without examination whatever reasons
for fighting are given to them? Do the young want war? Would they be
old before their time if they no longer wanted it?"

—journal entry, October 11, 1916

Kollwitz's search for a theme for Peter's memorial—despair, rage, blame, sacrifice, heroism, comradeship, futility, fatalism, waste, peace or grief—eventually led her to parenthood. Does it end when a child is killed? No, but neither of my two sons has gone to war, so really I can only wonder. In a war, do your children die only after you receive the notice of their death? In the case of my great-uncles, the notifications came by telegram. Or do you know only when you hear the knock on the door, the way some militaries now deliver the news? Does grief ever completely heal?

My great-grandmother's letters rarely mention the deaths of Joe and George, but by the end of the war, in the photo on the steps, she seems worn away. Do dead children keep dying in their parents' dreams? Personally, I dread the thought that my children might be buried before me. My grandmother Philippa feared the nightmares about her brother Warren Pemberton's pain-filled death after a Royal Flying Corps accident. Severely burned, he survived almost a day before succumbing.

Our blood clots in order to save us from bleeding to death. Likewise, reason and language can coagulate around emotional wounds. Leave a physical injury gaping and we may bleed out or die from infection. Clots help build the scab that seals the wound, and we survive. It is the same with language and emotional injuries. Left gaping, grief can pour out from the wilderness within us. Language can limit and contain the sorrow. If we can summon *reasons* for the pain, we stand a chance of closing the wound. Perhaps that is how Mary Elizabeth managed to endure Joe and George's deaths. After receiving the telegram telling her about Joe in the spring of 1918, she wrote to her youngest son, Rick:

"My little darling son Rick, I know with what grief you will get the telegram. These are terrible times and I suppose we cannot expect to escape sacrifices, but our dear Geordie and now darling Joe seems pretty hard to hear. Our family circle is growing smaller but we must ever bring it closer together with love and helpfulness one to another.

Though my heart is heavy and aching, I am well and making up my mind not to fret too much and to remember the loss is ours but theirs to gain . . . take care of yourself my dear and write often.

We have had some warm weather here and in raking off the borders I find lots of perennials sticking their heads up and full of promise. The spring always makes me sure of the Resurrection and that nothing is lost."

Extreme traumas need muscular reasons to contain them, and in Mary Elizabeth's case she reached for religion and the language of Christ's resurrection. When an entire nation is traumatized, as many postwar countries were, high ideals are used to thicken the language into an unassailable rhetoric. "Sacrificed for democracy" and "patriotic duty" are idealized sentiments meant to quell the despair (or dissent) that arises when we grasp that what was won may not have been worth the cost. No one and no nation can survive unabated grief, so to continue living, who wouldn't embrace lofty sentiments to close the wound and let the forgetting begin? Except for Kollwitz, who continued to probe her own grief, as well as that of other families:

"Just as I want to make these parents—simplicity in feeling, but expressing the *totality of grief.* Perhaps now a few other things will work out also, so that the lot will express what I have to say about the war. Perhaps 'Killed in Action'—the woman crying out, surrounded by the children. Or the young pregnant woman—or the old one with raised hands looking down upon her empty lap. Or perhaps what I want to do now, the woman floating in the water with her child."

—journal entry, 1917

The stone parents that she would eventually carve out of Belgian granite are on their knees. She wrote in her journal in 1916: "This frightful insanity—the youth of Europe hurling themselves at one another."

Dearest Isabel, I suspect that by 1918 you no longer fully believed the rhetoric that fuelled the war. The distraught Mrs. Turnbull's grief unnerved you, as well as Dr. Muspratt's reckless despair when he discovered that his son had been dead for almost six months before he was told. You asked your sister Mary Elizabeth how she coped with her sons' deaths. It would have been a betrayal of your loyalty to Britain to travel to Berlin in 1931 to see Käthe's *Grieving Parents* when their plaster versions were first presented in Germany's national gallery. As an artistic romantic, you probably would have dismissed Kollwitz's expressionistic statues, which hint at the betrayal of the young by the old. It was 1933 before the kneeling parents had been carved out of granite and installed in the Vladslo German War Cemetery in Belgium. But by then the Nazis had seized power and the injured pride of Germany's extreme right was looking forward to the next war.

"At the beginning it would have been wholly impossible for me to conceive of letting the boys go as parents *must* let their boys go now, without inwardly affirming it—letting them go simply to the slaughter-house. That is what changes everything. The feeling that we were betrayed then, at the beginning. And perhaps Peter would still be living had it not been for this terrible betrayal. Peter and millions, many millions of other boys. All betrayed."

—journal entry, March 19, 1918

"When I think I am convinced of the insanity of the war, I ask myself again by what law ought man to live—certainly not in order to attain the greatest possible happiness. It will always be true that life must be subordinated to the service of an ideal. But in this case, where has that principle led us? Peter, Erich, Richard [Peter's friends], all have subordinated their lives to the idea of patriotism. The English, Russian and French young men have done the same. The consequence has been this terrible killing, and the impoverishment of Europe. Then shall we say that the youth in all these countries have been cheated? Has their capacity for sacrifice been exploited in order to bring on the war? Where are the guilty? Are there any? Or is everyone cheated? Has it been a case of mass madness? And when and how will the awakening take place?"

—journal entry, October 11, 1916

Entering through the gate off the road from Ieper and Diksmuide, in the earth before me lie more than a thousand grey stones. Trees have been permitted to grow amongst many of the graves. Unlike the Commonwealth war cemeteries in France and Belgium, there is no Cross of Sacrifice here whose bronze broadsword, like King Arthur's Excalibur, is embedded in a memorial stone that stands guard amidst rows of white headstones. Instead, in the distance, kneeling by the hedge at the cemetery's far end, are the two parents.

At Vladslo, more than 25,000 German soldiers lie mainly in mass graves. The plot of land is so small that each stone marks a pit holding twenty bodies. After the Second World War, when a number of German cemeteries in Belgium were forced to close, thousands of soldiers' remains were transferred (the term used was "concentrated") to Vladslo. Belgium wouldn't give the German war graves organization any additional land to accommodate the growing numbers, so the solution was communal pits.

The stone figures are bound by neither time nor place, simply by universal sadness. While working on the sculptures, Käthe often felt she was speaking to her son. The woman and the man kneel before the buried remains of 25,000 children, in perpetual remorse for their generation's responsibility for the war, asking forgiveness. The father's arms wrap tightly across his chest, bearing down on the sorrow that threatens him from within. His gaze is fixed on a grave marker nine pits away, beneath which lies his son Peter. On Käthe's last trip to Vladslo, she was alone with her husband, Karl.

"We went from the figures to Peter's grave and everything was alive and wholly felt. I stood before the woman, looked at her—my own face— and I wept and stroked her cheeks. Karl stood close behind me—I did not even realize it. I heard him whisper, 'Yes, yes.' How close we were to one another then."

—journal entry, 1933

The power of the *Grieving Parents* endures for me, while the swords of sacrifice and soaring phrases on the British Commonwealth cemetery monuments remain trapped by their era's attachment for heroic expression. In her work, Kollwitz had moved beyond the nineteenth century's flirtation with Romanticism, while the designers of most other 1914–1918 monuments had not. Rudyard Kipling's recommended epitaph from the Bible, "Their name liveth for evermore," appears in the Commonwealth cemeteries, but it too cannot escape the sentiment of its time. I prefer his rueful couplet written after the battle death of his son: "If any question why we died / Tell them because our fathers lied."

Personally speaking, only the stacks of bones of more than 100,000 soldiers at the Douaumont Ossuary at Verdun or the brooding figure of Mother Canada standing at the Vimy Monument in France share the power of the *Grieving Parents*. But to borrow a little audacity from Kollwitz, the emotional impact of our monument at Vimy might have been completely transformed if the towering figure of Mother Canada had been on her knees.

The figures at Vladslo are simple and intimate. There are no words carved on them to repurpose the death of their children. Their silence endorses no ideals or rationales that might seal the wound and let the forgetting begin. At the far end of the cemetery, they have a solitude and an elegance that break my heart. Their kneeling in the name of their children's memory shows both courage and humility. As long as the stone endures, they will reflect on war—the how, the why and the harm of it. By the time I left the cemetery to return to Ieper, those parents had made me think differently about the memories that conflict creates.

"Now the war has been going on for two years and five million young men are dead, and more than that number again are miserable, their lives wrecked. Is there *anything at all* that can justify that?"

—journal entry, August 27, 1916

The weight of the mother's granite shoulders and the manner in which she pulls her shawl about her intimate that more war is to come. Even while working on the figures, Kollwitz knew that was possible. From her knees, this mother tells us that we cannot absolve ourselves from having acquiesced to the conditions that make wars possible—that the responsibility lies with ourselves.

"Tonight I dreamed there would be another war; another was threatening to break out. And in the dream, I imagined that if I dropped other work entirely and together with others devoted all my strength to speaking against war, we could prevent it."

—journal entry, June 1926

The next war came in 1939, and Käthe's grandson Peter, named after her son who died in Belgium in 1914, was killed in 1941 in the fighting in Russia. Near the end of the war, because much of her work had been destroyed by the British and American bombing raids, Kollwitz abandoned her house in Berlin, moving to a small town near Dresden, a city that soon after was infamously firebombed by the Allies. Käthe died in the spring of 1945, two weeks before Germany's surrender. She said that war had followed her for her entire life.

Buried first in a small cemetery in Moritzburg, Kollwitz's body was later reinterred with ceremony in Meissen. Replicas of the *Grieving Parents* are now in a cemetery in Rzhev, Russia, that holds both Russian and German soldiers from the 1939–1945 war. That is where her grandson Peter is believed to be buried—"believed" because he is one of the millions of unidentified dead. The monstrous losses of Russians and Germans in the Second World War overshadow the death rate of the First. The *Grieving Parents* now kneel before the results of two global conflicts, watching over the children.

Standing on the grass between the stone figures, looking out over the burial pits, permitted me to see a little of what Käthe saw. In my odyssey to persuade national governments to support a collective approach to memory and reconciliation, she would surely have understood what I was attempting. Käthe Kollwitz was a mother who stated what must be said about war and peace. I would discover that other women, including my grandmother Philippa and my godmother, Margaret, could also assist me, if only I would hear them.

CHAPTER 9

WHERE PEACE MIGHT BE MADE

. . . such a peace can be established only if it is based upon social justice . . .
And whereas conditions of labour exist involving such injustice, hard-
ship and privation to large numbers of peoples as to produce unrest so
great that the peace and harmony of the world are imperiled . . .
—Preamble to Part XIII of the Treaty of Versailles, 1919

my grandmother Philippa's photo of a former battlefield
in Belgium, 1919

On November 11, 1918, the armies halted and the Great War's death-on-demand economy crashed. Countries *had* agreed to stop fighting but had *not* agreed on how to make the peace. Emerging from the fever of the war, both winner and loser nations sweated and retched from their lingering infections. There were revolutions, angry veterans, communists battling capitalists, compensation demanded by victorious nations, violence against strikers, classic art forms being dismissed out of hand, self-serving histories written by war leaders, suicides of returning soldiers, and millions of grave markers being prepared. In Paris, the peace agreement, called the Treaty of Versailles, was denounced by the losers and questioned by some of the winners. And let's not forget the millions of military widows from all the warring nations, the children without fathers, and the German people impoverished by hyperinflation. In the midst of all that, the fascists fed on the turmoil.

While the peace treaty was being negotiated, my grandparents were living in Paris. Cuthbert Holmes, my mother's father, was a Canadian born in India; he'd moved to Victoria but was serving in the British Army. Cuthbert was posted to Paris as camp commandant with the British section of the Supreme War Council for the duration of the negotiations. The victors were keeping enough of their armies at the ready that, if the peace process failed, they could recommence fighting and battle all the way to Berlin. My grandmother Philippa (the one who bent her knees) travelled to join Cuthbert in France soon after the birth of my mother in Victoria. I suspect that Part XIII of the Treaty, which advocated for social justice and improved conditions of labour, would have been anathema to my grandfather, but I doubt that he ever read it. Shame on me for being so presumptive about someone I never knew well.

The newlyweds Philippa and Cuthbert spent almost two years in the French capital while the glassy-eyed Europeans, their bedsheets still wet from war fever, created giant military cemeteries and seemed surprised that Europe was losing its status as the centre of the *civilized* world. How could they claim to be the pinnacle of culture, science, intellect and governance when for the slimmest of reasons they'd engaged in a four-year war that killed roughly fifteen million people, after which the opposing armies ended up basically where they had begun?

At the Peace Conference, American president Woodrow Wilson proposed the creation of a League of Nations to inoculate against future infections. Because Europeans had spent centuries solving disputes with guns, the purpose of Wilson's league was to settle disagreements *before* a major war broke out again. It was, in fact, the first draft of the United Nations, but unfortunately it soon failed. In 1919, most of the victorious countries, cavalier in their disdain for Berlin, dismissed their chances of reinfection and insisted on making the losers (primarily the Germans) pay billions in reparations in both money and land. It was not only the Spanish flu that infected and killed millions in 1918 and 1919, but also the virus that would bring on the fever for the next war. As Adolf Hitler put it in his 1925 book *Mein Kampf*,

"What a use could be made of the Treaty of Versailles . . . How each one of the points of that treaty could be branded in the minds and hearts of the German people until sixty million men and women find their souls aflame with a feeling of rage and shame; and a torrent of fire bursts forth as from a furnace, and a will of steel is forged from it, with the common cry: *Wir wollen wieder Waffen!* (We want arms again!)"

Amidst all this, the Treaty *did* include "The Covenant of the League of Nations," as well as a remarkable statement in the preamble of Part XIII (named the Labour section), about social justice and "humane conditions of labour."

Both Cuthbert and Philippa had brothers who were buried in the war cemeteries being created near the battlefields in Belgium and France. When the newlyweds visited the graves, my grandmother took her camera, which has left the family a legacy of photos such as the one at the beginning of this chapter. If you look closely, you can see her shadow. What did Philippa and Cuthbert make of the Paris Peace Conference, which for its duration was essentially a world government, run by the leaders of the four victorious powers? Petitioners from multiple nations had come to Paris insisting that their country be given more territory, more seaports, and payments for their war losses. The Peace Conference's rearranging of borders, creation of new nations and redistribution of ethnic populations had the power to determine if *more* wars would be fought. The Conference was drawing up an accounting for the millions of deaths, among which were Cuthbert's older brother Wildy, killed in 1916, and Philippa's two brothers who'd died in the Royal Flying Corps. Her brother Fred had been shot down over a farmer's field in France, and Warren had endured a painful death following a flying accident.

Legal language often leaves me scratching my head, but not the preamble to Part XIII. I first saw the text on a ceramic mural in the entrance hall of the World Trade Organization (WTO) in Geneva, Switzerland. The building had originally been constructed to house the International Labour Organization (ILO), which was established in 1919 as a result of the peace treaty. But that building was taken over in 1975 by the General Agreement on Tariffs and Trade (GATT) and is now the headquarters of the WTO. Sorry for all the acronyms.

The mural is a multitude of colourful tiles. Designed by Albert Hahn Jr. of Amsterdam, it's basically a presentation of the preamble's text. Most likely the drafters of the Treaty of Versailles included Part XIII because of the influence Bolshevik anti-capitalist activities were having in multiple nations. I find the preamble's words inspiring.

The peace treaty had fifteen sections, most of which concerned taking German lands, stripping the German Empire of its colonies in Africa and elsewhere, and arraigning the Kaiser for "*a supreme offence against international morality and the sanctity of treaties.*" It also declared Germany responsible for the war and therefore financially liable for the destruction of French and Belgian farms. Even today, ghosts from the Treaty's let's-rearrange-the-border provisions haunt the nations of the Middle East, as well as Hungary, which had two-thirds of its territory spirited away. The document's financial-reparation phantoms—that had originally demanded $33 billion in today's US dollars—were *finally* exorcised only in 2010, when Germany made its last payment: $94 million for defaulted bonds dating from the 1930s.

Of the fifteen sections, Part I did create the Covenant of the League of Nations, and Part XIII, the Labour section, did address the social conditions needed for peace. The rest of the treaty was mainly about punishing the losers, so it's no wonder the Germans detested it.

Preamble to Part XIII of the Treaty of Versailles— Labour Section—1919

"Whereas the League of Nations has for its object the establishment of universal peace and such a peace can be established only if it is based upon social justice:

And whereas conditions of labour exist involving such injustice, hardship and privation to large numbers of peoples as to produce unrest so great that the peace and harmony of the world are imperiled; and an improvement of those conditions is urgently required: as for example, by the regulation of the hours of work, including the establishments of a maximum working day and week, the regulation of the labour supply, the prevention of unemployment, the provision of an adequate living wage, the protection of the worker against sickness, disease and injury arising out of his employment, the protection of children, young persons and women, provision for old age, and injury protection of the interests of workers when employed in countries other than their own, recognition of the principle of freedom of association, the organisation of vocational and technical education and other measures;

Whereas also the failure of any nation to adopt humane conditions of labour is an obstacle in the way of other nations which desire to improve the conditions in their own countries; The High Contracting Parties, moved by sentiments of justice and humanity as well as by the desire to secure the permanent peace of the world, agree to the following: A permanent organisation is hereby established for the promotion of the objects set forth in the Preamble."

The underlining is mine.

When I saw the mural—called the Delft Panel—at the WTO building in Geneva, I was surprised by how specific the text is about hours of work, living wages, the protection of children and prevention of workplace injuries. Aren't those just the simple social health practices needed to keep the body fit to better fight off disease? Don't they point to the kind of societal injustices that help spread the fever of war? Communities with robust social and labour standards have stronger political immune systems. Societies splintered by exploitation, internal disrespect, extreme disparities of wealth, and insecurity of food, shelter and income are less able to fend off the extreme political factions that come to feed on their frustration.

It was a sign of optimism that the Treaty's drafters included Part XIII—and yes, they probably did so because of the workers' strikes and political revolts springing up all through Europe. By June 28, 1919, when the treaty with Germany was finally signed, the Third International had been created in Moscow whose goal was to spread the communist revolution throughout the world. The Red Terror—the political executions in Russia—was under way, and the Red Army, having defeated the Whites, had invaded Latvia, Belarus, and Lithuania. Hungary had also declared itself a pro-Bolshevik Soviet republic. It is worth remembering that both totalitarianism and fascism, whether originating from the right or the left, are haters of peace and lovers of force. Both are corrosive to democratic instincts. Russia's and China's present-day manoeuvres on the world stage attest to that.

Amidst the turmoil, I am sure that Cuthbert, despite the recurring pain from a war wound, would have been sitting at his desk at the British section of the Supreme War Council in the Trianon Hotel grinding his politically conservative teeth at the socialists, Bolsheviks, fascists, communists, and anarchist agitators.

Conservatives in both Europe and North America (and fascists everywhere) abhorred the new social order that democrats, unionists and communists were proposing. In most democracies in the decades after 1919, social and labour policies—which could be as simple as employees' right to form a union—were strengthened. Yet each step forward was met by reactionary attacks through workplace intimidation, arrests, imprisonment, arbitrary firings, and physical assault.

Both state *and* private-sector violence were being used against union members and strikers. The Winnipeg General strike in 1919 was put down with force. At the Battle of Blair Mountain in 1921, which resulted from an attempt to set up a union, between fifty and a hundred striking West Virginia coal miners were killed, and almost a thousand arrested. Most of the charges were later dropped. The 1932 Ford Hunger March by unemployed autoworkers in Dearborn, Michigan, faced deadly force. First the police attacked peaceful protesters with tear gas and clubs; they responded by throwing rocks. The police were then joined by private security men, who fired on the protestors, killing four and injuring many more. This is not a recipe for peace.

But yet, in the spirit of Part XIII, gains were made in many nations with the introduction of minimum wage and old-age pensions. After World War II, progress continued with universal health care, the charter that established the United Nations, the UN's Universal Declaration of Human Rights, and laws against pollution. But by the late 1980s, reactionary forces, driven by conservatism and narrow corporate ambitions, had retaken the lead and were rolling back the gains—so much so that, by the 1990s, disparities of wealth that hadn't been seen since the 1890s were reappearing. The gap has been widening ever since.

If we *want* peace, we might consider what fuels violence. War fever certainly does, with ultra-patriots seeking to crush their opponents through state-on-state violence. However, nations also tolerate other forms of violence when they condone the economic repression of their people, usually the working poor, the disadvantaged and the marginalized. Both those *with* power and those *without* use social disruption to achieve their aims. In Western nations, the powerless use the direct route of demonstrations, riots, and looting, while the powerful use both direct and indirect means. Directly, in the name of keeping the peace, the powerful have employed riot police, water cannons, sound cannons, tear gas, pepper spray, stun grenades and rubber bullets against citizens. Indirectly, in the name of maintaining a strong economy, states can use the bare knuckles of biased economic and tax structures that often reward capital over labour. The legal grip of international trade and investment agreements has been used to set the wage-poor workforce of one nation against the wage-poor of another. If we want a peaceful world, then the pursuit of social and labour justice is just as important as either good diplomacy or putting down the guns. At least, that's what the treaty-makers thought.

"Whereas also the failure of any nation to adopt humane conditions of labour is an obstacle in the way of other nations which desire to improve the conditions in their own countries."

This sentence in the Preamble was prescient. Just decades after World War II, governments swung in the opposite direction, signing international treaties that gave social and labour reactionaries *more* opportunities to play off nation-states and the working poor against one another. Businesses armed with new rights gained through those agreements are now (mostly) free to shuffle investment, profit and production among nations to leverage against local levels of taxation, humane conditions of labour, and environmental standards. They do this to enhance their profit.[3] Labour costs (wages, insurance and retirement benefits) are a component of the price of most goods, and the trade, service and investment treaties enable corporations to shop the world for the lowest available.

---

3   A thread of hope was the 2018 renegotiation of the North American Free Trade
    Agreement (now called the United States–Mexico–Canada Agreement, or USMCA),
    which started to address the labour and environmental injustices ignored in the original
    1994 agreement. But only time will tell if the USMCA produces any meaningful results
    on these issues.

If someone in Bangladesh will sew T-shirts for fifty cents an hour rather than sixteen dollars an hour, as in Canada, and if the factory in Bangladesh isn't required to maintain the health and safety standards of a factory in Canada, then a business can easily move its T-shirt production to Bangladesh. At the Rana Plaza factory outside Dhaka, 1,134 garment workers lost their lives in 2013 when the five-storey building in which they worked collapsed. More than half the dead were women and children. An additional two thousand were injured. In the Rana Plaza tragedy, garment production *hadn't* moved from Canada to Bangladesh in search of lower labour costs; rather it had moved from China to Bangladesh because of rising labour costs in China. "Labour cost" is used by businesses to price their inputs, but I prefer the language of "living wage" and "safe working environ-ment," since that reflects the need for families to feed their children and not lose their jobs through workplace injury, sickness or death. Not only have our global disparities of wealth reverted to nineteenth-century levels, but the same kind of labour and political instabilities are returning as well. You might think we would have learned and would want to foster the conditions for peace.

The tradition has been around for a long time. The Triangle Shirtwaist Factory fire in New York in 1911 killed 136 textile workers (mainly immigrant women and girls) partly because the exits had been locked to prevent the women from taking breaks. In photos of rescuers searching for the injured and the dead at Rana Plaza, you can see a hand emerging from the rubble. It's part of the litter of exposed rebar, broken concrete and garment labels, complete with bar codes. The body attached to the hand is beneath the wreckage, along with perhaps a thousand other garment workers' corpses, an anagram of expendable articles of commerce in the building's collapse: sewing machines, cutting tables, pressing machines and people. The owners of the facility, like the crafters of most trade and investment treaties, had *ignored* the principle articulated in Part XIII, Article 427, of the Paris peace treaty: "that labour should not be regarded solely as a commodity or article of commerce."

I doubt that this legacy of the First World War would be much comfort to the families of Rana Plaza's dead and injured, but the principle must be kept alive, if for no other reason than to maintain some human dignity. After all, what was the "War to *End* All Wars" fought for, if not for principles?

In Geneva, the Art Deco Delft Panel, measuring about three by four metres, is in the entrance hall of the World Trade Organization. Incredibly, it had been *deliberately* hidden for three decades. The WTO, the organization that manages international trade and investment treaties and conducts the world's trade-dispute courts, had concealed the panel by constructing a false wall in front of it. The mosaic, a delight to the eye, is composed of about two thousand tiles spelling out the Preamble to Part XIII of the Treaty of Versailles in English, French, German and Spanish. It is fitting that once again it *is* on display at the WTO because of the ongoing tension between global corporate interests and the social and labour responsibilities that elected governments may want those businesses to assume.

The mural was covered over in 1975, when the General Agreement on Tariffs and Trade took over the building from the International Labour Organization. The director-general of the GATT had looked at Albert Hahn Jr.'s mosaic and considered that "the presence of this panel was inappropriate for a building which [is] now to be the headquarters of the GATT." It being impossible to have the two thousand tiles chiselled out and moved elsewhere, he had a false wall built to hide it. At the same time, many of the building's other murals whose themes were the dignity of working men and women were removed. The director-general *did* allow statues depicting Peace and Justice, which were outside the ILO's entrance, to remain, but not the colourful mosaic inside that spoke to the *conditions* for peace and justice. As with so much else, there can be support for principles but much less for the means of achieving them. The concealing wall was not removed until 2007, when a new director-general had a change of heart.

For me, this reflects the impoverishment of our ideas about how to achieve peace. After major wars, sometimes we do attempt to change course. Following the Great War, the treaty-drafters in Paris tried to address such issues, but progressive ideas such as Woodrow Wilson's proposal for a League of Nations were resisted by victorious countries that wanted cash, territorial security and a little revenge. I wish I could have heard the conversations between Cuthbert and Philippa on his return from the "office" each day.

Two hundred kilometres from Paris, the war dead were being consolidated into enormous cemeteries. When the German delegation travelled to the Paris conference, the French ordered their train to be slowed as it passed through Verdun—one of the war's slaughter fields. The ossuary that would hold the bones of the 130,000 unidentified dead from the battlefields had not yet been built, but the grave markers for the 100,000 others who *could* be identified were being made. The French wanted to force the Germans to *see* the waste of human life, yet the French themselves seemed blind to the consequences of their own vindictive treaty-making.

My grandmother's memories about 1919 are my only personal window to this world, since Cuthbert's disappeared with his death in 1968. He left no letters from his time in Paris. Philippa had married him in 1917, when he was in Victoria recuperating from a war wound that affected his sciatic nerve. To block the pain in his legs, doctors had tried everything, including electrical treatments, but the pain would plague Cuthbert for the rest of his life. By 1918 my mother had been born and Lieutenant Holmes (as his rank then was) had travelled back to France for the preparations for the Peace Conference. It was many months before Philippa followed him to Paris. Like the rest of her grandchildren, I adored her. In the spring of 1919, this tall, shy, beautiful young woman who'd spent a quiet life in Victoria, or at the family farm just outside it, left my infant mother with her parents and travelled to join Cuthbert.

Like many attending the conference, my grandparents lived for a time in a hotel close to Versailles. Philippa told me stories not only of the ghosts she had seen in the Versailles gardens but also of the laughter that had greeted her when she first arrived. Her husband had been in Paris for almost a year and had been having fun at informal conference gatherings with a running joke: he would introduce whichever woman he happened to be with by announcing, "Gentlemen! This is my wife!" When Philippa finally arrived, already out of place in such a prestigious setting, and always uncomfortable about her height, she was introduced with the usual "Gentlemen! This is my wife!" The laughter she heard, she misread as being a reflection on herself.

My question for Philippa, whose life spanned two world wars that killed an estimated 75 million people, is *where* did she situate herself in that canvas? Her older brothers, Fred and Warren, had been killed in the First World War and two of her sons had fought (and survived) the Second. The conflicts had covered practically the entire globe. How could Philippa approach the world with such grace when so much of the world about her had been graceless?

Her magic, like the bending of her knees, seemed to be that she absorbed most everything with patience, rarely losing her generosity of spirit. An exception was her story of the ghost, the general and the hair on the back of the general's neck. To say that my grandmother was a mystic would be an exaggeration, but she possessed a spiritual sense that there was more to existence than meets the eye. I was performing the play *Comedians* in Victoria and stayed at her house for the seven weeks of rehearsals and performance. During that time, I asked her many things. "How did you spend those long months in Versailles while Cuthbert was at work?" "Did you make friends there?" "Were you able to visit your brothers' graves?"

She said that as the months passed from spring to summer to winter, in the afternoons she often walked in the gardens of Versailles, which had been commissioned by France's kings and queens before the Revolution. She and Cuthbert had eventually moved from the hotel into an apartment so the young couple could lead a more normal life.

Her walks to the food markets often led her through the incredible palace gardens. Philippa took pleasure being amongst the hundreds of seventeenth- and eighteenth-century statues and other artworks that lined Versailles' vistas. She never mentioned that France's monarchy had been viciously pruned by the Revolution's Reign of Terror—but she knew: "*Oh yes, and if you happened to catch him, you might see a Monsieur walking among the statues.*" A monsieur? "*Yes, from that time. And walking quite, quite casually, though few noticed him before he disappeared between the hedges.*" She recounted this in her mercurial way, as if the mystery of things was a simple affair, though she herself was not. She had an observant eye.

Comedians is a play about would-be comics taking a night-school class in stand-up. A passionate and funny script by socialist playwright Trevor Griffiths, it addresses the casual bigotry that comedians can traffic in to please audiences. It also proposes that the *best* laughs are when a joke releases us from fear by addressing the truth (or untruth) that fuels that fear. The play's language is at times rough. Our performances were often punctuated by the sound of seats flipping up as some of the good people of Victoria walked out in disgust. Our cast photos in the lobby once had *GARBAGE* scrawled across them with lipstick. It was a strong play, not an easy one, and my grandmother attended twice. She seemed untroubled by the surface noise of the coarse language, for she'd surely heard worse. From the stage at one matinee performance, I caught a glimpse of her white-haired head as the seats around her emptied. My character, Gethin Price, had concocted a limerick, "There was a young lady called Pratt," that ended three lines later with "twat."

Perhaps Philippa stayed out of loyalty to her grandson, but I prefer to think that she was interested in the young man I played, an iconoclast anarchist who'd shaved his head (and I had) for maximum shock. We had a wonderful seven weeks together, and she *had* heard worse. It was the story beneath *Comedians* that she kept asking about. "Why was the young man you played so angry?" One afternoon, I asked if I could tape a conversation about her time in Versailles.

My grandmother had *gently* told the British Army general, who had become an acquaintance after he moved into their Paris hotel, that she *thought* his rooms *might* have a ghost. But the older military man had pooh-poohed the naïve twenty-one-year-old woman from a small city in British Columbia. As we sat at her dining room table, her aged-grandmother knuckles re-enacted the nervous *Knock—Knock—Knock* on their hotel room door that had awoken Cuthbert and her late one night. When they opened it, there stood the white-faced general in his pajamas, the hair standing up on the back of his neck, asking if he might come in and stay awhile.

In the wave of spiritualism after the First World War, perhaps brought on by the bereavement of millions and by the tens of thousands who toured the battlefields searching for graves of loved ones, Rick Stratford, the young brother of my five Stratford great-uncles, wrote his mother when he was in France in 1923 looking for his brother's graves.

"I can hardly describe to you the feeling I had. The presence of our soldiers seemed to fill the air. There were soldiers crowding into the trains, marching along the roads through the treeless country and yet there were no soldiers, and very few traces in the country of the war only five years ago."

And Rick was an educated man who had just finished his degree in chemistry.

While Philippa never told me, she and Cuthbert had visited the graves of Cuthbert's brother Wildy and her own brother Fred. I know because Rosemary, my clear-eyed cousin who had inherited our grandmother's observant eye, found the photos that Philippa had taken. Their gravesites were among clusters of burials in the rain-soaked countryside that had not yet been gathered into one of Fabian Ware's new Imperial War Graves Commission cemeteries. For as far as my grandmother's camera sees, the spindled trunks of trees stand with branches shredded by the storms of shrapnel. The sky appears perpetually overcast, as if the sun is reluctant to acknowledge where the killing took place. The earth's surface is pooled by winter rains, meaning that the bodies beneath are swimming in the Belgian bog. Her shadow appears faintly, bundled in a winter coat, her back to the dim sun directing the camera at some remnants of barbed wire. In others she observes rusting tanks, collapsing trenches and the occasional wooden hut built by Belgian farmers as they begin their long road back to normalcy. Where were her thoughts about this aftermath?

In 1917 my grandmother's family received a letter from a French farmer in whose field her brother Fred's aircraft had crashed when he was shot down. Philippa *must* have read it. The farmer, Louis Milhelm, had seen the impact. The following day, thinking that the Germans who found and buried the body had not treated it with enough respect, the farmer reburied the remains and carved a cross. This stranger wrote that he had cleaned the face, combed the hair and that, "I could tell that he must have been a handsome boy." Louis Milhelm *didn't* wish the family to know about the mutilations to the head, but he wanted to assure them of his good impressions of the corpse that had been Philippa's twenty-three-year-old brother.

What *did* my grandmother think about the world that the gravediggers and delegates at the Peace Conference were trying to tidy up after? The detritus of the war's fever was all about her. The major fighting had stopped six months before she arrived, but at least ten smaller wars were continuing in the territories of the collapsed Austro-Hungarian and Russian empires. Cuthbert, as camp commandant, knew that a standing army had to be kept ready in the event that Germany would not sign the treaty.

More than four million of France's soldiers—give or take a few hundred thousand—had been wounded. How many veterans did Philippa see on the streets? *Hundreds* of thousands of wounded had been classified as "mutilated." Just before her arrival, France's prime minister, Georges Clemenceau, had been shot by an anarchist angry that municipal guards had fired on striking workers. Paris was still living the elation of victory, yet a dread persisted that the war's mess would never be cleaned up. My grandmother *must* have seen the omnipresent black armbands worn by those in mourning. A pyramid of captured German cannons was still stacked up in the Place de la Concorde, and the French army's heavy field howitzers were lined up along some Parisian boulevards. She *must* have seen boys shinnying up their barrels with French flags in hand.

To reach the graves, Philippa and Cuthbert went by train to the battlegrounds near the border with Belgium. She *must* have seen the devastated towns in northern France. I know she saw the rubble of Ypres (Ieper), since her photos tell me so. Where Philippa pointed her camera reveals her eye for the desolation. She would have seen fields *still* being cleared of human remains, army equipment and munitions that had failed to explode. She must have seen the labourers—mostly Chinese—who did that work and bore much of the risk. From the train she may have heard the controlled detonations of live artillery shells that were still being dug out of the fields. In Paris she must have seen the war widows, head to foot in black, who were pressing the negotiators to make the Germans pay for their husbands' deaths. She must have seen the columns of marching soldiers as armies slowly continued to demobilize.

Even at home in Victoria, my grandmother had seen the amputees with stumps instead of legs, and a young man, his face severely burned, who spent his days walking the streets. Philippa had said to my cousin, "He was a bright fellow who used to have a future." But how many more of the mutilated were in Paris? Perhaps she saw the *Délégation des Gueules Cassées*—veterans with faces described as "broken" since the surgeons' early attempts at plastic surgery had merely turned them into movie monsters. The French government paraded the *Gueules Cassées* at the Peace Conference to shame the Germans. She probably did not see the funerals of the men—some from the Chinese Labour Corps but also farmers from Belgium and northern France—who had been killed when what they were clearing from the fields exploded in their hands. She would *not* have seen the bones of the 130,000 skeletons at Verdun being gathered for the proposed ossuary, sorted according to the section of the battlefield in which they had been found.

But Philippa had *certainly* heard about the unimaginable number of dead. It was in the air. It was the reason why delegates from thirty-seven nations were in Paris. She was *in* the canvas of the war's epilogue, but was she shocked by the insanity? Or had she found a way—as most of us surely would have—to distance herself from it? Or even to endow it with purpose? I know she had nightmares.

> *Turning and turning in the widening gyre*
> *The falcon cannot hear the falconer;*
> *Things fall apart; the centre cannot hold;*
> *Mere anarchy is loosed upon the world,*
> *The blood-dimmed tide is loosed, and everywhere*
> *The ceremony of innocence is drowned;*
> *The best lack all conviction, while the worst*
> *Are full of passionate intensity.*

W. B. Yeats addressed the aftermath in 1919, in "The Second Coming." Yet how many were ready to listen? The poem has many threads, and the destruction loosed by the Great War is one of them. My grandparents probably never read it; however, Cuthbert had a knack for spotting promising new artists, so perhaps I am wrong. Yeats was Irish, and his poem peels back the cover of conventional thinking about the aftermath of the war. At that time, leaders were looking for language that would normalize it and acclimatize citizens to the view that the loss of life had been necessary for achieving victory and freedom. In other words, they preferred language that made the horror less horrible.

Yeats and many of the war's soldier-poets never lost their shock about what had just happened—a condition necessary for remaining alert while the political and military establishments attempted to clean up after the catastrophe of the previous four years. The

respectful high language used in the remembrance liturgies and official accounts of the Great War soaked up most objections to the
waste of life and cloaked them within the priorities of patriotism. For
example, this excerpt is from the 1920 commemoration publication
by a Toronto bank:

"The fervour evidenced throughout Canada in the early days of
the war was infinitely more than the flag waving and the patriotic
exercises of peaceful times; it was a heartfelt desire to be at one with
the motherland in sacrifice and in the service of right. Nowhere in the
Dominion was the call of duty more resonantly heard than in the
Canadian banks."

The Canadian Bank of Commerce's *Letters from the Front* was a
two-volume record of its employees who had served in the war, and
of the 265 who'd been killed. The almost five hundred pages, however
well meant, are an ossuary of language that wishes to legitimize the
deaths of those who had given their lives on the "field of honour."
Phrases such as "in the service of right" and "the call of duty" render
the books mute on the conduct of a war that resulted in an estimated
sixteen million deaths. Such language was embraced in the hope
that, just like the bones in the vaults and the bodies in the cemeteries, the voters, next time they used a ballot box, might remain quiet
and not object to how the Great War had been conducted. Words
were tools—at least for the victors—for bestowing purpose, restor-
ing innocence and avoiding despair. Here is part of bank employee
R. Marshall Livingstone's letter:

"Do you realize that Christ was the first one to fall in the present war?
How? Well, simply this: the very principles for which Christ gave His
life are identically those principles for which Britain is to-day giving her
life-blood. It is an old struggle, and Christ Himself was the first martyr
to the cause. We are fighting for principles. Right against might. Would
the world be worth living in if might and might alone prevailed?"

Private Livingstone wrote that a short time before he was shot
in the head at the Battle of the Somme. The battle is infamous since
on its first day 17,000 soldiers (counting only our own) were killed
and as it continued—for *nineteen* more weeks—about 290,000 more
(from both sides) would succumb. The Somme neither changed the
course of the war nor achieved much in terms of territory. It was
R. Marshall Livingstone's first principal action, and his mother must
have known about the rising death toll because, week after week,
casualty lists were being printed in the newspapers. The young man
no doubt believed what he had written. He was killed in the final
month of the battle, shortly after sending this letter. In it, he reiterates
his inspiration.

"Mother dear, your letters worry me, worry me considerably. It is
evident that you do not understand, but I shall put it to you this way:
do you realize that Christ was the first one to fall in the present war?
How? Well, simply this: The very principles for which Christ gave
His Life are identically those principles for which Britain is to-day
giving her life-blood . . ."

Well, I think that Christ would have been appalled. R. Marshall
went on to say "we are on duty primarily for God," thereby shielding himself from seeing the waste of life and probably cauterizing his
conscience at the same time. If enough of us let such language sear
our consciences shut—a dark procedure—then it will be simpler for
manipulative leaders to persuade us to embrace the next war.

"The Second Coming" by Yeats might have bewildered Private
Livingstone, since it is not about the biblical return of Christ but
the return of the Beast. It bears including the rest of this astounding poem:

> *Surely some revelation is at hand;*
> *Surely the Second Coming is at hand.*
> *The Second Coming! Hardly are those words out*

When a vast image out of Spiritus Mundi
Troubles my sight: somewhere in the sands of the desert
A shape with lion body and the head of a man,
A gaze blank and pitiless as the sun,
Is moving its slow thighs, while all about it
Reel shadows of the indignant desert birds.
The darkness drops again; but now I know
That twenty centuries of stony sleep
Were vexed to nightmare by a rocking cradle,
And what rough beast, its hour come round at last,
Slouches towards Bethlehem to be born?

Words were at war over how to account for what had happened
between 1914 and 1918. Livingstone's and Yeats's might occupy the
extremes. The first sought refuge in a bunker of religiosity, while
the other wrote that there was no refuge, since the "centre" was giving
way, which would usher in new dangers. But there was also language
from the middle, such as that I saw carved into the stone at the Island
of Ireland Peace Park, near Mesen, Belgium. The words are passionate, observant and stubbornly rational about what lay before Private
David Starrett. Like Yeats, Starrett was Irish, and like Livingstone,
he also fought at the Somme. As the November 11 Armistice arrived
and newly promoted Captain Cuthbert Holmes became camp commandant in Paris, Private David Starrett of the 9th Royal Irish Rifles
was batman to a brigadier general. There was elitism even among
regiments, and the Royal Irish Rifles ranked lower on the social ladder than Cuthbert's Irish Guards. As a batman, Starrett was basically
a soldier-servant, and perhaps that's why he spoke a middle language
free of pro or con mythologies about war. After leaving the army in
1919, he worked in the building trades, so the Preamble to Part XIII
was meant to help David Starrett achieve a better life and to prevent
him and his children from having to fight a future war.

"So the curtain fell over that tortured country of unmarked graves
and unburied fragments of men: murder and massacre: the innocent
slaughtered for the guilty: the poor man for the sake of the greed of
the already rich: the man of no authority made the victim of the man
who had gathered importance and wished to keep it. Greed and lust
of power, that was the secret. We were said to be fighting to stop future
war, but none of us believed that. Nor ever will."

—Private David Starrett

And for myself—I would never repeat this to those who knew
and loved Philippa—in the midst of her quiet observance and grace
I think my grandmother thought this too. Such a raw and direct use
of language appears when you remain alert, abandon convention by
the side of the road and set out to find peace.

These details I do know. My grandfather Cuthbert's father was Anglo-
Irish and Cuthbert spent his childhood in India and Switzerland.
The family story is that, since he spoke a number of languages—
German, French, Tamil and Telugu—Captain Holmes was at the
Peace Conference as a translator. But his military files from the Public
Records Office in London reveal that he was there as camp commandant with the Supreme War Council. *Whatever.* That my grandfather
was in Paris when borders were being redrawn and the victorious
leaders were dealing with the war that had just ceased—*that* was what
interested me. The president of the United States and the prime ministers of France, Britain and Italy were literally creating new nations.
The conference, which lasted almost two years, became the centre of
the political universe. *What was it like? Did you stay near where any
of the delegates stayed? Did you see Lloyd George, President Woodrow
Wilson or even Ulrich Graf von Brockdorff-Rantzau, the German foreign minister, or any of the Germans when they finally arrived and were
told to sign what they hadn't agreed to?* The main negotiations were
held in the French Foreign Ministry offices at the Quai d'Orsay, but

the formalities and final document signings were held at Versailles, a few kilometres from the centre of Paris, in the residence of France's former kings.

My grandfather's memories disappeared with his death, so by the time I knew what questions to ask, there was only silence. As far as I know, no letters were kept from his time in Paris. I do remember an elderly man who walked with a cane, sometimes two, because of recurring troubles from his war wound. He liked to lunch at the Union Club, Victoria's establishment venue. The small city of Victoria was the provincial capital and still embraced the vestiges of the British class system. Having been promoted, Cuthbert was called Major Holmes even forty years after he left the army. He knew the importance of having served with a prestigious British regiment, the Irish Guards. As his grandson, my perception of Cuthbert's crust could be softened by the scribbled notes I sometimes received in the mail. After hearing that I had acted in a school play, in a late-night note written in a scrawl probably dictated by his pain, he wrote, "*Well done, Bobbie.*"

CHAPTER 10

FRANCE—THE CENTRE OF THE WORLD

*Le souvenir de la Grande Guerre est sur la France
comme la cendre du volcan sur ses pentes.
[Remembrance of the Great War lingers over France
like the volcano's ash on its slopes.]*
—Michel Bernard, *La Tranchée de Calonne*

Philippa Holmes in 1919

More than thirty nations attended the Paris Peace Conference in 1919, and roughly that number returned in 2013 for a planning meeting about the centenary of the Great War. The first conference was to deal with the mess left by *la Grande*

Guerre and the second was to discuss the collective memory of it. The meeting in 1919 dragged on for close to two years, redrew national borders and meted out financial punishments. The 2013 event, for which I received an invitation by the French government to pitch the *The World Remembers* commemoration, lasted two days.

My grandmother Philippa had told me a little about the Peace Conference. So, ninety-four years later, arriving for the meeting in Paris, I wanted to book the same hotel they had stayed in, but having neither the address nor the budget, I settled for a cupboard-like room in a lodging near the Gare du Nord. The photos from Philippa's camera helped me glimpse her time in Paris, since some of the war's aftermath had appeared in its viewfinder. The politics surrounding the aftermath of nations' memories of the war appeared in mine almost a hundred years later.

France's 2013 report on possible centenary projects identified *The World Remembers* as one worth considering. It was in that report that I read essayist Michel Bernard's observation about the ash of the war lying on France's shoulders. At the conference I was allotted thirty minutes in front of more than eighty delegates from the assembled nations. It was a high-stakes half-hour. Are performers nervous before auditions? Well, if you aren't, you should be. Was I nervous? Absolutely.

In 1919 Canada didn't have official status at the Peace Conference because we had not yet been weaned from our mother country Britain. But, with a growing appetite for independence, Canada insisted that "Mother" not sign the final peace treaty on our behalf because tens of thousands of Canadians had been killed, and we were old enough to sign it ourselves. So we signed, but, disappointingly, the signature appeared only in a list of nations that were "part" of the British Empire.

The 2013 meeting was held in the Salle Turenne, a former refectory for invalided eighteenth-century soldiers at the Musée de l'Armée. The Canadian delegation was headed by the then minister of veterans' affairs, who I'd hoped would champion my proposal.

Subgroups of nations were planning centenary projects, but *The World Remembers* would be the only *fully* international commemoration—a fact from which I still have to recover. Woodrow Wilson had crossed the Atlantic to urge the nations of the Great War to think as a collective. His goal was to prevent future wars by establishing the League of Nations. My journey's purpose was to create an inclusive memory about a war that I and others believe should never have happened. Both proposals set precedents, and both eventually encountered the rocks of xenophobic nationalism.

President Wilson's dream was, of course, exponentially more significant, but we both faced entrenched national reflexes. His proposal threatened traditional nineteenth-century nationalisms, since he wanted each country's instinct for self-preservation to defer (at least partially) to the League of Nations. My proposal asked countries to relinquish a little of their national story by becoming part of a shared remembrance of the war. Neither President Wilson nor I foresaw tribalism's intractability and the political interests that it serves.

I had already experienced the headaches of trying to get the British to participate, and ultimately suspected that their indifference towards displaying the name of *every* soldier killed might be a class-system hangover. Britain has a long history of regarding its common (lower-class) soldiers as expendable. After Wellington's defeat of Napoleon's army at Waterloo in Belgium, British merchants eventually collected any bones left abandoned on the battlefield. They were carted to the Belgian coast, shipped back to Britain, ground up by machines and sold as fertilizer—an odd business venture by an island that embellishes its history by elevating its war heroes. It's probably certain that no femurs or skulls of dukes, marshals or princes were in the barges coming back to England. Upper-class bodies would have been removed soon after the battle concluded and given proper burials. Only ordinary soldiers' corpses went into the grinding machines, and in a manner of speaking, that tradition had continued throughout the Great War we were meant to be remembering. I had repeatedly appealed to the British government to join *The World Remembers*, but the ministry responsible for commemorative events was content to leave the names of Britain's more than 800,000 dead World War I soldiers in the archives. The ministry also appeared strangely indifferent to the millions killed from other nations. At times I wondered if the seas surrounding their island weren't so much a barrier to keep foreigners out as a watery moat that hemmed their imaginations in.

France was another challenge, even though Joseph Zimet, the director of its *Mission du Centenaire de la Première Guerre mondial* had *specifically* asked me to attend the meeting. Around the long, U-shaped conference table sat more than thirty differing national interests. On a row of chairs behind sat the observers. La Salle Turenne was dominated by paintings glorifying France's military conquests in Holland three and a half centuries before. To enter, we had to pass the cannons used by Louis XIV's gunners to batter the Dutch cities into submission. On the barrel of each was inscribed *Ultima Ratio Regum*—"The Final Argument of Kings." Dashing seventeenth-century French officers on horseback were on every wall. The Dutch were surrendering at the end of the room.

Joseph Zimet sat at the head of the table, and I spoke from the opposite end. The names I was proposing to display might very well have been the relatives of many of the delegates there. I knew that Zimet and his team were ambitious, but I was learning that they lacked some of the plodding practicality of actual event producers. The painting above Joseph's head of Louis XIV declaring war on Holland while being adored by cherubs and semi-clad allegorical women was all myth and little action.

The challenges I encountered owing to the divergent, politicized memories around the table, whether Belgian, South African, American or Turkish, paled beside the difficulties of reordering the world in 1919. Of the more than eighty faces that looked at me, how much ash from how many wars still lingered on their shoulders? The Serbs sat next to the Croatians. Two places down the table, the Germans sat opposite the British. The Russians sat opposite the

Americans. The Turks sat between the Austrians and the Irish. How many times, over how many centuries, had their nations faced each other with bullets, bombs, pikes or swords? My own shoulders were dusted with ash from the wars of my father and great-uncles.

Solutions would be needed if *The World Remembers* were to survive the contradictory demands of some nations. Even a century after the Great War, the topic of civilian deaths could be contentious. Turkey would withdraw *if* civilian names *were* included, and Belgium would withdraw *if* civilian names *were not*. Non-military deaths, however tragic—and rarely acknowledged at commemorations—had often been a political football. And war departments had been even less concerned about civilian deaths than they were about their soldiers' demise. No 1914–1918 nation had bothered to accurately document non-military deaths. Remember, armies first began to record their battle casualties only because they needed to know how many troops were left to fight the next day. The Turkish/Belgian impasse might be avoided if I restricted the civilian names to those from historically documented and *verified* sources. The In Flanders Fields Museum in Belgium was the only organization doing that painstaking work, and only for those who had lost their lives within Belgium's borders. So, technically, Turkey's condition would be met. It was delicate. In the end, our designers tweaked our display software that would project the names so that Belgian civilians would appear only in displays *in* Belgium. That's just a taste of the complications around the U-shaped table.

I'd hoped that Zimet might champion *The World Remembers* and win a consensus among the delegates. No such luck. But he liked the project's boldness and I liked his ambition. The year before, he'd remarked that he wanted our display created on a grand scale in Paris. I asked if he meant projecting the names onto the front of the Musée de l'Armée. "No, even bigger," he replied. "Onto the wall of the Trocadéro, opposite the Eiffel Tower." So I sent him renderings of how it might appear at both locations, as well as on a large screen installed beneath the Eiffel Tower itself.

My audition went beyond its allotted time and I'd tried not to speak in my usual clatter. The questions that followed included how nations' names would be distinguished one from another. The Americans were concerned about security at display locations. The Russians inquired whether the commemoration would have music and if their flag could be displayed beside each of their names. Thankfully, few mentioned civilians or the challenge of obtaining the names of the millions of dead soldiers, because most delegations weren't aware of the state of their country's war archives. I closed my appeal with something like "The Great War was the first global war, and therefore I ask you all to agree that the centenary of *la Grande Guerre* merits a global response." Zimet thanked me, then asked that I leave so that the delegates could begin private discussions about what they'd heard.

Unnerved that the fate of my project was at stake, I emerged into the courtyard by the Sun King's cannons and headed to a park to walk off my adrenaline. Parks had been my grandmother Philippa's refuge as the Peace Conference dragged on. The Versailles negotiations had been expected to conclude after several months, but lasted almost a year and a half. Only when the dominant nations swallowed their disagreements and crafted treaties with each of the five central powers—Germany, Austria, Hungary, Turkey and Bulgaria—would Philippa and Cuthbert return home. The treaty with Germany was the first to be completed, but would they sign? Armies had been kept at the ready. The German delegation, presented with a document that damned them, responded with anger. Cinema newsreels revealed how they refused to put their names to the document and then quit Paris. The conference issued an ultimatum: return and sign, or Germany would be immediately invaded. Everyone waited for Berlin's decision. It was by then June 1919, and my grandparents had moved from their hotel to a small apartment close to the gardens of Versailles.

Almost two weeks later, Berlin dispatched two lower-level diplomats to Paris to sign. The French couldn't resist making a show of

Germany's capitulation. Tickets were next to impossible to obtain to access the palace at Versailles, where the ceremony would take place. Movie cameras were cranked for posterity. The two Germans, like prisoners paraded behind Caesar's victorious army, were taken to the Hall of Mirrors for the finale. The Hall opened onto the gardens, for which an official pass was also needed to gain entry.

It was late that afternoon, while preparing supper for Cuthbert, as she liked to do, that my grandmother must have felt the air shake as cannons were fired the moment Hermann Müller and Johannes Bell put their pens to their nation's humiliation. I should have asked Philippa if the detonations dispersed any of the ghosts she had seen. Not likely, since weaponry doesn't dispel ghosts but usually summons more. Heavy artillery was set off in many parts of Paris to signal that the "Peace" had been made. That evening Philippa walked in the city with Cuthbert to take in the music and street celebrations. Ninety-four years later, I wandered alone in the Champs de Mars, then sat in a café to drink two coffees before returning to the Musée de l'Armée to buttonhole whichever delegate might still be there. It would be months before I found out if those at the U-shaped table had come to any consensus about *The World Remembers*.

Had I inherited my grandmother's eye for ghosts? I'd presumed that only three wars were represented among the delegates in Salle Turenne—the First and Second World Wars and the 1990s conflict in the Balkans. But more had crowded into the room. Along the walls, on rows of phantom chairs sat phantom observers from other wars: the Franco-Prussian War; the Napoleonic Wars, whose Waterloo left-overs had fertilized English fields; the Seven Years' War; the Franco-Dutch War; the Thirty Years' War; the Hundred Years' War. Before being converted into a conference hall, Salle Turenne was where France's regimental flags had hung, complete with the collected dust of past glories. Before that it had been a dining hall for invalided soldiers who had defeated the Dutch in 1679, and crippled veterans from subsequent wars. With fewer teeth and probably fewer limbs, they sat as we had sat three hundred years later. It had been Louis XIV's Hotel des Invalides, but in a way we were all invalided.

But there were more.

Civilian ghosts from the massacres and rapes that trail in the wake of war were also present. Since no room remained inside, they had crowded into the courtyard outside, peering in at the windows. The invalided veterans had eaten their dinners not only under the paintings of their rulers' conquests but also under smaller prints on the walls that showed other aspects of soldiers' work: the burnings, lootings, killings and abuses of old men, women and children from the conquered towns. Blending with the scrape of their spoons were the inner sounds of that brutalizing violence whose epigenetic consequences spilled through succeeding generations. The courtyard soon overflowed with the beaten, the violated and the butchered, and so they poured out into the Esplanade des Invalides and the Champs de Mars, then along the banks of the Seine, across the bridges and into the streets and boulevards of Paris—millions and millions of them.

And there were even more.

These ghosts of the young, the old, women and children, peering in at the windows and filling the city were only from old Europe's conflicts. From across the oceans came more of the war-murdered, Indigenous peoples who had received the colonizers' bullets, blades, diseases, and cannonballs that destroyed them by the hundreds of millions. With no room in Paris, they soon filled France.

And more.

On the wall above Joseph's head, the god of war, torch and sword in hand, marched with Louis XIV's armies against the Dutch.

Yet in the sky above *our* heads hung a future holocaust. The majority of the world's nuclear weaponry lay in the hands of nations gathered at the U-shaped table.

The god of nuclear war is perpetually ready and willing. The sprint to his war will take mere minutes, and will burn, vaporize, poison, maim and shred at least 300 million people within an hour, and at least a billion within the year. There would not be room enough in all of Europe for the ghosts of ourselves and of our children, were we to join the legions from before. Where is the peace conference for that war? Chris Hedges is only one of many astute writer-observers who have considered the never-ending nature of conflict. This is his response:

"Until there is a common vocabulary and a shared historical memory, there is no peace in any society, only an absence of war."

CHAPTER 11

MARKING TIME—THE LANGUAGE OF STONES
OPTIMISM OR FOLLY

'Tis thus at the roaring Loom of Time I ply,
And weave for God the Garment thou see'st him by.
—Thomas Carlyle

Wildy Holmes's grave, 1919

Philippa's photos of the graves in Belgium show wooden crosses, because the headstones had not yet been cut for her brother Fred or for my grandfather Cuthbert's younger brother, Wildy. It took years for the Imperial War Graves Commission to consolidate the hundreds of scattered burial sites by constructing the cemeteries we see today, and provide each grave with a marker made of stone.

Joe Stratford, my great-uncle with the waxed mustache, would also eventually get a headstone, but there would be none for his brother George, since the body was never found. Instead, nine years after the war, George's name, along with 54,000 others, was carved on the Menin Gate in Belgium, a stone monument the size of a squat four-storey building, designed and paid for by the British. The names inscribed on it are of the men of whom never enough could be found. The Menin Gate will secure their memory against time for a few centuries, and maybe even longer.

Each gravestone will be maintained as long as governments wish the history to be kept crisp. The Commonwealth War Graves Commission (successor of the Imperial War Graves Commission) has calculated the fraction of a millimetre that the letters cut into headstones will wear away each decade, and replacements are made as necessary.

My love of sailing comes from my father. Setting a sail in a wind is a skill. If it is well set and secured, the fabric will fill and you will be carried along. It's a delight to be powered by the wind across a small part of the surface of the planet. But when poorly secured, strong winds make the sail unruly and it may take on a will of its own. If the wind is relentless, as the winds of time are, then eventually nothing can restrain the fabric, no matter how well it is set. Inevitably the sail will be torn from the ship and disappear across the water.

We are all subject to time's winds that will inevitably carry us away. We do our best to set our sail for the voyage of our lives. We create rituals to counter and contain the wind, presuming that our journey will be more bearable if we can find some meaning in it. Travelling the oceans, skilled sailors use rigging, rudders, stays, satellites, winches, keels, compasses, computers and chronometers to keep their ships on course and survive the hurricanes. Our devices are religions, histories, clocks, philosophy, prayers, poetry, memorials, family stories, seed vaults (to preserve the genetic heritage of more than one million plant species), libraries and art. Our rituals are often as ingenious as the sailors' navigational satellites, but so far no one has been able to sail forever.

We also secure our sails in simpler ways. Counterweights such as gravestones, statues, pyramids and other memorial edifices, which we hope are heavy enough to hold our sails in place, assure us that we are not completely subject to the whim of time. Like our religions, stories and histories, these counterweights are also about messaging the (possible) meaning of our voyage—and, indeed, of every voyage that has ever been. Yet no matter the attempt, no matter how massive the monument, we cannot hang on forever. Inevitably, like the sail torn from the ship, we will be carried away and a rubble of stones may be all that is left behind.

We live, breathe, fight our wars, and raise our children within the dimension of time. When our bodies return to the earth or are delivered to the flames, rituals again attempt to attach some meaning to it all. When multitudes are violently killed, as they are in wars, memorials and commemorative events try to address the relentlessness of that loss. November 11 is one such occasion.

Headstones are the most ubiquitous of life's counterweights. Knowing that memories of our lives will fade, we tie tombstones to graves. Large cut rocks are preferred, since they seem permanent. I want a stone to mark mine. My parents' graves are in a small cemetery near Ayr, Ontario, on the top of a hill, which makes them a little closer to the sun and the stars. When I stand on that hill, I remember them and contemplate growing old. When their names on their stones start to wear away, my family will have them re-carved. But if the family has been scattered or is unable to maintain the memorials, the writing will eventually be erased by the winds and the rain.

Because the First World War produced so many unidentifiable soldier's bodies, millions have *no* gravestones. This is part of the reason why the language of the war's memorials and cemeteries was so purposefully chosen. The Imperial War Graves Commission decided that all headstones would be identically cut from near-white Portland stone. For the Commission, the bodies beneath remained soldiers, and so the grave markers were placed at attention as if on parade.

Row upon row they stand, equally distanced and shoulder to shoulder. The troops had drilled for inspection many times when alive. At the command "Right Dress!" all heads turned smartly to the right, right arms raised till right knuckles met the next man's left shoulder. Small shuffles would bring the line into a precise alignment. And then, on "Eyes Front!", arms dropped and heads snapped to the front. At attention and in perfect order. So stood the soldiers and so stand the stones.

The Commission's thousands of cemeteries can be found in almost all parts of the world. Visitors walk the rows like officers inspecting the ranks. Names and dates of death are precisely placed, as if the individual soldier's buttons were polished and their caps at the correct angle. Because no trees are permitted to grow among the rows, the battalions of headstones stand with a pale vitality under the open sky. The messages seem to be *These deaths had purpose* and *Victory was ours*. In some cemeteries, this permanent World War I parade numbers in the tens of thousands.

The German cemetery designers chose a grey stone, and rather than purposeful precision, their burial grounds are places of sombre reflection. The bodies lie sometimes in mass graves whose marker stones are set flat in the ground. Trees *have* been allowed to grow, so that gravesites are often in shade. The German cemetery in Vladslo, Belgium, where Käthe Kollwitz's son Peter is buried, has the statutes of the *Grieving Parents*. The woman's head is lowered and the man's eyes gaze at a grey marker just a few burial pits away, beneath which Peter and nineteen others lie stretched out. The kneeling parents' rounded shoulders carry the weight of their generation's responsibility for the death of the children buried before them.

In British cemeteries there are no depictions of bereft parents, since their themes are respect, purpose and valour. The white stones of the victors speak of sacrifice, while the grey stones of the vanquished speak of perpetual loss. In each Commonwealth cemetery, Kipling's biblical epitaph, "Their name liveth for evermore" appears, usually on a centrepiece stone, as a presumptive stab at defeating time. For how many centuries will the Commonwealth War Graves Commission and Germany's counterpart, the Volksbund Deutsche Kriegsgräberfürsorge (VDK), spend money maintaining the graves? Already one century has passed since my great-uncles' names were inscribed. After another hundred years, weary with standing at attention, the headstones might lean on one foot or the other while the shine on their buttons fades. After three centuries, the old fellows, too ancient to wander off, might forget why they're there and lie down. After five hundred years, who knows what the parade of the fallen might resemble.

It is very possible that the Menin Gate, built almost a hundred years ago from hundreds of tons of stone, will fare no better. Even Khufu's five-thousand-year-old pyramid tomb in Egypt, made of millions of tons of rock and meant to last an eternity, is now just the disintegrating overbuild of an overreach for meaning. The Egyptian king *is* remembered, but mainly because of the pile of rock he left behind. His quest to outlast eternity was a fantasy. In contrast, the tiny headstones of Joe, Wildy, Warren, Fred, Peter Kollwitz and the others will be lucky to last a few hundred years. So, is leaving rocks behind a gesture of optimism or folly?

There are burial practices that don't resist the winds but dance with them in a circular way, the *recycling* of life and death. As our Earth was birthed from the ash of burned-out stars, so we too have emerged from the dust of previous lives. Perhaps, then, rather than a stone, I might ask my sons to carve a beautiful wooden marker that might endure a hundred years before settling back into the earth.

Making marks in space

Leaving marks is also about claiming territory. Shortly after I climbed the German trench mortar at my school and wondered if the Russians would invade, Moscow launched the world's first satellite in 1957. *Sputnik 1* was a small sphere, less than a metre in diameter, but it was a startling success that triggered a space race with the United States.

The Americans lost the next lap of the race four years later, when the Soviet cosmonaut Yuri Gagarin became the first human to orbit Earth. The third lap involved walking on the moon. Both hot and cold wars are about territory and eleven US and USSR space vehicles had either crashed or landed on our nearest celestial neighbour before anyone's boots actually made marks in the lunar dust. That time it was America and astronaut Neil Armstrong who won the race.

Bears mark their territory by scratching trees as high as possible. Until Neil's space boots met the moon's surface, our tallest scratches were the collection of abandoned or crashed space machines that we'd sent there. Working our way through the solar system, we have now left marks much farther away, dropping instruments on Mars and even on asteroids such as Eros. Of course, leaving Earth is also about exploring the universe, hoping to find information about our beginnings that might reveal the meaning for which we constantly search.

"The surface of the Earth is the shore of the cosmic ocean," said astronomer Carl Sagan.

My fantasy is to ride the Canadarm at the International Space Station, which would be akin to standing on the highest cliff of the highest mountain and looking out over what Sagan described as "the cosmic ocean." Better yet would be strapping myself into one of NASA's old self-propelled space-chairs and rocketing away from the station to drift alone and untethered in the near vacuum of space.

In the summer of 1969, while Neil Armstrong was stepping onto the moon, Americans draft-dodging a hot war in Vietnam were arriving in my college dining hall in Toronto. I watched the *Apollo 11* landing on a small TV in the kitchen of the house where I rented a room. The fuzzy black-and-white images seemed unreal. Later that evening, standing on the sidewalk still warm from the day's heat, I looked up and tried to connect what I knew intellectually about the landing with the actuality that at *that* moment, almost 400,000 kilometres above my head, Neil and his fellow astronaut Buzz Aldrin were asleep in their lunar module. I wondered how long it would be before Neil's boot prints in the lunar dust would be swept clean by the wind of cosmic particles streaming in from space.

Expressing meaning in a transitory world is challenging in the performing arts. When we tell you stories, we endeavour to be "entertaining," but only because we want to keep you listening. And since every night our performances vanish without fail, I ponder the marks that we seem intent on leaving behind.

Spaceships—or space*craft*—have now travelled beyond the solar system. In 2016, NASA's *Voyager 2* passed through the riptide 17 billion kilometres from our sun where the solar winds meet the interstellar winds. Riptides on Earth are standing waves seen most dramatically in places like the Bay of Fundy, where the water flowing out from the land meets the incoming ocean tides. It was a historic moment for *Voyager 2* to sail through the sun's riptide, the invisible demarcation zone in the cosmic ocean, and then depart in the direction of the constellation Andromeda. No one was onboard, although its high-gain antenna dish was large enough for someone like myself to comfortably stretch out in. If anyone *were* lying there, they would not be in complete darkness since our sun would appear as a pinprick of light among 300 billion other stars in our galaxy. And if that someone knew where to look, they *might* see minute smudges that are some of the trillion or so other galaxies.

Voyager 2 was launched in 1977, five years after the last manned moon landing. It then took thirty-nine years to leave the solar system and the region of space dominated by our sun and head off beyond the riptide into the space between the stars. The interstellar winds are gases of hydrogen and helium as well as the streaming rubble of dust and charged particles from ancient stellar explosions. Because of the radiation and ferocious cold, space is hostile to human biology, but not to our ideas and our art, both of which are transitory anyway. As well as exploring our fellow planets in the solar system, *Voyager 2* is also about leaving marks.

To prepare for the voyage, information was loaded onto the craft: *where* we are located in the Milky Way galaxy; the year *Voyager 2* was sent; *facts* about our sun and our planetary system; *samples* of our math and science to indicate humankind's degree of knowledge; and *pictures* of life forms. For all his tons of rock, Pharaoh Khufu was not mentioned. Also included were twenty-seven recordings of music, among which was Prelude and Fugue no. 1 in C by Johann Sebastian Bach, played by Glenn Gould. Adding the music was a visionary act by the mission's planners. There was also a message from the US president at the time, Jimmy Carter:

"This is a present from a small, distant world, a token of our sounds, our science, our images, our music, our thoughts and our feelings. We are attempting to survive our time so we may live into yours. We hope someday, having solved the problems we face, to join a community of galactic civilizations. This record represents our hope and our determination and our goodwill in a vast and awesome universe."

Carter mentioned survival because we were then in the midst of the Cold War, which, if it had turned hot, could have been a catastrophe for most of Earth's inhabitants. Following unimaginable loss of life by thermonuclear explosions and radiation poisoning, the planet would have endured several years of a cool, dim nuclear winter. Starvation would follow. In 1961, the American Strategic Air Command estimated that their *first*-strike nuclear plans could kill between 360 and 425 million people. It's safe to say there would be no cemeteries for them.

When *Voyager 2* left the launch pad, the combined atomic arsenals of the opposing sides was about fifty thousand warheads. It would take perhaps twenty minutes to transition from peace to destruction. For years, in order to prevent being caught by a surprise Soviet attack, squadrons of American bombers with nuclear payloads flew on a daily basis towards targets in Russia, only to turn back when a recall order was given. We survived on that recall's edge. That was the world in which NASA chose to include Glenn Gould on the piano, Louis Armstrong playing "Melancholy Blues," Senegalese drummers, the cavatina from Beethoven's String Quartet no. 13 in B flat played by the Budapest String Quartet, Blind Willie Johnson's "Dark Was the Night and Cold Was the Ground," and "Night Chant" by Navajo singers Ambrose Roan Horse, Chester Roan, and Tom Roan. The music and information about our world was embedded in analogue marks on a gold-plated copper disk—essentially an old-fashioned long-playing record—that was then bolted to the side of the craft. Hieroglyphic-like diagrams on the disk's surface provided instructions for playing the record and retrieving its contents. There were also the words:

"To the makers of music—all worlds, all times."

So here's the question.

It will be at least 36,000 years before the spacecraft reaches a region in Andromeda where there *may* be extroplanets that *might* have presences both curious and capable of playing the record. Was including the music and information an act of optimism or folly?

If things go well, humanity might still exist in 36,000 years, and at least thirty-six civilizations may have come and gone before the record is played. If things *don't* go well, through either nuclear confrontation or climate catastrophe, the planet may have lost its human presence—species extinctions happen, and we have been responsible for many of them. Neil's footprints on the moon will certainly have vanished.

Whichever scenario you choose, some remnants of us will probably remain: certainly not the Menin Gate, but perhaps the last rubble of Khufu's tomb, or the Svalbard seed vault, tunnelled into the frigid mountains of Spitsbergen Island near the Arctic Circle, or even some Paleolithic cave art that was painted long before Khufu ruled. After we have gone, those may yet survive the constant battering of Earth's surface by wind, water and ice. Whatever remains, *Voyager 2*'s gold-plated disk will still be a testament. Here we are, or were. This is what we know. This is what we saw. These are the sounds we made. By these marks, know that we existed.

Might there be *meaning* in any of this? Of course. Perhaps. Or not.

⌁

In Samuel Beckett's tragicomedy *Waiting for Godot*, a lonely Vladimir stands by a desolate road. It is the end of yet another day and he has been waiting in vain for the arrival of the mysterious, godlike Monsieur Godot. Even though he has been doing so every day since he can remember, Vladimir has forgotten *why* he was to meet him. Monsieur Godot *never* appears. A philosopher in his own right, Vladimir wavers between optimism and despair. Looking at his sleeping companion, Estragon, he wonders aloud to no one in particular:

"Astride of a grave and a difficult birth. Down in the hole, lingeringly, the grave-digger puts on the forceps. We have time to grow old. The air is full of our cries. (*He listens.*) But habit is a great deadener. (*He looks again at Estragon.*) At me too someone is looking, of me too someone is saying, he is sleeping, he knows nothing, let him sleep. (*Pause.*) I can't go on! (*Pause.*) What have I said?"

It is a wry, funny play and I once had the privilege of playing Vladimir. A comedic glow seeps out from around Vladimir's and Estragon's thoughts on optimism and despair and the mystery of having to wait each day for someone important you've never seen.

Besides the twenty-seven pieces of music, another surprise on *Voyager 2*'s disk is the recorded brainwaves of Ann Druyan. Being the creative director of NASA's Voyager Interstellar Message Project, Ann thought for an hour—to no one in particular—about humanity, ideas and love. Later she wrote about her hour of contemplation:

"I began by thinking about the history of the Earth and the life it sustains. To the best of my abilities I tried to think something of the history of ideas and human social organization. I thought about the predicament that our civilization finds itself in and about the violence and poverty that make this planet a hell for so many of its inhabitants. Toward the end I permitted myself a personal statement of what it was like to fall in love."

The winds of time may be relentless, but we sail them in remarkable ways and weave astounding garments for the universe to see us by. And despite everything I've said here, I am thankful that my great-uncles' names and a few million others *have* been carved on *stones.*

Some artists optimistic about time

Thirty thousand years *before* Khufu built his pyramid, in a cave in southeastern France, artists worked by the light of their torches. After scraping the stone walls clean, they painted bison, cave bears, leopards, horses, woolly rhinoceroses, lions and hyenas. They are compelling images. We know when the artists worked on those walls because, to rekindle their torches, they used the cavern ceiling to scrape off the dying embers. The flames again grew bright and they continued their painting. The embers fell to the floor and remained there undisturbed. The radiocarbon in the extinguished embers serves as the death dates on headstones do and as does the golden record on *Voyager 2*. It tells us that the painters were working as the Quaternary ice age was ending, 35,000 years ago.

We live almost at the midpoint between the possible witnessing of NASA's record 36,000 years in the future, and the artists' work in the Chauvet Cave in France, 35,000 years in the past. Placing myself on the timeline between the two events is dizzying. The vividness with which the Chauvet artists painted and drew with their ochre and charcoal humbles me, and I am giddy that *any* art has endured that long.

The dizziness comes because, the closer we examine time and its passage, the more mysterious things become. Just as with the wind, we see the effects of time but never perceive the thing itself. I can sense the *where* of the Chauvet Cave but not the *when.* I can visit its location in space but not its location in time. Even more mysterious is that time is inseparable from the three dimensions of space—height, width and depth—which is why it's called the space-time continuum.

What I have grasped is that, without motion, we can perceive nothing about the workings of time. Think of it. Time's passing is measured *only* through movement: watch hands turning, pendulums swinging, soldiers' bodies decaying, oscillations of cesium-133 atoms, names on headstones wearing away, conductor's batons beating and moon dust being blown smooth.

If all the clocks stopped ticking and all the matter in the universe suddenly stood still, does time vanish? Well, yes. Do we have evidence of that? Yes. It vanishes completely in the crushing gravity of black holes, fanatical gravitational pits that suck in matter, along with the space-time continuum in which the matter exists. Nothing is seen again.

We *know* that space-time warps and twists. We have *felt* it—or, rather, our scientific instruments have. On September 14, 2015, at 5:51 a.m., you and I, the Menin Gate, Khufu's rocks and indeed the entire Earth became slightly taller and then slightly shorter. An intense storm of gravitational waves rolled through us, created by the collision of two black holes more than one billion light years away, in the direction of the Magellanic Clouds. That collision created the equivalent of a cosmic hurricane that produced the waves that travelled the universe and landed on our shores. We *know* this because they were measured and recorded by the Laser Interferometer Gravitational-Wave Observatory (LIGO) instruments designed for that purpose.[4] What's more, LIGO's recording of the gravitational waves was transposed into its sound equivalent. If you listen to it, you hear the violent twisting of the fabric of space-time by a gravity storm generated a billion years ago. It's strange music, but it is where we live.

---

4   In Livingston, Indiana, and Hartford, Washington, LIGO detectors, funded by the US
      National Science Foundation and built and operated by MIT and Caltech, measured
      the waves at 5:51 a.m. Eastern Daylight Time. Given the slight time difference between
      the occurrences at the two detectors, it was inferred that the waves came from the
      southern hemisphere.

The closest I can come to comprehending time is to accept that the architecture of space-time may be similar to the mystery of music. Johann Wolfgang von Goethe put it this way:

"Music is liquid architecture; architecture is frozen music."

And be assured, I am still pondering whether it was optimism or folly to carve millions of names on millions of World War I cemetery headstones. And whether it was worth it to put anything at all on *Voyager 2*'s gold-coated record.

Resisting at Chauvet

Five thousand years *after* the first artists worked in the Chauvet Cave—roughly the same span of time that separates us from Pharaoh Khufu—a second group of artists reworked some of the paintings. For your thoughts, that is basically 29,000 to 30,000 years ago. The clay-like floor of the cavern shows the remains of their fires and a child's footprints. An ice tongue of the receding glacier probably still lay in the valley below the cave's entrance.

Our climate produces its own pendulums of time, in this instance the cycling of the ice ages. Every several hundred thousand years, glaciers advance and recede. At the height of the Quaternary age, the ice sheet in the French mountains near the cave was perhaps three thousand metres thick. The seas were so low that the Chauvet painters could have walked to Britain. Today most of our mountain glaciers are the final remnants of those ice continents, and most will completely vanish in our time. The pendulum swing of disappearing ice will then have reached an extreme, its motion accelerated by our burning of Earth's fossil fuels without conscience.

The artists' painting of cave bears, horses and other animals were conscious acts; the painters not only cleaned the walls before they began, but they also dipped their hands in red ochre and pressed them onto the rock. One artist had a crooked little finger, and today we see that misshapen finger among the handprints. That artist made a mural of multiple prints of their own hand. Here I am. This is what I made. This is what I saw.

Thirty thousand years ago the cave had a single entrance, one that now no longer exists. Everyone who entered would have encountered the first mural in which the hand with the crooked finger appears at least fifty times on the wall before them. The paintings of the animals were much deeper in the cave, where visitors would have been in complete darkness except for the light of their torches. Far from the entrance, the beasts would have been animated by the shadows cast by the flickering light of the burning brands. As the visitors and their torches shifted, so the animals shifted in the moving light and shadow, making them seem more present in time. When the visitors departed, taking their light with them, darkness and stillness returned, and the prehistoric horses and bears stepped once more outside of time.

It was only by happenstance that the Chauvet Cave with its animals were preserved and resisted the ravages of time. After the second set of artists had painted, the cave was accidentally sealed for 29,000 years. For an unknown reason, the cliff above its single opening collapsed, leaving the entrance buried. The paintings, footprints, dead embers and bones remained in utter darkness, practically outside of time except for three almost imperceptible movements: the glacially slow formation of calcite minerals from moisture seeping from the rock ceiling, the slow decay of the radiocarbon in the dead embers, and the ripples of gravitational waves moving through the rock.

In 1994 the long sleep was broken when three speleologists—those who study caves—were feeling for air coming from holes in the cliff face. They found a small opening that emitted a breath-like current. Enlarging the hole, they had just enough room to squeeze through. Exploring with their flashlights, they descended into the sealed cave some metres below. Standing in what 29,000 years before had been the original entrance, their lights caught the mural of fifty hand marks before them. The rubble of fallen rock that had blocked the entrance seemed fresh.

Deeper in the cave, the explorers found bones underfoot. They also saw the host of animals painted on the walls, again appearing to move in the light and shadow cast by their electric lamps. The paintings were so sophisticated and in such pristine condition that at first the explorers thought they were forgeries. They were not. Just as the glorious sounds of Louis Armstrong's trumpet in "Melancholy Blues," of Glenn Gould's playing Prelude and Fugue in C, and of all the other music on *Voyager 2* journeys to its future, so these exceptional works have travelled to us from their past.

Was the work of the person with the crooked finger optimism or folly? The Chauvet artists were witnesses to their time and the paintings reveal their awareness of the world and their place in it. There are no human remains in the cave, only animal bones, and those are mostly of cave bears. The bears too had marked the walls. Some of their scratches were over some of the paintings and others were on the bare rock. Standing on their hind legs in the darkness, they had made their marks to say *Here I am* and *This is my territory*. But never having had a conscious forethought about preparing the walls by cleaning them, and without torches by which to observe their work, their scratches in the darkness reveal no perceptions regarding the world about them. They did not say *This is what I saw*, and they could not say *This is what I am*.

But Glenn Gould, the artist with the misshapen finger, Blind Willie Johnson, the Navajo singers and even Ann Druyan thinking about love and civilization, they thought, painted, sang and played by the light and shadow of their awareness. They consciously reflected on the world both inside and outside themselves. Where inner and outer worlds collide, *there* is the artist's riptide. It is there that the conscious imagination can be at its richest. This is what I made. This is what I saw. This is what I am.

Time makes an appearance when either matter *or* imagination moves. Just as for thirty thousand years the paintings in a cave closed to the world were almost outside of time, so too will the art and information on *Voyager 2*'s record remain outside time until it is retrieved and spun, allowing the music and voices to emerge from the silence and darkness, and re-enter the *now* of whatever creature spins the disk.

~~~~~~

I practise an art that is the epitome of impermanence. Acting is neither hung in galleries nor studied centuries afterwards. In theatre we've even made our transience a ritual. When the play ends, we step out of our characters, banishing any illusion that our stage has presented anything "real"; we bow, the audience applauds (hopefully), the lights are turned off and we all go home. We make no marks on the walls. Yes, film and TV actors leave something behind, since their performances are collected in the small digital galaxies that reside in memory cards. Theatre's fleetingness is exhilarating because, after every performance, the walls are laid bare in anticipation of the next performance. To hang theatre on a gallery wall would be to drain it of blood.

On the way out the stage door, I sometimes slip back through the wings and go onstage. If the crew has gone, it will be dark except for a single light by which I will cast shadows. As I've said, theatres traditionally place one lamp—the ghost light—on a stand to burn all night to prevent people like me from falling off the stage. There is also a superstition that some theatres are inhabited by the ghosts of old actors, and the light allows them to continue their work. To stand in a dark theatre after so much life has been acted out is a thrill. The only motion is the beating of my heart, the photons fleeing the ghost light, and my shadow shifting on the walls. All the characters seem to be there still: Vladimir has contemplated the abyss and optimistically waits for the next day; Estragon sleeps on; Juliet, in her grief for Romeo, has ended her life, and their guilt-stricken parents have promised to find a path to peace.

But should we tell stories at all if everything is to vanish— the actors, the sets, the audience's memories, the shadows when the ghost light burns out, the names carved on the headstones, and even the Earth itself, from which all life will be burned away when our dying sun grows so large that it scatters our ashes and every mark we have ever made to the cosmos? *Yes.* Because the cycle of creation will begin again. The dust and particles will once again gather into clouds between stars. The clouds may again compact, grow dense, and form a new star with "earths" and moons. And perhaps there will exist everything needed for some entity to leave the next set of marks and tell the next set of stories—to no one in particular. But that takes courage.

———

A girl composed a poem in November, 1943. Since she had neither pencil nor paper to write it down, her name will be forever unknown. She *thought* the poem, and then she spoke it. Those working along-side her heard and remembered it. She was twelve years old; her job, along with three hundred other women, was to sort the shoes of the eighteen thousand Jewish men, women and children who had been executed during Operation Harvest Festival at Majdanek con-centration camp in Poland. The girl lived and worked on a desolate road until she herself was murdered some months later. Yet she saw, she thought, and then she found the words and painted with them. It was an extraordinary act.

Decades after her dying, her poem "Schuhe von Toten " ("Shoes of the Dead") came to light. It was at the public prosecutor's office in Duesseldorf, Germany, in 1972. A Majdanek camp survivor who had remembered the poem spoke it aloud and finally it was written down. Was the young girl's act optimism or folly? Her decision to create inspires me more than the revulsion I feel for the depravity of those who killed her. The poem was the light of her imagination in a cave whose every entrance had been blocked by a landslide of hatred. Her words, together with some of the shoes she speaks of, are on display in the Bundeswehr Museum of Military History in Dresden—but any footprints they left have long gone.

Shoes of the Dead
In empty spaces,
bound by wire as if by cobweb,
there grow piles of shoes, shoes of the dead:
small shoes, children's shoes, men's shoes, girls' shoes.
High riding boots
shine with black eyes,
ladies' boots made from morocco leather
speak a mysterious language of their own.
The rain pours over them without a sound, like tears,
they are burnt by the sun.
They are sorted by nervous, trembling hands,
the piles grow, piles like giants,
becoming pyramids,
rising above themselves,
thrust into the sky like columns
shouting: Why, why, why?

Here I am. This is what I saw. The unknown girl was also asking if there might be meaning in any of this. Of course. Perhaps. Or not.

There are stories about long slumbers that have allowed a sleeper to step away from time. I have another fantasy journey in mind. The animals in the Chauvet Cave slept for 29,000 years. The stage in the Drottningholm Palace Theatre in Sweden slept for 129 years. The diversity of much of Earth's plant life sleeps in the seeds stored in the Svalbard Global Seed Vault, halfway between Norway and the North Pole, so that should the need arise, they may be awoken again. Rip Van Winkle slept. He was an odd man in a Washington Irving tale who enjoyed meandering in the Catskill Mountains. While out wandering one day, he met some ghosts who gave him a mysterious drink and Rip stretched out on the mountainside and slept for twenty years.

I would like to wander like Rip Van Winkle, meet ghosts and stretch out for 36,000 years. The gently curved high-gain antenna dish on *Voyager 2* is almost four metres wide and would be the perfect place. Facing back towards the Earth to receive signals from NASA's Deep Space Network, the dish would comfortably accommodate my tall frame. I could snooze on my back with my hands behind my head. Somewhere above me would be a now-invisible Earth. I might still see our sun amongst the billions of stars, but probably not. Behind my back, in the direction we would be travelling, will be the constellation of Andromeda. I would slumber on.

From time to time I'd awake in the dimness of the billions of points of light of the Milky Way and smudges of some of the trillion galaxies around me. *Voyager 2* and I would leave billions of infinitesimal shadows. Travelling at 55,000 kilometres an hour, we would seem to be at rest. Except for the beating of my heart, the silence would be matched only by the silence in the sealed Chauvet Cave. A metre from my head would be the gold-plated disk bolted to the side of the spacecraft, and all about me would be the greatest cave of all.

Sadly, I would be alone, since I don't think my family would want to accompany me. And sadly, I would be without the company of the artist with the crooked finger, whose companionship I might have enjoyed. However, I would be travelling with my friends Glenn Gould, Louis Armstrong, the Navajo singers, Blind Willie Johnson, the Budapest String Quartet and all the other artists. Their silent treasures, protected from the radiation of space by the gold skin of the record attached to our ship, would comfort me. Their marks *were* worth making.

To survive the interstellar winds, I would wrap myself in one of NASA's golden foil blankets so that my memories of the lives I saw played out on Earth would also be protected. When, or if, the disk is finally played, my new Andromeda friends might be able to add some of *our* music to their cave, just as we actors painted stories in our theatres by filling them with exuberance, insight, pain, love, questions, poetry and passion—in fact, everything about the architecture of being human—and then leave not a trace behind.

The spacecraft's small generator will stop working by about 2030, after which we will not be able to communicate or receive anything from Earth until we are found. Drifting in and out of sleep, sheltered from the wind by my thin film of gold, I will have time to think—to no one in particular—about why any of us has ever left marks at all. I would treasure the unknown girl's poem, since its creation was one of humanity's most optimistic acts. Borrowing a little of her courage, I know that our optimism has been justified in this endless and mysterious universe. As Carl Sagan wrote:

"The surface of the Earth is the shore of the cosmic ocean. On this shore, we've learned most of what we know. Recently, we've waded a little way out, maybe ankle-deep, and the water seems inviting. Some part of our being knows this is where we came from. We long to return, and we can, because the cosmos is also within us. We're made of star stuff. We are a way for the cosmos to know itself."

CHAPTER 12

A ROMANTIC ATTACHMENT

Joe Stratford

"At last we have got some good news. We got instructions to mobilize as a cavalry regiment and proceed overseas at once. This will take about four weeks to equip us and then I think we are off for sure. Thank the Lord. Now all we have to pray for is a charge and of all the glorious things that will ever be pulled off in this world, it will be the best. Could anyone imagine a 100,000 cavalry in a charge—and that is what it will be. It makes my hair curl to think of it."

—Joe Stratford's letter to his mother, 1916

In the last decades of the nineteenth century, Romanticism was at its extreme, in poetry, painting, music and nationalistic fervour. That era might appear a curiosity, were we not in danger of returning to it. My great-uncle Joe was a fighter, a romantic and a man known for his "dash," right down to the twin tips of his waxed mustache. Yet, alas, his dream of a cavalry charge of 100,000 horses never took place. Unmounted units of his regiment did serve time in the trenches, and there were some smaller engagements on horseback, but his dream died in the Great War. However, in April 1918, when the Germans were on the offensive in France that nearly won them the war, Joe's actions earned him the Military Cross. Here is part of his citation for bravery:

"He commanded the Fort Garry Horse Squadron in the attack on Bois-des-Essarts. While he was heavily outnumbered, he drove the enemy out of this section of the wood, with great dash."

But a week later, while sitting under a tree having lunch, shrapnel from an exploding enemy shell entered his abdomen and he was dead within fifteen minutes.

The late nineteenth century's flirtatious romance with sentimentality inflated the aspirations of nationalists, encouraged indulgent romantic poetry, bred music that was often nothing more than a sloshing soup of emotionality, and filled galleries with grandiose paintings. The Romantic era's soaring and easy-to-digest idealism had a talent for drowning critical questions and challenging observations, whether from artists or politicians. It also glamourized war and warriors.

Military officers, no matter their ability or brains, wore uniforms as colourful and plumed as exotic birds; the newsreels of the time show us how they could strut and pose in a manner befitting their plumage. Military designers outdid themselves with fabrics and tailoring that could transform a potbellied major into a miracle of manhood. In the name of fashion, Kaiser Wilhelm tinkered with his army's uniforms, making thirty-seven changes in sixteen years, according to Margaret MacMillan in *The War That Ended Peace*. Officers dressed for gallantry, masculinity, prestige and power. Even today, dubious dictators, whatever their continent, costume up as nineteenth-century European officers, laden with medals but light of meaning.

Joe could not have known that the First World War would be the last hurrah for warriors on horseback. Mechanization was changing warfare, and not for the better if you cared about the body count. Joe was frustrated at being kept "out of the line" because the cavalry was being held in reserve for the long-awaited breakthrough in the gridlock of trench warfare. The thinking was that, after the infantry (and later the new tanks) had broken the enemy's line, mounted men would pour through the breach with swords drawn and rapidly advance against the foe. While waiting in reserve, from mid-1915 to mid-1917, Joe wrote home about teas, training, parties, playing baseball, playing polo, and going to the beach to see the "girls" in their one-piece bathing costumes.

Joe's sword hangs on my study wall. As much as I rail against the war in which he fought, when I slip my fingers round the sword's grip and extend it forward in the "slope" position—palm up above my shoulder but blade angled slightly down—I catch a little of the thrill of my great-uncle's dream. Heels angled down in the stirrups, thighs tight to the flanks of the horse in full gallop beneath me, reins in the left hand and sword raised in the right, the horse's nostrils wide and its lungs heaving, we would descend upon our enemy—an intoxicating act of aggression riding to victory.

Fighters on horseback had first appeared from the Asian steppes three thousand years earlier, bringing a new terror to warfare as they swept west into Europe. Horses meant speed, mobility and status, since wealth was needed to possess them. Like the men on their backs, horses are herd animals driven by adrenaline and susceptible to fear. The wilderness in a horses' eyes matched the chaos of the warriors on foot being swept aside by their stampeding power—unless the warriors happened to be seated behind machine guns. The ancient thunder of hooves was no match for the modern chatter of the German Maxims.

Two schlägers hang either side of Joe's sword. They were given to me by a relative who had no use for them. They are German duelling swords made from heavy iron and combine romance and masculinity with militarism. Schlägers were the fashion for students at some German universities in the late nineteenth and early twentieth centuries. Lacking the elegance of an Italian rapier or the finesse of a French épée, they have a brutish quality in keeping with their nation's reputation for steel and blood. The blade ends with a sharpened curve the width of your little finger, meant for opening the skin of your opponent's face. Used for duelling, schlägers weren't operated at chest height as in traditional fencing, rather they were held high, similar to Joe's cavalry sword work, and swung so that they could slash at your partner's head. For a duellist to dodge a blow was considered dishonourable, since it implied a retreat from the romance in the violence.

German duellists even *looked* fanatical, fitted in their padded protective suits with high collars and heavy gauntlets. Heads were exposed except for wire-mesh goggles and a leather nose shield resembling a beak. Post-duel photos show students glistening with blood and manhood. Scars criss-crossing temples and cheeks became badges of bravery. It smacked of sadism, and some were rightly alarmed by the extreme sport that seemed part of Germany's enchantment with its own military, industrial and scientific might. Joe's hair-curling cavalry charge was meant to defeat that.

A useful policy tool

What were my great-uncle's expectations of going into battle? To follow in the hoofprints of Britain's heavy cavalry at the Battle of Waterloo? He had certainly thought that war was a legitimate activity of *civilized* peoples. As an officer in training he would have studied the art of war and the tactics of that famous battle that defeated

Napoleon. To Joe, wars were ways that nations defined themselves. They were noble affairs—particularly if you won them. Kings and dukes had been accustomed to buckling on a sword and cantering onto the battlefield. For governments wars were useful policy instruments for dealing with aggressors. The two global conflicts in which my family participated are good examples, since Germany (and later Japan) was a reckless advocate of militarism and had been the aggressor in both. World War I's Kaiser Wilhelm was a warmonger and Hitler was worse.

I propose that war has played a central role in the history of nations because it contains four articles of faith: (1) that the destiny of nations can be determined on the battlefield; (2) that battle is where heroism and manhood are expressed; (3) that the warrior's pride *is* the tribe's pride; and (4) that you secure your right to *be* a nation through victory. Warlords and tyrants live by that last one.

In a letter home, Joe berated his sister Helen (my grandmother with the toy soldiers in her basement) for doubting some of the men in the Canadian forces, writing that the British had *initially* thought the Canadian army a joke until nine months into the war, when they held the line near Ypres against the first German gas attack.

"Don't you ever say anything against the Canadians, as you did in your last letter calling some of them nuts. It was those same nuts that made the greatest stand (at Ypres the other day) that any army has ever made in the history of the world and the English people are just commencing to realize it and appreciate what Canada is doing for them. They thought the Canadian Army was a joke when they first came over here but they think something quite different now. I could go on talking all night about the Canadians because no one talks about anything else over here just now . . .

Just the other day we rode through an old [British] gent's estate and asked him if we could take our men through his deer park and over his fields, and he said certainly not, cutting up his meadows and frightening the deer, not on any account. But when he found out

later that we were Canadians he said 'My dear boy you can ride your
men through my house if you want to, go any place you like, the place
is yours.'

—Your loving Bro. Joe"

Canada's victory at Vimy Ridge two years later *was* inspiring.
In 1917 Canadian troops (with British support) drove the Germans
off a ridge in France. It was a rare victory in the third year of the
war. Achieved under basically Canadian command, our accomplish-
ment at Vimy *was* notable even though the action was a sideshow to
the main Battle of Arras. Some Canadians have made much of the
achievement, but if you think our military success at Vimy was connected to Canada's coming of age as a nation, then you might reflect
on your definition of nationhood. Until we dismantle that connection, we are less likely to step away from the assumption that war is
a legitimate policy instrument.

War's association with "heroic" acts barely survived the obscene
violence of the Second World War, and was almost obliterated by the
awkward military adventures in Vietnam, Iraq and Afghanistan. Yet
despite being shaken, the idea that warriors can be glamorous persists.
Yet again I am reminded of my father's fighting on the North Atlantic
and how little glamour or heroism he associated with it. *Necessity,* yes.
Bravery, yes. *Fortitude,* yes. *Drudgery,* yes. But *glamour?* No. Honour
can reveal itself in battle, but there is a quiet and deeper honour in
those who build peace. Yes, wars need champions, but they are more
urgently needed for peace. The fact remains that the popular war
stories with which we surround ourselves today—usually blockbuster
action films and first-person shooter games—continue to be violent
enchantments for many.

War's usefulness also went unquestioned because armies can be
tools for rulers in troublesome domestic situations. They were (and
are) the dictator's weapon against dissenters or the insubordination
of the underclasses. Soldiering in the nineteenth century was promoted as a manly profession that could get the idle lower classes away

from their drinking establishments and the fermentations of political agitators. Joining the army would turn them into *real* men, thereby ridding cities of degenerates while socially "cleansing" the nation.

In any war it is the lower and middle classes who do most of the actual fighting. Getting them into uniform and onto the parade square created the opportunity to re-instill their obedience to their betters, which the political activists had been wearing away at. Taken to its extreme, war was considered the storm that could purify and purge the tensions and disorder of societies. At the First World War's outbreak the promise of great battles was intoxicating, and the populations of belligerent nations revelled in a heady brew of patriotism . . . unless you were of German or Austrian heritage living in Canada.

Getting out of hand

And finally, conquest satisfies the temptation of financial or territorial gain. Until the Great War got out of hand, a successful battle-field adventure might make your kingdom and your elites richer by acquiring the loser's territory, their fertile lands, castles, slaves, works of art, their gold, their colonies, their coal (and later oil) fields and—in the case of Britain—by securing dominion over the seas to benefit your traders and bankers back home.

But when industrialized warfare got up to speed as it did in 1914–1918, victory only seemed possible by "wearing down" the enemy—meaning the attrition of men and materials. The *costs* became uncontrollable and big wars got expensive. In 1914, European bankers thought the war would last only a few months, because no nation could finance a longer one. It then continued for four years. Fear is difficult to conquer and expensive to maintain. Belligerent nations took out loans and sold off their family silver. Special taxes were created, which in Canada's case was a tax on income that was meant to be only temporary. Even today, small wars in small places might turn a profit as long as the nuclear weapons remain in the pantry. They always make money for someone.

In the 1950s, when I was balancing on the barrel of the trench mortar in front of my school, the world was strapping on its nuclear suicide vest. Yet few people thought that our stories about the uses of war *had* to change. There have always been pacifists and anti-war advocates, but the peace movement came of age only with the buildup of atomic arsenals after World War II. The early "Ban the Bomb" activists in the 1950s could be, and were, dismissed by their detractors, who reverted to calling them names—except for US president Dwight Eisenhower. As a five-star general he was no "peace-nik," but he was a realist who saw that war had reached a tipping point. After being presented with a federal committee report on the probable consequences of a nuclear confrontation with Russia, Eisenhower, former World War II supreme commander of Allied forces, said, "You can't have this kind of war. There just aren't enough bulldozers to scrape the bodies off the streets."

This was the possibility I grew up with. I was aware that a terrible bomb existed, which is why my father made sure that our basement could be a shelter as well as a playroom on rainy days. I knew that two cities had had atomic bombs dropped on them, which was all fine and good for the US commanders who wanted to showcase their new weapon for the Soviets, as well as achieve a quick wrap-up of the war with Japan. In their minds it helped that the tryout cities were both in Japan, whose army was known for its atrocities. However, I was only dimly aware that throughout the 1950s our Earth was being dusted with strontium-90 from atmospheric testing of successive generations of nuclear weapons. The detonations were conducted in the Pacific Ocean as well as at a test site in Nevada.

It was the dust from the tests that finally disrupted the story that wars were fine to fight as long as you won them. By the 1960s, in places such as St. Louis, Missouri, that were downwind of the testing sites, enough radioactive dust had accumulated in the food chain to increase by more than fifty times the amount of a cancer-causing isotope in the teeth of children born after 1950. The material had migrated from the test explosions to the pastures, to the cows, to the milk on the breakfast table, and finally to the bones and teeth of children. However, the radiation poisoning still wasn't enough to change the narrative of our *need* for war, but leaders were sufficiently alarmed to move the tests underground.

Movements grew to restrict nuclear weapons, yet few advocated for outlawing war. More than seventy years later, we *still* haven't changed the narrative that sustains the institution. Instead of gathering every November 11 to commemorate wars we did well in, perhaps we might explore other ways of acknowledging our war dead, while also asking serious questions about the institution itself. Nuclear non-proliferation treaties *were* signed to reduce the number of weapons in the national pantries, but according to military historian Gwynne Dyer, we really only tweaked the language by creating a category called *nuclear* war, in effect further normalizing what we refer to now as "conventional" war. Nuclear-tipped missiles are now "non-conventional" weapons. Language has the power to change the way we think, yet in this instance it increases the danger we have put ourselves in. The dust from our primordial past continues to drift down and accumulate in lethal amounts in our storied imaginations.

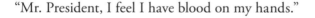

"Mr. President, I feel I have blood on my hands."

The physicist Robert Oppenheimer, referred to as the father of the atom bomb, is reputed to have said this to US president Harry Truman, who in 1945 ordered the nuclear attacks on Hiroshima and Nagasaki. He apparently said it several months after Japan's surrender, while in President Truman's office. Nagasaki had been hit only because on the day of the mission, the primary target city, Kokura, was under smoke and cloud cover that blocked the bomb aimer's sighting. So the B-29 loaded with the nuclear device named "Fat Man" flew on to the secondary target, Nagasaki. Fat Man went off about five hundred metres above a tennis court and generated temperatures approaching four thousand degrees Celsius.

We live in a casino, a house of odds in which we play every time we cross the street. To believe chance favours us, we take precautions against being hit by buses *and* we tell stories about how "good" people, by and large, survive the odds and "bad" people usually don't. But for the 35,000 children, women and men killed in the kilometre surrounding the tennis court, neither precaution nor story applied. The casino was ruthlessly rigged against them, with even the clouds and smoke over Kokura conspiring. Those individuals were among the more than 100,000 to, basically, instantaneously perish from just two nuclear devices.

We have run out of stories to justify an institution called war that can now destroy with sunlike power. Ironically, the odds weren't completely bleak for the people of Nagasaki, since there were fewer deaths there than at Hiroshima three days earlier. Fat Man's destruction had been somewhat muted by the valley in which Nagasaki lay. President Truman had become the casino dealer with the stacked deck. There are several versions of what he is reputed to have said in reply to Oppenheimer: "Well, here, would you like to wipe your hands?" is one, as he offered the physicist a handkerchief. There is also "The blood is on my hands. Let me worry about that," after which Truman told his secretary of state never to bring "that son of a bitch into this office ever again."

The year 1945 was the tipping point for the legitimacy of war. Germany, as World War II's warmonger, had brought a venerable institution to the brink of disrepute, but it was our side that pushed it over the edge. Before August 1945, wars were destructive, pain filled and often irresponsible, but they were what nations sometimes had to do to solve problems. But while we were defeating Germany for the second time that century, our imperilled goodness seduced us into pushing *everyone* across a line of no return. Ultimate weapons are extensions of ultimate war, and at least in the warmaker's logic, success on the road to victory means overcoming consciences concerned about collateral damage.

Hitler was such a menace and so morally bankrupt that our side decided to develop the "ultimate" weapon, which, for the first time, turned war into a *real* problem. Despite seeing ourselves as the good guys, we built it, tested it, witnessed the horror of the test detonations, and then dropped two atomic bombs on Japan anyway. Soon after the war ended—it was close to concluding anyway—my father returned home from the navy. Soon after that, I was born into the nuclear age.

It was our enchantment with the institution of war, which we believed could deliver us from the Nazi peril, that put us in ultimate danger. It took time for scientists to understand the consequences of the radiation poisons the new bombs produced, as well as the political repercussions of the weapons themselves. But whatever was understood at the baptism of nuclear weaponry at the test site in New Mexico, some, like Robert Oppenheimer, the lead scientist for the Manhattan Project, realized it was a point of no return. Twenty years after, this is what he said about witnessing the first detonation:

"We knew the world would not be the same. A few people laughed, a few people cried. Most people were silent. I remembered the line from the Hindu scripture, the Bhagavad Gita: Vishnu is trying to persuade the Prince that he should do his duty and, to impress him, takes on his multi-armed form and says, 'Now I am become Death, the destroyer of worlds.' I suppose we all thought that, one way or another."

Being a concerned man, in 1949 my father built the earth berm around our basement. He saw what some American military strategists were also seeing, that the new weapon's sunlike power and the radiation it released would turn battlefield attrition into mass civilian attrition. But what neither my father nor the strategists could see— since climate science didn't exist in the late 1940s—was that atomic war would also bring nuclear winter, after which would come the end of a lot of living things.

Observing dust storms on Mars in the 1970s, some space scientists became curious about how planets cooled. They explored how much the surface temperature of our red neighbour might be reduced by the storms of dust they saw through their telescopes. They concluded that temperatures would drop. Their calculations started others thinking about the climate consequences of a nuclear war on Earth. As with the storms on Mars, dust from nuclear explosions, combined with the soot and ash from the cities and forests that had been set alight, would be carried into the upper atmosphere by the mushroom clouds rising from the detonation hypocentres. The sun would be shuttered for possibly years, bringing crop failure and starvation to those not already dead from the blasts or dying from the radiation. War had become a *real* problem, yet, remarkably, too many of us remained enchanted by it.

Is it fear that makes us continue like this?

Perhaps some hardier species, such as the multi-legged cockroach, might survive such a holocaust, but not the two-legged vertebrates. For millennia our storytellers have told us how remarkable humanity is, and how in our brief history we have conquered so much: the challenge of making fire, competing religions, garden pests, the extraction of fossil fuel from rock formations, remarkable aliens in unremarkable movies, the storage of galactic amounts of data in microchips, instant global communication, space travel and most infectious diseases. But there have been few stories about how we conquer the fear with which we continually infect ourselves— because we never have.

"The only thing we have to fear is fear itself" was what US president Franklin D. Roosevelt said at his 1933 inauguration. He was referring to America's fears about the 1929 stock market crash and their limping economy, that if allowed to drive their decision-making would only make the economic depression worse. Fear can trump every other emotion. It can wrench the steering wheel away from rationality and reason. It *was* fear that steered us towards developing nuclear weapons.

To survive our fear, perhaps we need a vaccine with which to inoculate ourselves. Or, to get the ball rolling, maybe we could try reprogramming the "victory or perish" stories with which we dose ourselves. Our narratives must expand to include ourselves as part of the problem. In this regard, the German mortar in front of my school wasn't helpful, since having an enemy simplifies any narrative. Vilifying Germans in both wars as brutes in uniforms not only made them easier to kill but also made it more likely that *we* would develop nuclear weapons. Our attention is too often galvanized by the enemy from without, while the enemy within is ignored. The monster in *our* uniform makes a good war story challenging to tell.

The historical watershed created by nuclear weapons was assembled from our hubris and fear. The Americans built and dropped the bombs, but the Germans played their part by scaring us. Physicists had already calculated the unearthly amount of energy that would be released if one uranium nucleus could be split, uranium being the first and easiest choice of atom for the job. Things got rolling when European scientists fleeing the Nazis in World War II sounded the alarm that the Third Reich was developing a bomb that would use nuclear fission. Their alarm helped convince the United States to spend billions to create an atomic weapon, using uranium from (please note) Saskatchewan. The first device, named Trinity, was detonated in July 1945 in the New Mexico desert, and witnesses such as Robert Oppenheimer felt that they had seen the power of the sun. No military could turn down being the first to have the biggest bomb—certainly not America's, and certainly not when many felt we were in peril from a possible Nazi nuclear program. There is a lot of truth in that last sentence, but not enough for me.

It turned out that the fleeing scientists' fear was misplaced, since the Third Reich had abandoned its plans for atomic bombs and wanted instead to build nuclear motors. To be fair, intelligence about

Germany's nuclear ambitions was shrouded by the fog of war, but fear hurried us along, elbowing aside calls for caution and reason. More tragically, President Truman gave the order to use the bombs on Japan three months *after* Germany had surrendered. Even more tragically, a suggestion to detonate the first device off the coast of Japan rather than *on* the people of Hiroshima was rejected. Demonstrating the world's first nuclear weapon to the enemy in a non-combative manner, by exploding it over the sea near Japan, would be a warning about America's new capability, not a history-changing use of it. The coastal option was discarded, and more than 100,000 people were issued tickets to the rigged casino. The committee whose job it was to determine the targets for the first nuclear bombs was reminded that the US Air Force had only two devices ready for use in early August 1945. Because their cost was essentially in the billions, if one of them was used only for demonstration purposes, that would be expensive.

We are now past the point of no return: nine nations currently have nuclear weapons. In our collective atomic pantries there are about fifteen thousand devices, sufficient to finish off most of us and much of the biosphere several times over—if they are used. But heck, what's an *if* doing in a good war story?

Can we ever change our narrative about war?

In trying to bring Germany into *The World Remembers*, I realized that after the Second World War the Germans had already changed the story. Throughout World War II, mass civilian killings remained an acceptable policy tool, even after our side had firebombed Tokyo, Hamburg and Dresden. In Tokyo's tornado of fire of March 1945, 100,000 people burned to death, yet, despite the body count, neither side would relinquish what they thought was gained through war.

The very first change was made after World War II, when the casualty tally for both wars approached an estimated seventy to eighty million. Governments began to amend the nomenclature. Before World War II, governments had ministries of war, but after a rethink, the language was changed to ministries of defence. That was a start.

When victors tell war stories, they win again with each retelling. If being a winner is a must-have for your identity, then you may be deaf to stories that involve futility, tragedy, loss and failure. It takes a confident victor to tell stories of their own cruelty or incompetence. Of course, it made sense for our side to fear the Nazis, who wanted to murder their way to becoming the master race. Forty thousand British men, women and children died in 1940 and 1941 from Germany's bombing of English cities. Yet if we follow the facts, we also learn that 593,000 German civilians were killed by our bombing of *their* cities in the final years of the war. Those German civilian deaths are part of *our* story. Tailoring our uniforms to only question the morality of others does not serve the purpose of amending our narratives about war.

And when commemorating a war, if you *don't* take sides you can end up in a no man's land where it's not only the bullets that fly both ways but also the stories that each side launches to rationalize their behaviour. *The World Remembers* was going to be a project in which the names of those who killed my great-uncles would appear alongside those whom my family had killed. What would my great-uncles have thought about that? But the larger question about what to do when speaking about war is to ask how fighting changes us. The challenge for anyone who considers themselves to be on the side of *good* is to avoid thinking that you ever have licence to do evil. The mushroom clouds over Hiroshima and Nagasaki were illustrations of that darkest of transformations.

Our addressing of World War II's nuclear devices and firebombings means that the deaths we are remembering are most likely human ones. Has anyone ever tried counting the lost animals? Having Joe's sword, I wanted to know what happened to his horse. He never names his mare in his letters, but he does speak of her when he writes to his mother in August, 1916.

"Brigade sports starts tomorrow and I have entered my mare in the jumping class and expect to do rather well as I have been putting her through some pretty stiff training the last two weeks. She is now hard and fit. I wish you could see her all dressed up in white bandages on all four legs and just ready to take the jump. The minute I get in the saddle she starts to prance and play to the grandstand. She is such a pretty thing she at once wins over all the queens and naturally gets all the cheering and backing from the ladies . . ."

Over the years I have grown to like Joe. His élan radiates through his words, but his principles remain too brittle for me. If he had grown old, would he have become pompous and disillusioned? If I knew more about how he used his spurs when riding, I might have a better idea. The mare's flanks would have borne the scars if he had been cruel with his spurs.

There is no accurate number for the horses lost in the First World War; most likely it was around eight million dead, but that includes donkeys and mules. We can assume that many had gruesome ends. It is said sixteen million animals worked the war. Of those that survived, some were shot in 1918 because of their age or illness. Or, if they were not worth the expense of shipping home, they were sent to slaughterhouses in France and Belgium, since, like the soldiers who had attested to join the army, they were considered the property of the King. That is one of the uglier aspects of the romantic's idealistic face that is usually kept hidden.

CHAPTER 13

GERMANY AND THE ENCHANTMENT

a German naval officer with his sisters, 1935

I had been invited to the Volkstrauertag, the People's Day of Mourning, at the Bundestag, the modern German parliament building that had been built *within* the historic Reichstag. Walking Berlin's streets, I still had the eyes of the victor. The geography of my imagination overlay the city. Here was where our bombs had met the Nazi infamy. Hitler's bunker had been *here* in

Gertrud-Kolmar-Strasse. In those basement rooms on Niederkirch-nerstrasse, torture and interrogations had taken place. Do we ever escape the stories we've been told?

The Reichstag is a building infamous for having been burned by arsonists in 1933. Both the flames and the political accusations that followed helped the Nazi dictator consolidate his power. During the Cold War, the Reichstag sat largely neglected; only after Germany's reunification in 1990 was it fully rebuilt to include the new Bundestag. It was a symbol of Germany's modern and unified government *inside* the country's historic and troubled past.

The event was a gathering more than a ceremony, and again I wished that my father could have been with me. There were speeches, a German Second World War veteran spoke and a youth choir sang Mozart's "*Ave verum corpus.*" Arne Schrader, my contact at Volksbund Deutsche Kriegsgräberfürsorge, the German war graves organization whose motto is "Reconciliation above the Graves," had gotten me the invitation.

Commemoration rituals are brief visits to history. In Canada we dip into ours by remembering our wars and sacrifices in the reaffirming light of our victories. But for almost seventy-five years Germany has looked at its history of guilt and loss without that light. I watched veteran Heinrich Pankuweit's eighty-six-year-old face as he read his speech. He spoke of the death of his brother, who'd been shot down over England. It appeared that he and I agreed on the meaning of military cemeteries.

"The last German offensive caused immeasurable sacrifices. Within just one month, tens of thousands of young people died on both sides: Americans, British and Germans. Nor was the Belgian population spared in the bloody fighting.

The war on so many fronts, associated with such high losses, was part of our youth. It did not spare anyone—neither mothers nor children, neither the elderly nor the sick—war found its victims everywhere. Millions had been murdered, had died in ghettos, concentration and prison camps, lost their lives on the run, fell victim to hunger and deprivation, found a horrible death in the bombings and firestorms.

Their graves are irreplaceable memorials against war and forgetting. Every grave is a memorial to peace and reconciliation."

Heinrich was helped back to his seat and I can't recall if there was applause from the sea of uniforms present, from Germany's forces of land, air and sea. My father would have been 101 had he been beside me in his naval uniform. Would he have applauded? At Cambridge University in Britain before the war, he'd had German friends. After the war he shared a passion for sailing with a former member of the Luftwaffe. Yet for more than three years he had hunted Germans on the North Atlantic and had been hunted by them. I longed to glimpse his thirty-four-year-old face on the corvette's bridge—on winter watches, survivor watches, mid-Atlantic watches; firing warning shots at our own freighters that were slow to extinguish their lights; sighting suspicious oil slicks—or just reading Spinoza in his bunk while waiting for sleep before battle. Or having to abandon ship. When the war ended, he took custody of several German naval officers in the Channel Islands. Perhaps those men had been the fathers, uncles or cousins of those seated around me now in the Bundestag. And what might Woodburn have thought of his curious son and his First World War project of reconciliation?

The only photos at the ceremony were of French soldiers, appearing on large screens at either side of the speaker's platform. The assembled heads of grey and white hair carried a tincture of despair, for they, or their fathers, had lived through the 1939–1945 war. But the blond- and brown-haired heads of the youth choir that sang the Mozart were less encumbered, since the Nazis were from the world of their grandfathers. On the prowl afterwards for helpful German contacts, I took the elevator to the reception in the Reichstag's atrium on the top floor. It was lavish yet sparse, and the earnest talk and alcohol couldn't conceal the fact that Germany was the most prosperous and powerful nation in the European Union.

Near the Reichstag is the Brandenburg Gate, a triumphant stone monument built in 1790 by a Prussian king, topped with the goddess of victory in her chariot pulled by four horses. In Europe's relentless wrestling match of history, the goddess had been dragged back and forth. In 1806 Napoleon had her crated up as a war trophy and taken back to Paris; then, after Napoleon's defeat in 1814, the Prussians carted her back to Berlin. Now, for a price, buskers dressed as Cold War Russian or American soldiers will pose with you for photos in front of the goddess and the gate. Money is made and the cafés are full, but besides being prosperous, Berliners have chosen governments that keep alive the disturbing stories from their past.

Germany's history of authoritarianism and extermination camps has led it to reimagine the institution of war, since winning or losing really *isn't* a good reason for telling tales about it. VDK's motto, "Reconciliation Above the Graves," was chosen with this in mind. They prefer their stories as warnings about what can happen when a culture loses its conscience. Many Germans tell these stories, and those who don't are the white supremacist descendants of the Nazis who once more are beginning to take to the streets.

Not far from the Brandenburg Gate is the Memorial to the Murdered Jews of Europe, which resembles a miniature city of plinths. You can lose yourself walking in its four acres of pathways between the almost three thousand eyeless, concrete slabs. Placing this monument of Germany's murderous past in the centre of its capital city made it hard to look away. There is also the Topography of Terror Museum, built on the remains of the former Gestapo Secret State police headquarters. The remnants of its basements still have rubble from the Allied bombing in 1945. Neglected for decades, the site was finally excavated for public display. In those subterranean rooms, political prisoners were tortured and executed in the name of German nationalism. These places of past horrors are on public display to remind us that the future must be better.

Occasionally I've been asked if I would expand my reconciliation project beyond the First World War and include the names from 1939–1945. Would we name the Nazis who had lost their lives? Casting Germans as faceless villains certainly helps the victors write their narratives. It makes the storytelling simpler. But if the individuals were ordinary men who had drunk the fascist ideology and then worked the triggers and trains that ran the camps that murdered millions, could they be part of the commemoration story? Usually my reply would be "Not yet, if we ever can," and certainly not while anyone remains alive from that time who might be reinjured by the act. We have no right to trespass on the emotional memories of those who lived through the Second World War.

But perhaps by 2035, or after the last surviving witness has passed on, then, no matter how our narrative imagination rebels, we *must* name all the dead from World War II and face down every victor's war story ever told. Should I be alive in 2035, to start the ball rolling I'd first approach Germany, since its memories of 1939–1945 are perhaps the most complex. My final appeal would probably be to the United Kingdom since, if my experience with *The World Remembers* is anything to go by, it would join only if every other nation did.

The *Sunday Times* in London included an article about my plans for *The World Remembers* in 2013: "Cenotaph Tribute to German War Dead . . . The Red Baron is among the war victims whose names could be displayed at the [British] Cenotaph." The Red Baron was the World War I German flying ace who shot down eighty Allied aircraft. I had initially welcomed the British press coverage, presuming it might help persuade their government to join. But the English can have a subtle way of looking down on people not-from-the-island. Despite the Nazis not having existed in 1914, the article called the project "a controversial gesture of reconciliation." Its writer, Nicholas Hellen, had invoked tribalism while trolling for readers. Indignation gathers an audience, which is, of course, what publishers want. Omitted was the fact that our commemoration would respect the integrity of the British Cenotaph as being only for British names. Why was the victor-or-vanquished narrative still locked in the imagination of the *Sunday Times*?

"The name of every German soldier killed in the First World War could be displayed at the Cenotaph side by side with the British dead as part of the centennial commemorations. Under the proposal, the name of the German flying ace, Manfred von Richthofen, known as the Red Baron, would appear as part of a roll call of the 9.5m military fatalities from all combatant nations. The Cenotaph, focus of an annual wreath-laying ceremony led by the royal family, has come to represent all British war dead and opening up the hallowed ground to acknowledge former enemies would be a controversial gesture of reconciliation."

Ninety-nine years after 1914, the British newspaper remained bound by a narrative from the past. In the German media in 2008, there had been mention of the death of Erich Kästner, Germany's last living First World War soldier, but his dying went basically unrecognized. In contrast, the final British soldier, Harry Patch, who died a year later at 111, was feted and filmed. Mr. Patch presented an opportunity for Britain to burnish its history, and a state funeral was proposed. But Harry's thinking had been ahead of his government's, and they had to be careful about showcasing him. The world's *final* veteran of trench warfare had referred to Remembrance Day as "show business," adding, "If any man tells you he went over the top and wasn't scared, he's a damned liar." Among Harry Patch's other offerings was that war was "a licence to go out and murder." Before he died he let it be known that he had no interest in a state funeral.

Arne Schrader of VDK was familiar with the challenge of naming dead soldiers, whatever their history. Germany's First War narratives pale beside Hitler's moral swamp of the Second. Publicly remembering *any* dead German soldier from the Great War might be seen as honouring them and *possibly* condoning the nightmare of 1939–1945. Arne reminded me that my project was about naming individuals, not armies or nations, and VDK's policy of remembering the past in order to prepare a better future was a good fit with *The World Remembers*.

⁓

I was surprised by the young man from the 1930s whom I saw in a German photo album. The collection had been donated to the Bundeswehr Museum of Military History in Dresden by the family of a German naval officer. The young man looking at me from the photo was the spitting image of my father. There *he* was in a blue-black double-breasted naval officer's jacket, tightly tailored with his lieutenant's gold rings circling the cuffs of his sleeves. I stared at the young officer who was looking back at me.

Of course, my father *wasn't* in the album, but his double was. Both men were trim and fit, with handsome seafaring faces atop almost identical uniforms. Both were heading to sea to serve their nation. The young Deutschlander's sisters, glowing in their white summer dresses, are either regarding the camera or adoring him. The photographs catch the calm before the oncoming storm. My parents' wedding picture, taken just a few years later, at the beginning of the Second World War, also shows a trim naval officer beside a young woman in white. Woodburn is a single-purposed young man in uniform with a new bride by his side. My mother glows in her wedding dress.

Their officer's hats—one German, one Canadian—would have been basically identical, with naval insignia in gold thread and crowns above their visors. They would soon be worn at sea, saturated by salt spray, and perhaps years later would appear on the heads of small sons flying orange-crate Spitfires. The collection of photos shows the German officer sailing yachts and small sailboats as part of his sea training. In my mind, there again was my father standing by the mainmast shrouds. In preparation for the approaching war, my father told me, he'd sailed whatever he could lay his hands on. Fate for both men might mean battles at sea and shipmates sewing them into canvas naval hammocks for burial beneath the waves. But my father survived the war, and on his return home was back on the water, sheets and tiller in hand, teaching me about the unpredictability of the wind and how small vessels must be handled in rough seas.

Seeing the German officer *was* seeing my father. Their two worlds seemed almost interchangeable. Their faces carried identical ambitions. Their families were sending them on similar national adventures—that is before Germany turned toxic with fascism and history turned the two young men into victor and villain. Sections from Käthe Kollwitz's 1916 journal come back to my thoughts:

"Now the war has been going on for two years and five million young men are dead, and more than that number are miserable, their lives wrecked. Is there anything at all that can justify that? People who could be friends under other conditions now hurl themselves at one another as enemies."

—journal entry, October 11, 1916

The young naval officer's pictures also address the power of the seas and the ships that sailed them. Unlike the army, the navy doesn't really do parades. Intricate formations of marching men have never helped sailors win battles on water. Yet after I read the instructions on page thirty-four of my father's *Royal Naval Handbook of Field Training*, I knew that he had taken both sword and cutlass courses. Naval traditions run deep. But the bravura of parade-ground precision doesn't fit well with navy uniforms. Seamen had the practical responsibilities of operating complex ships to do battle in any of the world's oceans. Both lieutenants experienced the greatest expansion of naval power the world had yet seen. And on the eve of the Second World War, both Canada and Germany were young federations that had existed for less than one hundred years, the one formed in 1867 and Germany four years later, in 1871.

But there the parallels end. Canada (and my family) remained in thrall to Britain's imperial ambitions, whereas Germany became Europe's major power and a militaristic nation. By 1910 the German land force was unsurpassed in size and strength, and they were racing to build their sea power to compete with the immense British battleships nicknamed dreadnoughts. Weighing in at twenty thousand tons, their launchings fed the nationalistic cravings of their leaders. Yet countries such as France and Britain, while alarmed by Germany's military buildup, were blind to their own embrace of militant nationalism. Napoleon's armies had kicked their way across the continent to the outskirts of Moscow before being defeated by a coalition of Britain, Austria, Prussia and Russia. The British were particularly brutal with their sea power, policing the world's oceans in their own commercial and imperial interests and never hesitating to punish another nation's sea trade through blockades. Yet it was the new Germany's Prussian-driven militarism that rang alarm bells for many. And, in hindsight, rightly so, given that an estimated 75 million lives were lost dealing with Germany's aggression in the twentieth century's two world wars.

But in 1945, just thirty-one years after the Kaiser's army invaded Belgium and France in 1914, Germany awoke from its militaristic nightmare and began recasting itself as a post-heroic nation, turning away from the great-leader, great-pride, great-nation exceptionalism and becoming a land of antiheroes searching for peace rather than the flag-waving domination of others. Only in response to the deaths of German soldiers serving in Afghanistan was a memorial built in 2009, and its purpose was *only* to acknowledge troops killed *after* 1955. Its architecture is neither grand nor a statement of national purpose. Even its location, in a parking lot behind the defence ministry in Berlin, seems post-heroic.

Inside the cubelike structure, soldiers are individually remembered. The interior darkness is broken only by light from the entrance behind you and from openings at the top of its ten-metre-high walls. In the dim silence of its contemplation room, the names of the German dead are projected one at a time on the wall above your head, their anonymity being withdrawn only for a few seconds each, to suggest the transitory nature of their lives. The absence of statuary avoids any glorification. Preconditioned as I was by the memorials of the victors, it took time to appreciate this alternative language of memory.

During a conversation I had with Arne Schrader about Germany and *The World Remembers*, he said VDK's energies are mostly spent recovering the identities of soldiers who had been lost in Russia. You may recall that a copy of the Kollwitz *Grieving Parents* sculpture was recently installed in a war cemetery in Rzhev, outside of Moscow. Arne estimated that VDK was searching for more than 500,000 unknown First World War soldiers.

The loss implied in a sequence of zeros staggers me. The millions of World War I deaths from Germany, France and Russia never fail to put Canada's history in perspective. How *do* people absorb the immensity of that loss? Do we wrap our imaginations so tightly to our bones to avoid being overwhelmed by the pain? Does horror numb us into fatalism? Russia's arbitrary destruction of Mariupol, Ukraine, in 2021 or, through its support of Syria's Bashir al-Assad, of the city of Aleppo in 2016, can drive the peacemakers to despair.

However much I challenge the grand, heroic First World War monuments of the victorious nations, their grandiosity *does* in a way set the lives lost in an appropriately large landscape. As Canadians we don't create heroic portraits of our national dreams, since we distrust the myth-making needed to inspire any grandiose brushstrokes. However, for more than three centuries the malevolence towards Canada's Indigenous peoples *was* played out on just such a mythic scale, and only now are our non-Indigenous peoples beginning to see that.

Germany is still finding thousands of lost soldiers' remains each year in western Russia and eastern Ukraine, Belarus and Lithuania. One of the methods of locating the burial sites is by speaking with local village elders about their childhood memories. *Yes, there was fighting over in those fields and there will be graves in that part of the forest.* Where their stories lead, the searchers dig. It is similar to the First Nations' desire to find their lost children, long passed over by Canada's history. The elders remember and the ground-penetrating radar probes. There is urgency in both cases. The elders in western Russia, Belarus, Lithuania and Ukraine are mostly in their nineties, and when they die, the whereabouts of perhaps 400,000 German ghost soldiers may disappear with them. But in Canada, a dark luck is buried within the tragedy, since the graves of the Indigenous children are mostly located near the residential schools where they died. Canadians are now exploring how to live with the immense pain of those historic losses.

⌒

At the Bundestag ceremony, France had provided their soldiers' photographs that were displayed on either side of the speaker. The collaborative remembrance rituals of the Germans and French had begun thirty years before at Verdun in France; before that they had followed the usual "us-versus-them" playbook. You will recall that Verdun's Douaumont Ossuary holds the bones of perhaps

130,000 *unidentified* French and German soldiers. The *identified* Verdun dead, who number 132,000, are buried nearby. If you have a moment, let your imagination loose on how it came about that those two numbers are almost the same. But such was the insanity of the fighting that neither number is really accurate—just as when you look through the ossuary's small basement windows, you see mounds of bones inside, yet you cannot tell which belong to any particular body. Some piles are a jumble of vertebrae, fingers, femurs, toes, jaws and pieces of pelvis. Others are thighbones stacked one upon another like a log cabin. Skulls are lined up as if on parade.

A significant page was turned in the evolution of remembrance rituals at Verdun when in 1984 French president François Mitterrand and German chancellor Helmut Kohl held hands as they laid two memorial wreaths. It was a moment that bridged their nations' divide. They remained silent, making *no* political speeches, but stood hand in hand for several minutes as the anthems of both nations were played. The gesture was so simple, yet so important. The catafalque before them held a coffin draped on one side with the French flag and on the other with the German. Since then their countries' commemorations emphasize unity. Heinrich Pankuweit made a reference to it as he ended his speech in the Bundestag:

"I would like to thank the Luxembourg prime minister, Jean-Claude Juncker, for his words 'Those who doubt Europe, who despair of Europe, should visit military cemeteries.'"

⌒⌒⌒

Some Eastern European nations are now exercising a self-interested nationalism as they slide towards authoritarianism, restricting the free press, politicizing the courts and marginalizing the opposition. But German governments, both federal and local, resist the tide of intolerance even as far-right groups in their nation grow. Germany has made it illegal to question the existence of crimes against humanity.

It is a criminal offence to deny the Holocaust. The swastika symbol is forbidden. These laws restrict freedom of expression—a liberty so broadly defined in the United States that hate speech has become a legitimate currency—but are intended to contain the horror that Germans know too well.

Several days after the Bundestag ceremony, Arne Schrader and I were finishing our coffees before attending a meeting at the German foreign office. We had been exchanging views about the security cultures of different nations when Arne rose to his feet, impersonating an American ambassador's personal protection detail. Arne was a former soldier whose injuries while in training for the Kommando Spezialkräfte had ended his military career. In the large public lobby of the foreign office he performed a security ballet that might have been titled "As The World Menaces We Are Strong and Free." As head of VDK's commemorations, he had just returned from a ceremony at one of Germany's war cemeteries just outside Cairo. I'd been telling him about the remembrance events in Belgrade where I'd observed the Serb, American and Russian security services at work protecting their diplomats.

Slipping on his sunglasses, Arne was on his feet in a bob-and-weave waltz, his imaginary automatic weapon poised before him in the alert-and-armed position, as fetishized by action films. America no doubt has its enemies, but it's a sign of self-importance if you presume that *your* freedoms are under perpetual threat. Knees slightly bent, Arne's choreography pivoted him round the small tables in the foreign office lobby, tracking how the protection detail had to declare the cemetery *SECURE* before the ambassador could emerge from his armoured SUV and join VDK's commemoration. It was a pleasure to watch the former German paratrooper's performance, his finger pressed to an imaginary earpiece for threat updates, his body turning, sector by sector, in a minuet of masculinity. Finally, Arne paused and said with amazement, "It was a *German* cemetery! Who was going to attack them *there*!?"

My father had always encouraged me to read the French philosopher Simone Weil, and only recently did I open the pages of *The Iliad, or The Poem of Force* and read:

"Force is as pitiless to the man who possesses it, or thinks he does, as it is to its victims; the second it crushes, the first it intoxicates."

CHAPTER 14

SAILING WITH MY FATHER

The difficulty lies not so much in developing new ideas
as in escaping from the old ones.
—John Maynard Keynes

the German trench mortar in front of
my school in Richmond Hill

At twenty, while wondering what to do with his life, my father
studied economics at Cambridge University in Britain in the
early 1930s. At our dinner table he sometimes talked about
his friendship with German students at the university and the lectures given by John Maynard Keynes. In 1934 Woodburn was on

his college's rowing team (the year after the Reichstag was burned and Hitler took power) and sailed down the Bay of Biscay in a boat named *The Windflower*, which he and fellow students had rented that summer. They had no problems on the open ocean, but *The Windflower* sank after being accidentally rammed by a fishing trawler while moored in a Spanish port.

Keynes, you may remember, was the economics delegate for the British Treasury at the Treaty of Versailles negotiations—the British Treasury is the institution that American nurse Mary Borden will throw a rock at in the next chapter. Keynes's team had been asked to calculate how much the losers *could* pay the winners. They concluded that financially punishing Germany the way France and Britain wanted would damage the German economy, bankrupt Berlin and that the world would be worse off. Keynes eventually quit the Peace Conference in protest and wrote his book *The Economic Consequences of the Peace*, which brought him renown—not all of which was positive. His views about the difficulty of escaping old ideas, especially in the aftermath of wars, were spoken about at our dinner table. I mention all this since, in a sense, I've spent my life looking for my father. Of course he was the man who helped raise me, but it's the person, not the parent, that I want to know. The act of searching for *who* he was has tightened my embrace of his memory.

Stories told in the aftermath of wars

Woodburn encouraged me to look at familiar things in unfamiliar ways. After attending plays I was in at school and later university, he would ask what I *thought* about the story beneath the drama. What was really concerning the playwright? Therefore my father *is* in my thoughts when I propose that each war carries with it a hierarchy of stories—those told before, during and after—each set with its own purpose. The *before* stories create the conditions in which nations decide to fight and provide the megaphones for patriots. The middle set of stories are told *during* a war, when communities are under fire. These stories are usually fragmented, censored, self-interested and at times desperate, as when Isabel told my great-grandmother of the atrocities against the Belgians when Germans "brought out the nuns from a convent & outraged them." Anxiety stalks these tales since their endings are not yet decided. The middle stories search for meaning in the continuing violence since we all dread a world without meaning in which people are killed for no reason.

The third set—and the most important—try to understand the conflict or, some would say, to shape it to a particular point of view. These stories produce the histories and the memorials. They are significant not only because factions want *their* versions of history to prevail, but also because what is written afterwards may determine if wars will be fought again. These stories can be as important as the fighting itself. Of course, wars must be won on the battlefields, but their legitimacy must be secured by the stories that come after.

———

While John Maynard Keynes never visited Richmond Hill, in my mind he has a connection with the enemy trench mortar on which I climbed after school, in that the war trophy was an *old* idea that the town had difficulty escaping from. Astride its barrel, I rode the winner's version of the three major historical narratives that prevailed after 1918—namely that Canada had won a great victory and that peace was achieved only through our noble sacrifice of lives. The second is the loser's narrative, namely Germany's, in which it *hadn't* been defeated; rather, its army had been politically betrayed, "stabbed in the back" by Bolsheviks, Jews, republicans and an unpatriotic populace. The third historical narrative is the Russian revolutionary's: that the 1914–1917 war was perpetrated by capitalist imperialists, a catastrophe for the proletariat and best forgotten since the glory of the Soviet Socialist Republic lay ahead. All three versions have been challenged during the century since, yet still they persist.

I don't recall my father ever telling any victor's stories; rather, he would speak about the frustrations of convoy duty, what the corvettes' crews had to endure, being under the command of an

objectionable commanding officer, and the four-day battle off
Greenland. But Richmond Hill had been eager to tell the victor's
story. Following the Great War, communities across Canada were
commissioning monuments, building memorial halls and asking
the government in Ottawa for war relics. The Imperial War Trophies
Committee in Britain had collected and then distributed battlefield
booty throughout the Empire. Canada received its share of the loot
and set aside funds for "the cleaning, repairing, transporting and
distributing of war trophies throughout the Dominion."

Ottawa had received hundreds of captured trench mortars,
field guns, machine guns, several dozen German aircraft, five thousand rifles and bayonets, and five thousand "empty brass shell cases
of various sizes." Arthur G. Doughty, the Dominion archivist in
charge of trophy distribution, wrote, "When our tears are dried and
Time has assuaged our sorrow, then shall we seek for memorials of
this momentous event and regard them as our *ancestral heritage*."
Richmond Hill's request for a relic was granted and on July 9, 1919,
the 170mm German mortar arrived by train to become part of our
"ancestral heritage"—that of being the noble defenders of freedom.

Yet commemoration stories that centre on valour, victory and
sacrifice bring danger with them. When war memorials reference the
carnage in such selective ways, they are incurious about what *really*
happened and what, if anything, we might have learned. I know of
no Canadian monuments that depict amputees or corpses. I know
of no memorials that attempt to portray the mental wounds of veterans. The Tomb of the Unknown Soldier in Ottawa comes closest to
raising questions, since we only know that someone's bones lie within
it. Part of the Unknown Soldier's power is in his silence. I think perhaps the postwar storytellers counted on the millions of dead remaining silent, lest the view from the graves overpower what they wrote.

Consider the killing at the Battle of Verdun in France in 1916.
The voices of the 262,000 who lie in Verdun's war cemeteries and
ossuary have never been heard, but for one remarkable exception.

The French silent film *J'accuse!* was shot in the final months of 1918 as the armies were still fighting. The movie was completed in 1919. In it, a shell-shocked French veteran summons the dead soldiers from their graves to remind the living of the catastrophe of the war. In the fantastical scene that follows, thousands of French *poilus* leave their cemeteries and march into town to confront the inhabitants about their amnesia concerning the human cost of the war and their complicity in the killing. The soldiers leave their graves to accuse the living of believing in the fraudulent peace that was made in 1919. The character of Jean Diaz, the shell-shocked veteran, even condemns the sun for its complicity in the crime of the war.

And yes, the victory achieved in November 1918 and the peace that followed are a form of fraud, because twenty-one years later the same sides were at it again. In 1938, the year before that next world war broke out, the director of *J'accuse!,* Abel Gance, shot the film a second time and because by 1938 movies had sound, Jean Diaz, the French veteran, could speak:

"I accuse yesterday's war of creating today's Europe. And I accuse tomorrow's war of preparing its destruction. I accuse mankind of failing to learn any lessons from the last catastrophe, of waiting with folded arms for the next war. I accuse the careless, the short-sighted, the egotists of having allowed Europe to be divided instead of building a permanent alliance. And I accuse the men of today, not only of failing to understand, but of laughing when reminded of the most beautiful expression on earth: love one another. And I accuse you same men of ignoring the voices of the millions who died in the war who have cried out to you these past twenty years: 'Stop, you're taking the same terrible path!'"

My town's trench mortar bolstered our patriotism until I was in Grade Six, when it mysteriously vanished. Some say that pranksters turned it around one night and fired it at the school, but that couldn't have been possible since its layers of paint meant that *none* of its mechanisms moved. My friends and I knew this because we had banged away at its frozen parts with sticks of wood. Another tale told of a gang of boys who got it rocking on its wheels until, unexpectedly, it broke free and rolled out onto Yonge Street. Richmond Hill being appropriately named, the mortar rolled down the hill before coming to rest at the bottom. Who knows?

However, the instrument of death *did* disappear. Peter Wilson, at the town's library, thinks it spent years in someone's garage until it vanished for good. Perhaps the paint gave up and it fell to pieces, or else it was sold for scrap. But whatever happened, the town persisted with the narrative that the war had brought meaning to Canada, that settling disputes on battlefields was a legitimate government policy, and that it was only a tragic fact that millions had been killed in the process.

The stories told after a war are doubly disturbing because, for the most part, they are created by those who never saw combat. Ask yourself what might have been memorialized if commemoration committees were composed *only* of those who had done the fighting? In 1934, the *Toronto Star*'s Gregory Clark, a decorated Vimy Ridge veteran, wrote about the gulf between the attitudes of those in combat and those at home. For the newspaper's World War I photo series, Clark produced this caption for a picture showing Canadian and German troops waiting together at a medical dressing station in Belgium.

"There seems to be little hate here. But of course these are just common front line soldiers. Every mile you went back of the line the hate grew stronger, until at last, when you got right back to civilization, there you found hate in its pure unadulterated essence. These boys called him Jerry. Back home, they called him the Hun."

What might have been the meaning of war monuments if memorial committees had been made up of combat veterans from both sides? I mentioned the film *J'accuse!* since its director had served in the French army's film section and his assistant, the veteran Blaise Cendrars, could only use his right arm, having lost his left in the war. Ernest Hemingway described Blaise Cendrars in *A Moveable Feast,* "with his broken boxer's face and his pinned-up empty sleeve, rolling a cigarette with his one good hand." The scenes of the *poilus* rising from their graves were filmed just weeks before the Armistice in November 1918. The roles of the dead summoned to warn the living were played by two thousand French soldiers who were on leave from the fighting at Verdun. After their appearance in *J'accuse!* as "special business extras," they returned to their other business of war. The director Abel Gance described it this way: "The conditions in which we filmed were profoundly moving. These men had come straight from the Front—from Verdun—and they were due back eight days later. They played the dead knowing that in all probability they'd be dead themselves before long."

I wanted *The World Remembers* to take its cue from Jean Diaz and ask each of the First World War dead to *stand* and *state* their name. We had the technology to individually display the millions of names around the world. All that was needed was for "the careless, the short-sighted and the egotists" not to block the project.

～～

My father, the wind and the sea

The story of who my father was is bound up with his sailing of anything onto which he could attach sails, including canoes. Wind and water were his elements. From design plans he found in a magazine, he once constructed a small dinghy that the family christened the *At Last*, because of the years it had taken to complete. Woodburn found old boats in fields and trailered them to our cottage to repair. He bought a used one-person iceboat—basically a wooden cross with a seat, a sail, a mast and three steel skates on which the craft was capable of high speeds if the ice conditions at the cottage were right—which, sadly, they never were when he got there in the winters.

When I was five, my father bought an aging fishing trawler in which Estonian refugees had recently escaped the Soviet occupation of their Baltic nation. We marvelled at its one-cylinder diesel engine, whose flywheel was the size of a set of encyclopedias. The beast, which sat just behind the ladder leading up from the trawler's cabin to the stern deck, was started by heating its cylinder head with a blowtorch. Together with its sails, the vessel had carried the refugees to South America before it ended up in Toronto's harbour, which in the 1950s smelled of dead fish and bilge oil. We didn't marvel at the crusted paint on its wheelhouse that my brother and I were recruited to chip away. Despite its paint-lift, age eventually took the *Baltic Belle* to the harbour bottom, but by then my father had moved on to his next boat.

In the Second World War, Woodburn was on convoy duty (without sails) in corvettes. Having been brought up reading boys' adventure stories and occasionally hearing our town's air-raid siren, I was curious about what fighting was *really* like. Who was my father when he was at war? Even then I wondered if the man who had made life-and-death decisions on a warship was the same dad who tucked me into bed at night. I was in my twenties when he bought a second-hand Olympic class catamaran. The *Tornado* had two long, thin hulls that made it seem like a racehorse. While crewing for him, I thought I glimpsed my father at sea. The *Tornado* was about power, risk and speed.

In my short-pants years, my older brother John and I shared a bedroom. When our father came to say goodnight, he would give us back rubs while he told us stories. I have forgotten how much I yearned for security then. Those stories might be about the battle off Greenland when Allied aircraft from Iceland appeared to attack the German U-boats, forcing them to submerge and giving the convoy my father's corvette was escorting a chance to make it home to Halifax. When my brother and I complained that our bedroom was too small, he described how more than forty sailors slept in shifts in hammocks hung in the cramped seamen's mess in the bow of the corvette, and how there was only a quarter-inch steel-plate hull between the crew and the cold ocean. And that led to the tale of the Liberators that had flown out from Reykjavik to come to the aid of the combined convoys ON 202 and ONS 18 on the third day of the battle. The warmth of his hands rubbing my back as I drifted to sleep told me that I was treasured.

Sea skills became family games on road trips, with my father acting the part of a naval rating and steering the car according to our orders. We had learned the terms that described the position of the corvette's rudder. We knew that *midship* was navy talk for going straight ahead, and that *port* and *starboard* were navy talk for left and right. But we were just learning that the number after the port or starboard command would determine the degree that the rating turned the ship's rudder. The greater the number, the sharper the turn. My brother, sister and I were the bridge officers, and the family car was ours to command. To a chorus of "Port 10, no, midship, starboard 15, wait NO starboard 5, midship, starboard 5! midship! MIDSHIP!", we weaved down the highway, our father insisting that he was just following orders. Such were the responsibilities of young men who commanded 950-ton corvettes.

Would we have enjoyed the games so much if my father's navy had been on the side that lost the war? After he tucked me in and turned off the light, I thought about what he'd told us from beneath the warmth of my blankets. But it would be years later, on heavy-weather days when he and I took out the *Tornado*, that I saw something of him *at* war. In gusts reaching seventy kilometres an hour, with sails, steel rigging and sheets hard tight, we might cross the four-kilometre-wide lake in four minutes. At that speed, the *Tornado*'s rigging rang like a giant cello. Shouting to make ourselves heard over the wind and spray, the rising notes in the shrouds meant we were closing in on top speed. Ever faster meant even less time for decisions, and a miscalculation with either tiller or main sheet might capsize us or worse, bury the tip of the catamaran's lee hull in an oncoming wave. The boat's hulls were designed to cut *through* waves rather than ride over them, and the cold water that had been cut became, an instant later, what was flying at our faces. Exhilarated by the speed, we drove into the heavy winds wild enough to capsize us.

Travelling at close to fifty kilometres an hour, should a miscalculation with the tiller bury the tip of the lee hull, that tip would be driven down *into* the lake and come to an abrupt halt. Then everything else—my father, me, the two six-metre hulls and the eleven-metre mast with its sail locked to its top—would continue in a cartwheel *over* the water. Speed *was* risk since when catamarans cartwheel, they end up upside down, the top of the mast pointing at the bottom of the lake. Heavy winds shorten your breath, as well as the time you have to make decisions. At the rate we were going, our bodies jacketed with rain gear, capsizing was not danger-free. That was when I caught a glimpse of him at sea—one hand on the tiller, the mainsail sheet in the vise grip of the other, his eyes to windward watching for whatever might descend on us next. His voice warning, "Never wrap the sheet around your hand, because you'll never be able to react fast enough in an emergency."

Glancing back at him in those moments—winds running at us, water streaming from our faces, my aching hands working the jib sheet, leveraging my body far out over the windward hull to force it down to gain even more speed, the lake flying past beneath my back-side—I saw my thirty-four-year-old father on the bridge of his cor-vette. Immersed in the elements but not yet at their mercy, decisions were made with instinct and sea-experience, yet things could always end badly. Clinging to our thoroughbred wind-horse, hanging on to the speed as squalls rolled over us, eyes squinting to windward, my father would shout out, "Put her to it! Put her to it!" as we sped on over the darkening lake.

He knew what the wind's fists could deliver. When Woodburn was young, he'd been taught to sail by a navy veteran named Jock, and in heavy weather Jock had *insisted* that the course be held and that the boat be "put to it!" During the war years, with convoys of forty to ninety freighters, all restricted to the speed of the slowest ship, my father welcomed foul weather because storms kept the submarines beneath the surface, where they would be less likely to attack. I marvelled at the strength of his hands which, long after mine were numb with cold, handled sheets and tiller without complaint.

After two serious accidents when I was in my twenties, the *Tornado* was sold. No lives were lost but both had seen lives threatened. The second was my fault, since when out in late October with my sister and (then) brother-in-law, I was at the helm and I had miscalculated. The wind was strong, cold, and restless, sheering down without warning. I'd wanted speed and I got it. And yes, the top of the mast did end up pointing at the bottom of the lake. As I stood on the overturned catamaran, the squalls drove the waves over me while frequently burying those trapped in the water, making it risky for any rescue boat to approach. Hours later, when it was over and everyone was safe on land, I no longer cared what damage had happened to the *Tornado* since my sister's life had come close to ending. Alone by the shore that evening, the cold of the October water still in my bones, the lake looked at me—*hard*. As if speaking, it regarded *me*. There was a voice, but it had no sound, warning that I had *not* respected its power, and that it didn't care about life and could take it in an instant.

What then was being on the North Atlantic, bracing yourself on the bridge of a nine-hundred-ton corvette while being tossed about in heavy weather? HMCS *Sackville*, with my father as first lieutenant, would roll *forty* degrees to one side and then *forty* degrees to the other. On a blustery trip up Georgian Bay in a two-masted ketch—another old wooden sailboat that he'd bought—while fighting seasickness on deck, I watched him through an open hatch making sandwiches in the galley below. Rolling and pitching while under sail in weather which meant few were interested in eating, without a thought he'd jammed his legs and knees against the counter and bulkhead so that no matter how the ketch veered about, he could finish making lunch. He was a child of the open water.

After my father died, I found a small instruction book titled *How to Abandon Ship* in his study, so thin it could be slipped into your pocket. It had been published in 1943, which meant he had acquired it when he was in the navy. Did he read it in his bunk or while ashore on leave? There are pages and pages about lifeboats and it has passages on panic. "Prepare Yourself" is the first chapter and it comes straight to the point:

"The *Harry F. Sinclair, Jr.* was still afloat and burning a week after she had been torpedoed. Her fo'c'sle was free from flame. Yet men were burned to death because they jumped overboard, and they jumped overboard because they were not prepared. William Caves, the bosun, safe in a water-borne lifeboat, saw an A.B. [able-bodied seaman], who had leaped over the side, struggling in a sea of flaming gasoline. It was impossible to reach the man. Caves saw his shipmate suck fire into his lungs. The A.B. was still fighting when he was being cremated. Then his head nodded briefly as though he were dozing, and Caves watched the charred body float deeper into the flames. A needless death. The A.B. died because he had no faith in his own seamanship."

Clearly my father was interested in preparation. There are sections in the booklet on lowering lifeboats, casting off lifeboats, rainwater, rationing, overloaded lifeboats, sea anchors, torpedo fumes, rowing lifeboats, medicine, navigation, shrapnel wounds, fractures, burns, sunstroke, frostbite, suicide, recreation, burial at sea and hysteria. A slim volume. Chapter 8 is "Open Boat Seamanship":

"The important fact to remember about sailing is that the average double-end lifeboat, in good condition, is exceptionally seaworthy. It is far better equipped to fight a storm than you are. In any kind

of gale, do not try to sail a lifeboat. You will only be offering resis-
tance against a greater force, thus inviting disaster without getting
anywhere. But if the men keep down on the bottom boards, creating
a low center of gravity, the boat will be able to take a terrific pounding
without capsizing."

When crossing an ocean by ship, there comes a moment when
the land disappears. Days pass as you creep along the surface of our
watery planet before it appears again. The sea is vast and we are not.
Even the continents become minority players. Ships appear from
over the horizon, slowly emerging from behind the long slope of
the ancient seas. The slope is the curve of a planet that is indifferent
to our presence. The oceans that power our atmosphere can generate mythic storms that destroy practically anything we can create.
To survive hurricanes, ships head *to* sea, since staying in harbour
means being caught in a merciless conversation between typhoon
and land.

What did First Lieutenant Woodburn S. Thomson feel on entering Halifax Harbour on HMCS *Sackville* in late September 1943,
after the loss of nine ships from ONS 18 and ON 202? The crossing
had taken eight days and seven nights and he'd seen sailors survive
the sinking of ships and those who had not. Lists of lost crews would
be prepared and telegrams would be sent to new widows. More than
four hundred had drowned from the convoy's loss of a destroyer, a
frigate and two corvettes—and how many more from the stricken
freighters? Proceeding at eight knots (fifteen kilometres an hour), the
entire sixty-five-ship convoy had zigzagged at predetermined times
to make themselves difficult for the torpedoes to target. My father
recounted that on the first day of the battle, the destroyer *St. Croix*
was sunk. Its 57 survivors, from a company of 149, were rescued by
the frigate HMS *Itchen*. Two nights later the battle intensified and
Itchen itself was sunk. HMCS *Sackville* was ordered back at 4:45 in
the morning to search the ocean for anyone remaining alive, but they
would not dare stop to collect dead bodies.

Woodburn never knew seaman William Fisher, the sole survivor of *St. Croix*, the first ship to be sunk, or at least he never mentioned him. William was one of only three who survived the subsequent sinking of the *Itchen*. His account begins forty-nine hours after *St. Croix* went down and he was rescued the first time. He describes being by *Itchen*'s funnel when a German torpedo hit the magazine. As the ship exploded, William dove a second time into the ocean south of Greenland. Three hours later he was pulled from the water by the crew of a freighter that had lowered its motorboat. William Fisher's tale is from a world that I knew only through my father's stories and my own dread of what it could have been like for him to be yet another cold body in an indifferent sea.

"Around four o'clock action stations sounded. The *Itchen* dropped a few charges . . . Then around eight we had action again. We dropped charges and made another sweep around . . .

We all went down below and tried to sleep. About a quarter to nine, 22nd September, action stations went again. We went to the upper deck where it was quite cold and very dark. About nine our searchlight went on and there was a sub in the beam. I was standing by the funnel and had hold of the railing around the funnel.

I looked past the bridge and could see the sub about three hundred yards ahead. It was cutting across our bow. Then the forward gun went off but the shell landed short and the bridge gunners started to fire. There was an explosion. We had been torpedoed. I was blown about thirty feet and landed against a gun deck. I got up, the ship was listing and I could hear water rushing in. I couldn't see a thing. I got the davit of the skiff, reached out with the other hand to get the railing. Just before I jumped over the side I called for my chum Mackenzie, but there was no answer. So I dove over the side.

As I hit the water there was a terrible explosion. I was sucked under and nearly lost consciousness. My insides seemed to be squeezed out of me. I was choking as I struggled back to the surface again, got a breath of air, and a wave took me under. I came up and started to swim away from the ship. I swam about thirty to forty feet and looked back at the propellers of the *Itchen* which were just disappearing. She had gone down in about forty seconds.

It has been forty-nine hours between the torpedoing of the two ships. I started swimming around and started to take my shoes off. I reached down to take my right shoe off but it was gone, I reached and took off my left one. I had on a big duffle coat and I unbuttoned it but forgot to undo the mouth piece. It slipped under my chin and started to choke me but I finally got it off. There were quite a few star shells in the air; the water was rough.

I saw a lad holding onto a board, and swam over and took hold of the board with him. The water was very cold . . . Then the lad passed away and I started to run into quite a few bodies. I could hear a few of the boys hollering.

Then the convoy started to pass us. The wash from the ships would wash us back and forth; we would go under and choke and there was a lot of oil and small boards that would slap us in the face. Then the star shells stopped going up and it got very dark. I saw a small flare and hollered out to a fellow and asked him what he had. He said he had a float, so I swam over towards him. He had two life savers. He gave me one, the one with the calso flare on it. I put it round me, then a wave parted us.

There was a splash and I could hear voices. I looked and there was a freighter [SS *Wisla*] which had dropped one of its floats, I tried to swim to it but I was too weak . . . Then I felt something hit my face and heard someone say grab the rope. Then I saw the motor boat when it was nearly on top of me.

They threw me the rope again. I caught it and was pulled up to the side of the motor boat. A hand grabbed me and pulled me inside. I lay there coughing and too tired to move; I was cold. I couldn't understand what they were saying. I finally moved beside the engine and tried to get some heat. They circled round and picked up two more boys.

They pulled alongside of their ship and as they pulled the motor boat up, I felt a lot of hot water go over me it certainly felt good. It was the exhaust from the engine. One of the lads they had picked up was doing a lot of groaning. Finally they got the boat up and put blankets around me and helped me into the officers' wardroom. They gave me a full glass of rum. I drank it all and it warmed me up.

I was a frightful looking sight covered with oil from head to foot, but they got some towels and rubbed the oil off and put my feet in hot water. I had been in the water 3 hours when I was picked up for the second time. The other lad lay on the floor groaning. They were rubbing him with whiskey and trying to get him to drink some.

I asked the other chap who he was and he said he was off the *Itchen*. The lad on deck was off the *Itchen* too. I had been saved for the second time but all our boys were gone."

I am thankful these were not my father's words, but neither were they from *any* of the four hundred from the convoy who passed away in the water—the dead continuing their habit of remaining silent. Three submarines, each with a crew of about fifty German sailors, had also been sunk in the battle off Greenland on September 22–25, 1943, making it close to six hundred who experienced the death I had always feared for my father.

"Remembering the war is not new in itself. During, and definitely after the war, its victims were already commemorated. . . . For public recognition as a war victim, first and foremost another identity had to be proved." These words preface the list of names on the website of the In Flanders Fields Museum in Ieper, Belgium.

Identity through a group didn't appeal to my father. I don't remember him ever standing with other veterans on Remembrance Days. Perhaps it was because he didn't care for speeches with platitudes. Some of his closest friends were navy veterans, and it was

always an occasion when HMCS *Lunenburg*'s chief engineer arrived
at our house. In the final year of the war Woodburn had left *Sackville*
to take command of the corvette *Lunenburg*. He and "the Chief"
would swap stories while the whisky was poured. Only their time
at sea could account for the bond between them. My father's war
memories centred on individuals rather than groups, and I think that
is why he wanted to find the names of the Liberator aircrews who'd
appeared in the skies over the sea battle off Greenland, coming to the
rescue of ONS 18 and ON 202.

I am my father's son and my own uneasiness with any group
identity was part of my determination to create *The World Remem-*
bers. As the In Flanders Fields Museum goes on to say, identifying the
dead by nation, race, rank, gender, politics, social status, regiment or
cemetery can become tools for those who wish to divide us.

"Victims needed further qualifications as members of specific groups:
football teams and companies, schools and railway companies, villages
and nations endeavoured to compile a list of their own dead. Each
register would always therefore be limited to a list of 'proper' names,
a list of Our Comrades, Nos Enfants, Our Heroes, or Unsere Toten.
Public remembrance continued the dividing logic of us versus them.
Unconsciously, perhaps. But it is clear enough that the Names List of
Our Own Dead afterwards was intentionally used as a powerful and
sharp weapon against new enemies."

In May 1945 the war in Europe was over and *Lunenburg* and
a second corvette, *Camrose*, were ordered to the Channel Islands,
just off the coast of France. They were to take charge of a group of
German destroyers, minesweepers, other warships and their crews
and escort them to the French naval port of Lorient, 450 kilometres away. After that they were to bring several German naval
officers back to England for questioning. James Lamb, a former
first officer from the *Camrose*, described it this way in his book
The Corvette Navy:

"It was a fascinating performance: Woody Thomson of *Lunenburg* and I went ashore in each of the little island ports—St. Helier, St. Peterport, St. Anne—and were met by the mayor and a deputation of authorities, who in turn introduced us to the German commanding officers. It was all most awkward; how after all, did one behave to the vanquished enemy on their home ground, so to speak. Complicating matters was the disparity of strength: during the months following the [Allied] invasion, all sorts of German craft had sought refuge here, as the other Channel ports had fallen to the Allies. How were two small corvettes to enforce their wishes on dozens of heavily armed destroyers."

As the Germans were boarding *Lunenburg* under armed escort, my father recognized one of them. The surrender of the German ships to the outnumbered corvettes was completed, and the convoy of impounded warships set sail for Lorient.

"Our Germans strung out in a long line-ahead formation, with the tug and assorted trawlers bringing up the rear, and Woody [*Lunenburg*] cavorting on one flank and us on the other. We shepherded our little flock, a gaggle of ugly ducklings if ever there was one . . ."

Once on course for the French naval base, my father released the man he'd recognized from confinement and they met in his cabin. Eleven years before, he and Michael Michaelus had been undergraduates at Cambridge University. Together with other students they had skied in Austria during the winter break. Having just spent the war years regarding each other through their respective metaphorical gunsights, what would they have talked about?

And sixteen years *after* that meeting on HMCS *Lunenburg*, I was introduced to Michael Michaelus, at his house halfway up an Austrian mountain. I recall little, since my family was only passing through on our way to a skiing holiday further east in the mountains. But my father had made a point of visiting him. I was twelve and *think* I remember Michaelus as being tall and speaking with an accent. At Cambridge in the 1930s, both students would have known that another war was likely, and that they would be on opposite sides. In fact, my father understood from their *Lunenburg* conversation that Michael had attended a British university to familiarize himself with English ways. In the event that Germany invaded, young Germans would be needed who knew how to keep the place running.

Should *Lunenburg* have encountered Michael Michaelus's warship, my father, as a dedicated navy man, would have welcomed the opportunity to send it to the bottom. And there I was staying in the house of an enemy who had remained his acquaintance. Later, at home in Canada, Woodburn would strike up a friendship with Helmut, who had served in the Luftwaffe and might have been part of Nazi Germany's invasion force of England. My father had little nationalistic or patriotic logic, just personal logic—opinions being based on who a person was rather than the group with whom they were associated. The identities that civilians superimpose on veterans are perhaps not those the former fighters themselves would choose.

James Lamb describes his disillusionment near the war's end with the shore-based naval personnel who did their tasks from behind desks. He contrasts the onshore navy with the sailors who did the fighting at sea. In my father's copy of Lamb's book, words are circled and comments have been pencilled in margins. It seems that much of *The Corvette Navy* also describes Woodburn's years on the North Atlantic. As the war was finally being won, Lamb writes about his bitterness on seeing the celebratory, boastful language used by onshore authorities about the Allied success as the histories of what had happened were beginning to be assembled. He writes what I think I remember hearing my father saying. The two underlined words in the following are what Woodburn circled with his pencil:

"Ironically, we found ourselves almost envying our old antagonists, the U-boat crews: they, at least, had been able to maintain their integrity and firmness of purpose, and had fought bravely to the end against hopeless odds. I can remember the real admiration <u>we</u> felt on visiting after VE day, the surrendered U-boat that we had hunted, with no fewer than thirty-one other ships, right in the approaches to Plymouth where it had just sunk a small fishing vessel. The guts of these German kids, shaken and shattered by bombing in port and depth-charging at sea, impressed <u>us</u> deeply; their demeanor robbed me of any savour in our triumph, now usurped and corrupted by boastful politicians, both service and civilian."

My father attended a screening of a television mini-series in which I played Dr. Frederick Banting, one of the discoverers of insulin in 1921. The opening scenes portrayed Banting as a fresh-faced First World War army doctor sewing up soldiers in France. Medical schools at that time often fast-tracked the students so newly minted doctors could get to the war to save lives. And owing to the abundance of patients and the savagery of their wounds, the young surgeons gained unique surgical experience.

There then followed scenes of Fred Banting's return to the family farm in Alliston, Ontario, where he is welcomed and given a celebratory dinner. Fresh from suturing and sawing in field hospitals in France, Banting sets about to carve the family roast—yet another bleeding piece of meat—while maintaining a casually crude commentary about the procedures he performed on men on operating tables. His family, unaccustomed to such surgically graphic and blue language, don't know where to look. As he loads their plates with beef and bangs them down on the table, it's not only the china that rattles but also his parents' propriety. In the shocked silence that stares at him from around the table, Banting begins to realize that Alliston is a long way from the brutalized world of war, and that he has brought some brutality home with him.

The film continued, insulin was discovered, diabetic children were saved, and the screening ended. There was applause. At the reception afterwards my father, who didn't often share his feelings, told me quietly, almost shyly, that the scenes round the dinner table had been *him* when he returned from the navy. He had shocked his mother (his father had died years before) with the language and manners he brought home from the sea. I think he was also trying to tell me that he liked my acting. But revealing the part of himself shaped by the war was the most meaningful for me. It lay within both of us till the end.

I feel I betrayed my father when I lost the wristwatch he had worn while on convoy duty. Woodburn never said how much his family meant to him, yet his gestures gave him away. Before we visited Michael Michaelus in his house on the mountain, my sister and I had been placed in a small boarding school outside Geneva, Switzerland. My father had planned to spend the year studying at a French university. Just twelve, I was inconsolable, having never before been parted from my parents. He removed his watch and put it on my wrist. It wasn't fancy; the crystal was scratched and its leather wrist strap was worn. He said that he'd used it to time the zigzags of his corvette while escorting freighters across the ocean. Small daubs of luminescent paint on the hour and minute hands meant it could be read on North Atlantic nights when all ships' lights were extinguished for safety. It had kept time off Greenland. Salt water had not seeped into the workings and halted its hands as its wearer lay lifeless in the sea. There was much to be thankful for in that watch, including my father's faith in me as he fastened it around my wrist. It had seen him through dark times, he'd entrusted to me, and I had lost it.

My last touch of him was a cold one. He was almost eighty and I was forty-two. While driving north to the cottage, he had been killed when his car went off the road and rolled into a ditch. Thrown from the vehicle, his neck broke on impact. Since he'd died away from us all, my sister Janet and I decided that we wanted his body *in* the family home rather than the professional impersonality of a funeral parlour. My mother agreed, and the undertaker found a way to manoeuvre my father's coffin into his study, next to the bedroom

I'd shared with my brother. For four days visitors could, should they wish, sit with him. For those uncomfortable with corpses, we kept the study door closed. He was *ours*, and it was deeply satisfying to have my father in the house. I chose my time to be with him. The photo of the *Tornado* in full flight was on the study wall.

The language we use to speak with the dead is the language the lake used with me. Simply being still, body *by* body, beside someone or something of long familiarity carries its own meaning. Stillness summons the space into which the unspoken language comes. Thoughts follow, many of them self-conscious. And after thought comes touch. I placed my hand along the side of his face. I was prepared for the chill but not for the indifference. I had gotten past the shock of seeing the residue of makeup that those who'd prepared the body had brushed on his face. But I could not get past his body's remoteness.

But he had been *my* father and the body was *ours* to care for, on every step to his grave. Yet Woodburn's years at sea, the stories he'd told, the winds we'd faced, all had no acknowledgement from the indifferent corpse beside me. The books lining his study's shelves, the notes and papers everywhere, the bazaar of items hanging on the walls, from Cambridge photos to pictures of the *Windflower*, *Sackville*, *Baltic Belle* and *Lunenburg*, the ceremonial key given him by the Town of Lunenburg, the brass "C.O.'s Cabin" plaque on the door—all those possessed more meaning than his dead body. I kept my hand along his cheek, my fingertips pressed to his temple, thankful at least to be returning a little of the warmth that he had given me.

Having crossed the Atlantic the final time in June 1945 in his "vehicle" HMCS *Lunenburg*, Woodburn arrived in Halifax. He sent a telegram to my mother, who was staying with my grandparents in Victoria and who by then had given birth to my older brother and sister. I was yet to be a gleam in his eye. *Lunenburg* would soon be stripped down and sold for scrap, which was the fate of most of Canada's corvettes. He'd been invited to the town of Lunenburg to meet the mayor and receive the key to the city.

While voicing someone else's words, sometimes you can slip round the barrier that separates you from them. As the sounds live in your mouth, you can slide *into* their thoughts. The telegram's words are silent on the page, but when I speak them, they ever so slightly become my father, who sailed away from this planet more than thirty years ago.

GREETINGS   BACK THIS MORNING   EXPECT BUSY ABOUT
ONE MONTH WINDING UP THIS VEHICLE   THEN RELEASE
POSSIBLE BUT DOUBTFUL AS NO PROVISION APPARENTLY
BEEN MADE   AM INVESTIGATING   HAD MOSTLY GOOD
TRIP AND BROUGHT JACK ROSS BACK   VISITING LUNENBURG
TOMORROW WITH THE OLD BUS AT SUGGESTION MAYOR
AND PALS   SHOULD BE GOOD SHOW BARRING SPEECHES

LOVE TO ALL   WOODBURN

CHAPTER 15

FOUR MINISTERING ANGELS

Margaret Killmaster at a military hospital in England

The first angel—my godmother

Margaret Killmaster's silence ended when I opened her photo album. For some forgotten reason, I now have her 1916 Kodak camera and the photographs she took with it. Through them I follow Margaret's gaze as a war nurse. There is even the intimation of her voice before it was coarsened by years of smoking, saying *Mac, Geoff! Look up!*

In their army invalid uniforms, two men with only two legs between them sit in the sun outside the Queen's Canadian Military Hospital in Britain. Mac and Geoff look up at my godmother holding the camera. Somehow I am now *in* the lens and they are also looking up at me. Margaret's finger touches the shutter's trigger and catches two more smiles for the nurse who had welcomed them into the operating room before surgery. Being in the lens, now their smiles are directed at *me*. A few photos later, no longer a still life, the men begin to move as the camera is passed to an unseen third man: *Would you mind taking one?* Margaret steps into the frame, joining Mac and Geoff with their pinned-up pant legs. She stands at first, the third man winds the film to the next frame, takes another picture, and then she sits between Mac and Geoff with their crutches and cigarettes. She doesn't smoke in these photos.

Turning to her patients, Margaret is earnest, engaged, shielding her eyes from the sun, her head at a slight tilt as she listens. I'm not sure I can quite hear what is being said in this moment. Their invalid jackets are buttoned up and she wears a sweater, so it is cool despite the sun. They are on the grounds of a country house close to the south coast of England, donated to the army to use as a hospital for the duration of the war. The third man must have said, *Sister, look up.* Now she looks at *me*, first with the observing eyes of a nursing sister, but after another shutter click a smile breaks out and a warm young woman appears.

My godmother gazes at me, her heels hooked over the bottom rung of a garden chair. She isn't tall. The Kodak is handed off a second time and the third wounded man joins them. They are all dead now. But the warmth Margaret directed to those she cared for now comes to me. Perhaps she gazed this way at her godson as he played on the carpet with his toy soldiers, and then he looked up at the lady with the cigarette voice bending over him. I confess that *that* boy never really saw her.

In another photo it's dusk—or dawn, it's hard to tell—and Margaret and a fellow nurse are sitting astride the peak of the hospital's roof. Tops of trees appear in the distance. Her friend, fully dressed in her Sister's uniform, perches and smiles. Her leather-soled shoes probably made the clamber up the roof tiles a challenge. The camera is passed across and now Margaret, in the company of chimneys and treetops, balances on the peak. In the heat of summer the two of them have come through a top-floor window and climbed up from their war work below. My godmother wears a nightie that might be almost off one shoulder, her body freed from the responsibilities of the undergarments, overgarments, head coverings and aprons-over-everything that the Sisters wore to fight the war. One hand gripping the tiles and her nightclothes gathered around her, my godmother looks off into the distance. They are near enough to the English Channel that France is visible from the hills behind the hospital. The fighting is seventy kilometres away. At that height and with little to hold on to, her fellow nurse must have been nervous about being entrusted with the camera and operating its sliding accordion bellows to focus the picture. The chimney pots behind Margaret's head are sharper than the pleased smile on her face.

The convalescing soldiers below all smoked like chimneys and Mac and Geoff *were* the two soldiers' names, since in her album she attached their pencilled note directly beneath their photos: "Miss Killmaster, Beachborough—Good night Sister—Mac & Geoff."

My godmother gathered the patients and her fellow nurses in groups, gathered them on free afternoons when walking in the fields, recorded the wounded arriving in ambulances, and assembled her Sisters for formal photos. The photographs are her way of speaking about them. The hospital's matron agreed to pose beneath a picturesque tree, but wouldn't smile. Here is a Sister behind a bush, both of whom seem to be in bloom. Here are five nurses blowing two sets of bagpipes and banging three drums borrowed from a visiting regimental band. The wind off the Channel turns their head veils into sails. Here is the head surgeon, Colonel Armour, and his surgical team. Here is Margaret's operating room, a new extension built onto the back of the Beachborough Park mansion that had become an army hospital. Here, behind the operating table and other surgical equipment, is the "big window." And here, since some of Margaret's letters survived, is that window in words:

"I am enclosing a picture of my operating room—an op. going on. I am the one with the X on the back of the picture and Col A is the one with an O. Isn't it just a lovely room? You might send it on for Aunt Elizabeth to see when you have seen it. The thing on the wall is not a tapestry picture—Oh! No!—It is just our big window with a view of the back garden on the other side. It shows how clean I keep my windows!!"

She celebrates her patients, remembers them and leads me along with her.

"Well, I got back from Bournemouth in time for Xmas and a jolly one we had here too. My cold is quite well now and I am feeling very fit. For Xmas we had all our wards decorated and they did look so pretty. My men were all bed patients at Xmas time so I had most of the decorating to do myself. While I was in Bournemouth we made 122 stockings for the men that I bought with money sent me for the soldier's Xmas—filling them with nuts, raisins, cigarettes, sweets, fruit and a book and puzzle. I had a whole steamer trunk full of things and filled the stockings Thursday night. On Friday I labeled them and took them to each ward after the lights were out—for the night Sister to put on the beds in the early morning. It took me till about 1 a.m. to finish it. Then we all wakened up about 6 a.m. and had our Xmas.

About 7 a.m. I went down to the wards to see the men, they were having a lovely time with their stockings. At 7:30 there was church held in our sitting room and I went. We went on duty at 8 am as usual and hustled through the work in order to get ready for the patients Xmas dinner. This was given by Princess Mary—they had turkey, ham, vegetables, plum pudding, sweets, raisins, cigars, pully crackers and fruit. The Queen sent them each a box of taffy . . ."

I ask your pardon, because this godson requests a pause. *Taffy?* That the Queen of England offered her soldiers chewy candy while they offered their lives sums up the top-down world of the time. It was a hierarchy that few, except anarchists, republicans and revolutionaries, questioned, and certainly not Margaret. *Taffy?* Really? The old world order, like my galloping dragoons with matchsticks for necks, was past its prime. Kings and queens perched on pyramids of power while tens of millions fought, were mutilated or died in their name. Living off the leftovers of feudalism, the royal family thought it fitting to send food and candy to their fighters at Christmas. And, most bizarrely, many in the maze of Europe's warring monarchies were cousins. Remarkably, the British Princess Mary, the Queen of England, Princess Louise of Argyle, and the others still occupied their royal residences after the war, but that was probably because their side won. By 1919 the thrones of Russia, Germany and Austria-Hungary were all empty while the Ottoman emperor was dethroned in 1922. Taffy?

" . . . and Princess Louise of Argyle sent each man a box of cigarettes with a message with her signature on it. After they had their dinner we had a hasty lunch and then began moving them on stretchers to the recreation hall where they had a wonderful tree and each got another stocking and about three parcels sent from Canada. After the tree there was a concert, given by some professionals from London, very good. Then began the moving back to bed. By the time we had them ready for the night we were dead bunnies!! I never have been so tired in my life but it certainly was worth it. I heard several men say that they had never had such a Xmas and never expect to have another like it.

We had our Xmas dinner at 8 and it was a good one. I disappeared as soon as I politely could and crawled into my little bed. Good night now.

Lovingly Margaret"
—January 7, 1916

There then follow photos of the Beachborough Park gardens covered in snow, then some taken in the spring in which Miss Killmaster has yet to appear any older.

"We are having beautiful spring weather here and I have taken off my flannels. By the way, may I pack up my furs and winter things and send them down to B. [Isabel Osbourne's house in Bournemouth] for the summer? I have nowhere to keep them here and they will only get dusty and horrible.

. . . don't know how much longer I can stick it as I am getting awfully tired and losing pounds in weight—latter part most delightful!—The other night we operated until 2.30 a.m. and then up and at it again at 6 a.m."

Another year passes, with the tides of wounded still washing in, filling the wards again and again as the generals continue their war of attrition. There are more photos of ambulances offloading at the front door and new faces in invalid's jackets, always some with pant legs or sleeves pinned up. There are pictures of groups assembled by my godmother by the tennis courts—and always the smoking. Perhaps on-duty Sisters weren't permitted, but even in photos of off-duty outings, a cigarette never appears between Margaret's fingers. Perhaps she had not yet reached for that habit.

"Excuse this scribble but we are awfully busy and haven't much time. Wounded come in almost every day now—about 30 to 50 at a time and we are putting extra beds in all the wards and are so crowded that we can hardly move about. It is very interesting. Word has been sent that England is to get 40,000 wounded this week, and to prepare all the beds we can.

I've asked for work and I've got it! Our beds are now full of the most awful cases we have ever had—and lots of operations. Last Saturday we operated from 8.30 a.m. till 4 Sunday morning—then up and at it again at six Sunday morning—got off at four in the afternoon and staggered to bed. The Matron was away last week so I had to take her place besides my own work—also helped on the wards as they were short there."

—December 14, 1917

The weeks that Margaret is describing followed the meat-grinder battle at Passchendaele in Belgium, which had been processing its way through British, Canadian, German and Australian soldiers for months. Margaret's cousin, my great-uncle George Stratford, was ground up there.

And still, I wonder if there was a "love" in Margaret's life. Then, the following spring, in a sequence of fourteen photos, a man who *isn't* a patient appears. They come near the end of the album and of her time at the Queen's Canadian Military Hospital, before she transferred to France to be nearer the fighting. Margaret was always nervous about the quality of her nursing, so I want you to know what the surgeon, Colonel Armour, wrote to my great-aunt Isabel about her:

"I want you to know under what a debt of gratitude the Queen's Canadian Hospital and my own humble self, are to you for giving us the services of your niece—she is one of the finest women I have met in a long time and it is an inspiration to work with her. She is a great source of strength to the nursing staff, both actively and passively."

The man in the fourteen photos is older than the other men. He is never in uniform, so perhaps he was too old for the army. Together with several other couples, Margaret and he are out walking in the fields. The photos are really snapshots, and since Margaret appears in thirteen of them, I doubt that she took her Kodak with her. The shadow of a woman in a sunhat holding a camera appears at the bottom of several pictures, and then a man's shadow taking more snapshots.

Wanting "to hear" the scene, I work the images backwards and forwards, searching out the relationships between the six of them— three couples. On their walk to the field, how did the five "on camera" arrange themselves? Now leaning on a gate, who stands beside whom? A picnic blanket is on the grass and *who* sits on it with Margaret and the man? The other two women are Sisters who I recognize from other photos, and all three wear summer dresses. On the blanket, the man reclines on his right side, leaning towards Margaret. Where is *she* looking? He seems more interested in her than she in him. Yet in the next three pictures, while her body may face the camera, her head turns completely towards him. My godmother had a way of fixing her eyes on others that was attentive and caring, but was there more? In fun, the three men are now wearing the women's hats. Who has Margaret's? Did the unnamed man wish to inhale the smell of her hair? Again and again he is by my godmother's side, and I am happy about his attentions to her. A smile radiates across her face, revealing her beauty in a way that the family's genealogy has not.

I wonder about the moment when Margaret laid out all fourteen photos in her album. Was *that* the man who'd caught her affections? She endeared herself to the surgeons whose operating theatre she ran, to Mac and Geoff, to her fellow Sisters, but was she *loved*? I am curious because I want her to have been happy.

After a midday meal in Beachborough Park's dining room, they crowd into the frame. The soldiers turn their chairs towards her, leaning on elbows and peering round shoulders. With no space left at the tables, they gather at the back with a Sister and several kitchen staff, enjoying having their photo taken by the twenty-seven-year-old operating-room nurse. The remains of tea and biscuits are on the tables. Their enjoyment of her is *my* enjoyment. As the sun streams in through the windows, they look up, look at Margaret and then at *me*. It is still in the sun.

I often return to this picture for the warmth of their company. Where are the grandchildren, the great-nephews and great-nieces of those people now? There is no way of knowing how many in the dining room didn't live out the war. While preparing *The World Remembers* project, my graphic designer, Marta Ryczko, asked, "Robert, do you have a photo that would speak for the project?" I'd learned that foreign officials became interested in my proposal if they felt personally engaged. So the materials I provided to embassies in Ottawa and the thirty nations at the World War I centenary planning meeting in Paris always included Margaret's gathering of her patients. I wish I could thank her for including them in my life.

Almost forty years after my godmother took that photo, I was the little boy on the carpet packing away my toys before going with her into my grandmother's dining room. My lead soldiers and nurses could be played with another day. I look up since I *think* Margaret has lightly touched my shoulder. I don't recall putting my hand in hers, but we went in together to join the others. I can't recall *ever* having spoken with her beyond a shy hello and "Thank you for my Christmas present." I feel now that I know her a little. It seems Margaret waited years to break her silence, and perhaps it was on the way to the dining room that she wondered if she might leave her photo album on the carpet, for when I eventually returned.

Two forthright ministering angels

Sixty-five Canadian nurses lost their lives in the Great War, some from the bombing of hospitals and sinking of ships, but mainly from a variety of diseases picked up in the wards. It was a time when the world was just on the cusp of developing antibiotics. The estimate is that fifteen hundred Allied nurses died, mostly from infections the wounded had brought with them into the hospitals, which were exacerbated by the nurses' exhaustion. In keeping with the habit of listening to history with only one ear, I don't think there's been an estimate of how many German, Austrian, Russian, Turkish or Hungarian nurses lost *their* lives. And while much has been made of the Germans executing British nurse Edith Cavell in 1915 for espionage, nothing much has been said about the British and French executions of German nurses Margarete Schmidt and Ottilie Moss, also in 1915 and also for espionage.

Few soldiers ever admitted that they cried—but they did. We know because the nurses told us. Courage, fear, elation and boredom inhabit us all. The particulars of soldiers' deaths were tidied away with phrases such as "killed instantly," "succumbed to his wounds," "fell doing his duty" or "died a hero." Sometimes those words were true, but mainly they were deployed to prevent the living from understanding the pain, inconsequence, horror and sometimes suicide that were part of the men's lives at the end. Margaret wrote about none of this. Perhaps in the name of loyalty she self-censored her criticisms of the war and graphic descriptions of the savagery. Or perhaps she didn't want to alarm her aunt Mary Elizabeth, the mother of the four Stratford boys in the fighting. Or perhaps it was simply that Margaret's sense of propriety prevented her from expressing those feelings. She would have put her camera away if ever her patients were distressed. Yet, unlike her aunt Isabel, Margaret never dressed up her letters in patriotism.

Had my godmother lived into her nineties, she might have sat down with me and told her darker stories. In old age, why not look someone straight in the face with such tales? But then again, why would she ever wish to revisit the night that she wrote "Our beds are now full of the most awful cases we have ever had"? Had she ever staggered to bed and cried at the hopelessness of a hideously injured man? It is too late now to know either whom she loved or what she dreaded.

Searching for words that might lead me into the emotional lives of nurses in the Great War, I found them in Lyn Macdonald's book of interviews from the 1970s, called *The Roses of No Man's Land*. The women were mainly in their eighties when Lyn Macdonald spoke with them. Their honesty about their concerns for the wounded in their wards resembles a photograph from the war that is in sharp focus.

"There was a very young lad who was badly wounded. He had all his genital parts blown off. Bad as he was, he was always cheerful about it. I used to wonder how he stood it. It was a terrible dressing to do, and very, very hard on him. We used to see him watching us as the dressing trolley came down the ward, and you could see that he was dreading the moment we would get to him. The wound—it was just a hole—was packed with gauze with just a silver tube coming out of it; that was the catheter that led into his bladder. Every morning all the packing had to be pulled out bit by bit, the hole cleaned, and the gauze packed back in again. It was agony. We all used to dread it because it was so very hard on him. He used to cry. He couldn't help it but he felt very badly about crying, and we used to cover his face with a handkerchief so that he wouldn't be embarrassed about it. He just lay there and we would give him a drop of brandy or a glass of champagne. He was about twenty-five. He recovered. Eventually, we were able to send him back to England and I expect he was discharged from the Army, but he'd never be any good as a man after that."

—Christina Hastings, Queen Alexandra's
Royal Army Nursing Corps

"There was a man with one side of his face blown away. The skin had grown over it, but he was still bandaged and I was told to syringe his face and to put a screen round him while I did it. I chatted to him while I was taking the dressing off and I must have smiled. He said, 'How can you smile when you look at me, Nurse?' It must have meant a lot to him, because later he wrote in my autograph book: 'Remember, dear Nurse, to keep that sweet smile. It helps us lame dogs over many a stile.'

—Grace Bignold, VAD, No. 1 General Hospital

What differentiates Margaret's words from those of Christina Hastings and Grace Bignold was that my godmother wrote them *during* the war. Christina and Grace were interviewed in the safety of afterwards. Writing *while* a conflict is raging is different. Risk and uncertainty pervade the telling. Endeavouring to survive becomes the priority. If the complete truth isn't helpful, then so be it. It isn't lying, it's trying to navigate the danger and the unpredictability. If omissions are made—such as Margaret's silence about the despair she may have felt over the wreckage of some of the young men under her care—that is understandable. Just as letters home were censored by officers, nurses and soldiers self-censored what they themselves wrote. How forthright can your stories be about the danger you are in? Firing a pistol at tin cans is a different kind of shooting than firing while being shot at. When a war is on "the wind is up" under the storytellers, who don't know who will survive or how it will end. Had Christina or Grace been interviewed during the Great War, they might never have said what they did. Stories told afterwards can take more risks.

Here are some full-frontal recollections from Nursing Sister Bignold, including the suicide of disfigured soldiers. I am grateful to Lyn MacDonald for her observations about the intimacy that can accompany pain.

"'Always look a man straight in the face,' one Sister instructed her staff. 'Remember he's watching your face to see how you're going to react.' It was easier to smile, to catch a man's eye, to look him straight in the face when you were doing a dressing before the wound had healed. Hideous though it was, in a raw, bleeding state it was not much worse than similar horrors on an arm, a leg, an abdomen, a back. A little more unpleasant to dress, perhaps, because the patient's breath, mingling with stale blood in the mouth and passages before the raw flesh healed, was peculiarly foul, and it was hard to sustain a smile during the close-quarters business of adjusting drainage or feeding tubes. Professional detachment helped. But the real difficulty arose much later when the wounds had healed, when the surgeons had done their best, when soon the man would be discharged from hospital, and he was still a gargoyle. Then, when one searching eye watched for a nurse's reaction, it was difficult for her not to drop her eyes in natural embarrassment. . . .

The hurly-burly of the ward was all very well for men with bandaged faces, but when the concealing dressing eventually had to be removed a disfigured man could hardly be exposed to the torture of the pitying or horrified scrutiny of the outsiders and visitors who were constantly coming and going. He could not be hidden behind screens forever. It answered only part of the problem to move him to a single room when one was available, where only sympathetic doctors, nurses, orderlies or companions from the main ward would have the right of entry, and which could be darkened, if the patient chose, when visitors came to see him. Often he preferred not to have visitors at all. When they did come the nurses dreaded the scenes that occasionally took place, where in spite of Sister's gentle preparation in the case of mothers and her occasionally stiffening lectures in the case of young wives and fiancées, some girls had to be brought out of the room in fits of hysterics. Restored with brandy in Sister's office, they would sit wringing their hands: 'Oh Lord, help me, what am I going to do? What am I going to do?' It was a natural reaction that struck little sympathy with Sister, who was rather more concerned about what her patient was going to do.

In the quiet single rooms there was time to brood. Despite the care and vigilance of the staff, and despite their support and assumed cheerfulness, there were occasional suicides, discreetly hushed up by the hospital authorities, and in cases where the patient lost the will to live and quietly died. The standard telegram was used in either case: REGRET INFORM YOU PRIVATE SMITH 10TH —SHIRE REGIMENT DIED THIS EVENING AFTER A RELAPSE."

The outraged angel—the one who threw the rock

I met Mary Borden on one of my visits to the In Flanders Fields Museum in Belgium. She was long dead, but her words squeezed my hand and urged me to listen. It was surprising that *any* nurse from that era would even think what the museum in Ieper quoted her as saying. What Mary said stung, yet it was invigorating, as if my principal in Grade Six had announced that the German mortar in front of the school was an abomination and would be melted down into frying pans and bicycles. Mary Borden asks what those who have never been in a war zone could never ask: What is the meaning of womanhood in an activity that could dismember its participants physically, emotionally and sexually?

You may recall my suggestion that war stories written by men offer only seven roles for women. Mary Borden, like Käthe Kollwitz, refused all of them. Instead, Mary was a *protagonist,* the outraged angel. Like my great-great-aunt Isabel, she had wealth, being an American heiress from Chicago. She had gone to Belgium in 1914 as a Red Cross volunteer and then used her resources to set up a hospital in France. There Mary nursed French soldiers until 1918. Before the war she'd married a Scottish missionary, moved to England, had three children and become a suffragette. During the war, she had an affair with a British officer, whom she eventually married.

The American heiress had also spent time in 1914 in the custody of British police, having been arrested for throwing a rock through a window of His Majesty's Treasury at 1 Horse Guards Road, London—which is where the economist John Maynard Keynes had worked before he was appointed to the Peace Conference in Paris. As the representative of the British Treasury at Versailles, Keynes's own rock-throwing was his warning about the crushing level of debt that the Great War's winners wanted to impose on the losers.

I detect no self-censoring in Mary's writing about her time as a war nurse. Here she describes how the language of the guns could be written on the bodies of men:

"There are no men here, so why should I be a woman?
There are heads and knees and mangled testicles. There
are chests with holes as big as your fist, and pulpy thighs,
shapeless; and stumps where legs once were fastened."

War stories that speak about sex come in different flavours and
can be arranged from the most to least told, from the sweetest to the
most bitter. First are the romantic stories, where the man departing
for battle falls in love with a woman who will wait for him. The marriage of my parents was such a sweet romance. The women in the
painting *Before Waterloo*, adoring the soldiers leaving for the battle,
are that romance writ large. Next come the tales of the war brides,
women courted by soldiers visiting foreign fields who later will make
a new life in a new land with their veteran husband. Among the least
told are the fighting man's hasty affairs stories that leave both mothers and offspring behind.

Also in the territory of least told are the sex-for-sale sagas about
the need of armies to procure women to—as the World War II
Japanese termed it—"comfort" their soldiers. In return, the women
either received money or, in Japan's case, enslavement for their services. At the bitterest end of the range are the rape stories and war-
and-sexually-transmitted-disease tales in which armies lose men
to hospital beds that they'd prefer to keep on the battlefields. At
the time of the First World War, venereal disease was considered
mainly a manpower problem since for six weeks or more soldiers
were in hospital and unavailable for war work. The stories of these
men, left with stigma, scarring, sterility or worse, are rarely told—
and even more shamefully, the stories of their women partners are
never told.

Mary Borden writes beyond *all* those flavours. She takes the
truism that war turns boys into men and drives it back upon
itself. In her book *The Forbidden Zone*, she speaks about nursing at
Roesbrugge, in Belgium. Here she continues about what she faced
and what she felt forced to be:

"There are eyes—eyes of sick dogs, sick cats, blind eyes, eyes of delirium; and mouths that cannot articulate; and parts of faces—the nose gone, or the jaw. There are these things, but no men; so how could I be a woman here and not die of it? Sometimes, suddenly, all in an instant, a man looks up at me from the shambles, a man's eyes signal or a voice calls 'Sister! Sister!' Sometimes suddenly a smile flickers on a pillow, white, blinding, burning, and I die of it. I feel myself dying again. It is impossible to be a woman here. One must be dead."

Mary Borden saw with such burning focus that it hurts my heart. I wonder about Margaret and the other nurses, and about my godmother's reticence to describe what the war had done to the wounded who kept washing up on the shores of England. If she *did* have thoughts like Mary's but contained her feelings of outrage, that might account for why she eventually became a serious smoker.

CHAPTER 16

BELGIUM AND GEORGE

"They shall receive a crown of glory that fadeth not away."
—inscription on the Menin Gate, Ieper, Belgium

George Stratford

Georgeorge was my link to the lowland nation tucked up against
France's northeastern shoulder. Apart from Belgian beer, the
country meant little to me, yet it was in its Flanders region
that my great-uncle George was killed. Because the location of his
battle grave was lost and his remains were perhaps "dispersed" by the

war's ongoing shelling, his name appears on the Menin Gate in the small city of Ieper. Also carved on the gate are the names of 54,394 other British Empire soldiers with no known grave.

"I suppose that Georgie wrote you that we went to quite a few movies, the last one was at the Electric Theatre and afterwards we walked down to the Rink, where Mother [Isabel Osbourne] was having a 'wounded's' tea. We were rather late and about a quarter to six, Mother and Jessie left but we sat on—Mother kept turning around every six steps and saying 'Aren't you coming?' and every time Geordie would stick his head forward and grin like Charlie Chaplin, then pull it back again quickly— you know the way, and OH! it was funny!"

—George's cousin Margaret Osbourne to
his mother after his death in 1917

Recalling the funny bone of the dead can be a fragile experience. My father had a wry sense of humour, but apart from his becoming breathless with laughter over a "Beyond the Fringe" comedy skit about a coal miner who wanted to write the exam to become a judge, I have few memories of it. If I heard my father's laughter again, I might remember him better. Photos of George reveal the clown in him. His nineteen-year-old cousin Margaret liked his comedic commentary on Isabel's questioning, as well as his poking at the seriousness of the world about him. "'*Aren't you coming?' and every time Geordie would stick his head forward and grin like Charlie Chaplin.*"

Humourists rarely survive beyond their time. Chaplin, a world-famous silent-movie comedian, barely escaped his era and few of us laugh at his antics now. Humour is fashion-bound and as slippery as the slope on which absurdity sits, chirping away at our presumptions. Just as incoming gravitational waves speed through us, slightly distorting everything we presume to be physically immutable, so too can comedy twist our perceptions—whether it's the dark absurdities in *Waiting for Godot* or Chaplin's antics as Adolf Hitler playing with his inflatable globe in the film *The Great Dictator.*

George stood six foot two, as I do. The gangling mimicry of his joints is also mine. In reading the correspondences of the five Stratford brothers, George's letters are what I would imagine myself writing if I had been in his uniform. We both took science degrees at the University of Toronto, and Chaplin, the diminutive clown, awakened the slapstick in both of us. Go figure.

"[We] have a good laugh every now and then at the places and conditions under which we sleep. It's a barn this time, some of the boys are in the loft, others in box stalls, another Corporal and myself have a stall in the cow-stable. There are a number of big guns so near that every time they are fired you think the old barn is coming down around your ears. At another time when we were billeted in a Chateau and some of us even had the luxury of a bed, I wish you could have seen us, our bedroom apparently belonged to 'My Lady' for the bed was covered with a pretty chintz, there were a few pretty pictures still left on the walls and the chintz and lace curtains were still on the windows. Well I bet we looked a sight the three of us crowded in that dainty little bed, with our equipment and shoes still on and covered ourselves up with spare curtains. We may have looked a little out of place but I may say we slept remarkably well . . ."

—George to his sister Mayden, May 1916

In parts of Flanders there are still more undiscovered war dead beneath the ground than living souls in the farms and villages above. George is one of those still below. In 1914 the German army, on its way to Paris, invaded Belgium. The country earned a reputation for being plucky for resisting the Kaiser's incursion, but it also had a reputation for cruelty. When George enlisted in 1915, the Belgians were still extricating themselves from the genocidal horror committed by their previous king in the Congo Free State. Still, many regarded the small nation as innocent and courageous for standing up to Kaiser Wilhelm's army and his demand to capitulate.

". . . that the Kaiser wired to the King of Belgium that if Liege didn't surrender at once he would be obliged to take it by force. The King of B. wired back 'Try.' Haven't the Belgians been glorious, they have won for themselves a place in history that will never be forgotten."

—Isabel Osbourne to her sister, August 1914

Two days after Isabel wrote that letter, Liège was lost. The Belgian king's defiance was widely admired, yet six years earlier his predecessor, King Leopold II, had been found complicit in the butchery and murder of the Congolese, thereby enriching both himself and his nation through slave-labour profits from the harvesting of rubber in Africa.

"One's heart bleeds for the poor Belgians, it is the country, that for no reason on earth, which will suffer the most for this cruel war— It is awful to think how that brave unoffending country has been devastated."

—Isabel to her sister, October 1914

The British Empire, and my great-uncles, came to the rescue of that "unoffending country" despite its brutality. Why had its notoriety in Africa gained so little attention? Well, racism. Humanitarian groups in both Britain and America had campaigned against the Belgian barbarities in the Congo with rallies, press coverage and publications. Missionaries who had witnessed the atrocities encouraged those groups to raise the issue with Brussels. People *were* aware, but the thousands of hands (and sometimes heads) that the Free State's private army had chopped off had black skins. (The Free State had no status as a nation and employed a private army paid by and reporting to the company that harvested the rubber.) Black was also the colour of the men who wielded the knives that did the chopping. The brutality was inflicted for business reasons, as an incentive to the labourers to collect more rubber. The private army's officers were, of course, white.

The number of deaths in the Congo Free State, whether from execution, exhaustion or disease, has never been agreed on, but estimates range as high as the entire population of Belgium in 1914—around seven million. The area that is now the Democratic Republic of the Congo was *owned* by a private charity run by King Leopold II—it was primarily his property. Wild rubber was gathered by men and women who were essentially economic slaves and whose hands would be cut off if they didn't achieve their quotas. The wealth from the rubber harvest flowed back to Belgium. The severed hands were collected to provide proof to the rubber company that the bullets used by its army had indeed killed recalcitrant or rebellious labourers. But in 1914 it seemed the world had no eyes for the barbarity. This is not to denigrate Belgians, because their nation has since pushed back against war and brutality—just as Canadians are working to emerge from our own dark racialized past.

George's letters offer no hint of any of those injustices, and perhaps that's not unexpected. At sixteen I viewed the world through a gauzy film, aware of little beyond my insecurities and insurgent hormones. As a teenager I had visited Belgium but only because my grandfather Cuthbert had sent me on a Commonwealth Youth Movement tour of First World War memorials and battlefields. I recall being only half awake during the days I spent in that small, trilingual nation that put mayonnaise on its french fries. The tour also involved an all-night vigil in a First World War soldiers' chapel in Talbot House, in the town of Poperinge. Fifty of us from different Commonwealth nations travelled on two buses; our jackets were scarlet and my shoulder patch said CANADA. Considering my daily depression about my romantic ambitions, it is not surprising that the vigil summoned few insights for me on remembrance.

Before embarking on the tour, Great-Uncle Art (George's younger brother, who taught us about throwing snake-eyes at Christmas) had attended the family gathering to see me off. Thinking that I might be hormonally tempted, as he had been as a twenty-year-old in Belgium in 1914, before I left for the train station Art took me aside and said quietly, "Let them buy you a drink, Bob, but don't let them take you upstairs." I understood completely, but pretended not to, while turning pink at the same time.

For a quarter of an hour, holding a vigil sword, I knelt in the attic of a Belgian house. At the top of three flights of stairs was an improvised chapel where Great War soldiers had prayed for solace and guidance. Poperinge, a few kilometres behind the front lines, had also offered entertainments with alcohol and women for hire. But the attic of Talbot House was a place for reflection and momentary peace. Rising from my knees at three a.m. to hand off the sword to the next Commonwealth Youth member—would it be the girl with the short, dark hair who I was sweet on or Molly with the glasses, with whom I was infatuated?—I was oblivious to the fact that my great-uncle George's remains might be somewhere in the vicinity. Afterwards, out on the street in the stillness of the night, I was lost in my desire to be dissolute with Molly under the spell of the Belgian moon.

"Dearest Mayd . . . We haven't been doing much fighting lately just enough to let everybody realize there is a war on. Our last trip in the line I got lost twice both times are quite worthy of telling—The first time was at night, I and my runner were coming back from the front line when we got tangled up in the numerous communication trenches leading back from the front line, after a short consultation with my worthy runner we decided to try our luck overland, so away we went. We struck a railway and traveled along that for some time until we struck a village, or at least what used to be one, where I thought surely we would run across someone who could put us on the right track. It was a bright moonlight night, the guns were very quiet and hardly a shell disturbed the stillness. We wandered around those ghastly ruins and shell craters for about an hour before we struck a machine gun post where the boys put us on the right track. I felt like the man who visited the moon, and felt as if there wasn't another soul on earth..."

—George to his sister Mayden, September 1917

Yet that all-night vigil in Poperinge eventually became one of the seeds that created *The World Remembers*. Flanders is a region now anchored in the destruction of the First World War. Visiting Ieper was the first time I experienced history *without* an overlay of Britishness. The thousand-year-old town had been bombarded for much of the war, and by 1918 not much was left standing. There *is* a British presence because Ieper's central monument, the Menin Gate, was paid for by Britain; the Commonwealth War Graves Commission has an office there; and St. George's Memorial Church offers services only in English. But it was refreshing to experience a Belgian view of history, unfreighted with Britain's imperial self-centredness. After the war, Winston Churchill had suggested that the town *remain* in its almost completely ruined state: "I should like us to acquire the whole of the ruins of Ypres. A more sacred place for the British race does not exist in the world."

The Belgians disagreed, thinking that the town's inhabitants deserved to enjoy a normal life. Yet even in 1919, as the postwar recovery began, curious visitors—including my grandparents, Philippa and Cuthbert—came to see where the fighting had been, to look for graves and perhaps find a souvenir to take home. Battle-field guidebooks were printed and the tour business began. Amidst the rubble, weeds and skeletal remains of churches, Ieper put the curious on notice by erecting signs that said: "This is holy ground. No stone of this fabric may be taken away. It is a heritage for all civilized peoples."

What exists now is a small city rebuilt with German reparation money, surrounded by farms and war cemeteries and visited by buses filled with battlefield tourists. Compared to the bureaucratic con-volutions of the British and French governments about *The World Remembers*, the Belgians took a practical approach. Meetings were straightforward and solutions were found to any differences that might have existed between us. They have to be practical since one hundred years after the fighting, farmers are still removing unexploded artillery shells that have been turned up by their plows. Belgians are overachievers with their array of official languages and jurisdictional layers, yet they remain practical. Ieper, as a City of Peace, is twinned with Hiroshima. Others in that group include Beirut, Berlin, Coventry, Dresden, Leningrad, Nagasaki, Recea, Srebrenica and Kigali. Because of these cities' shared experience of extreme destruction, war doesn't interest them—but the prevention of it does.

———

"All afternoon I sat on the side of a hill and watched the bombardment which was taking place. From my point of vantage I could see for miles, the ruined towns where only part of some church steeple or broken wall showed up white in the sunshine, the German trenches which stretched away into the distance and over which our shells broke incessantly. It sounded like a terrific thunder storm, and lasted all afternoon . . . Love to all at home, Your loving son, George"

—December 22, 1915

George lived out his last two years on the front lines in Belgium, in the reserves, or in England while recovering from wounds or on leave. His letters are clear about the context of the life he was leading. He and I both enjoy the collision of contrasts that sometimes produce unexpected perceptions. I admire his awareness of the visual richness or poverty of his surroundings. He was twenty-four and never mentions a girlfriend from back home, or—apart from his nineteen-year-old cousin Margaret, whom he made laugh on the way home from the Electric Theatre—a woman's friendship in the war. Visiting him through his letters, I like his musings and understatements. Of my eight warrior great-uncles, I feel that my easiest conversation, should I ever have had one, would have been with George.

"You don't know how good it is to get back among the green fields after putting in a week or so among rotten sandbags and debris. The first thing I noticed on coming out was the sweet smell of the hawthorne which was in bloom all along the railway track. It was

funny the other night when we were in the front line, there was a
nightingale, the first one I'd heard, in a bit of woods between the two
lines, which were about 200 yards apart, although it was anything
but quiet with the rifles and machine guns cracking away, bombs and
trench mortars bursting every now and again, that bird sang incessantly the whole night through. It didn't appreciate the value of wings
or it wouldn't have been where it was . . . Your loving son, George"
                                                                    —May 1916

"I have a recollection of a number of your letters that I intended to
answer some time ago, I put them safely by in my haversack await-
ing a favourable opportunity, but haversack and most of my personal
belongings are no more, as a shell hit the dugout they were in, and
I didn't think it worthwhile to look for the pieces. Also I had other
things to think about as that particular dugout was not the only place
the shells were bursting, so help me! I didn't expect to come out of that
place alive—it sure was hell! But here I am with a lovely little bullet
wound in the shoulder and across the back of my hand. The hospital
which was opened a few days before I got here is a dandy, I just lie in
a bed with a big contented smile on my face while about a thousand
pretty sisters come around every ten minutes to see if I am comfortable
or want anything . . . Love to all, Your aff. Bro George"
                                                                    —June 1916

"You must forgive me for not writing . . . but with a bum thumb and
sore arm one doesn't feel much like writing . . . when I got here they
couldn't do enough for me. Everybody, doctors, sisters and all had to
have a look at the Princess Pat men in Ward 6, and I never had such a
fuss made over me before or since . . . I was afraid some of the sisters
were going to kiss me, awful predicament for a wounded man to be
in. It took me about a week before I could look at one without getting
hot around the collar . . . Your ever affectionate brother George"
                                                                    —July 1916

And then he changed. War wore him down. It was remarked how much older he was looking. "Susie" was what he called his oldest sister, Helen.

"Dearest Old Susie . . . It is one of those clear, cool glorious days where if you look heavenward there's nothing to remind you that there is a war on at all except a few small puffs of anti-aircraft shells bursting in the distance, but you can't keep looking heavenward all day and your gaze comes down to earth again and then it all comes back with a big thud. There are acres and acres of fertile land full of shell holes, weeds and barbed-wire and in the distance once pretty little villages torn and wracked by shot and shell until they resemble nothing but a pile of brick dust.

The men are sitting around smoking and playing cards in the sunshine. It only needs one shell and they all scurry like a lot of rabbits for their dugouts, where they are comparatively safe many feet below the ground.

Well Susie, this sounds too much like a cheap novel so will have to ring off. Will write again soon. Your loving brother, George"

—September 1917

Then four days before he was killed, he wrote his eldest brother, Graham.

"I spent all my time on leave at Aunt Isabel's, believe me it's good to have a place like that to go to, otherwise I don't know how I would manage at all. This Belgium mud is something fierce. You absolutely can't stir out of your billet without getting plastered with it. That was a fine letter I got from you some time ago, I hope you come across with another soon. We expect to go up the line for a day or so and then back for a good old rest which we Greatly need after the show the boys have already gone through. Give my best love to Nonnie and everyone at home. Your affectionate brother, George"

—November 13, 1917

George's regiment had just concluded the Battle of Passchendaele when he rejoined them after being away on leave. While under fire, the newly promoted lieutenant was up "on top," directing the guide of the relieving regiment. Both he and Sergeant Stanborough were buried by the explosion of an incoming shell. It was a "Minnie," soldier's slang for Minenwerfer, that had been fired from a trench mortar like the one in front of my school. George was dug out alive, then carried over someone's shoulder to a casualty dressing station in an abandoned concrete German machine-gun post called a pillbox. It was about a twelve-minute walk. His tall frame bouncing along on a fellow soldier's shoulder, he was mortally wounded and probably unconscious.

Why the details? Because that's where the life is. The footsteps to the place where he finally died were ones I felt I could find. On one of my last expeditions to Belgium to try to create *The World Remembers*, I decided to remember George. Using Canadian and German military maps, I found the exact spot where he'd been hit just west of Passchendaele, and then I looked for the remains of the pillbox.

The shoulder that had carried George belonged to Private Ross, whose description of what happened is in the regiment's records:

"I asked Sgt. Stanborough for a snort of rum at Passchendaele. I did not get it. I went down the trench to dig a hole. Coming back I saw a Minnie coming over. I watched it. When I got back, well, it landed right on top of them. You know you're not to move in daylight, but ten minutes after a Corps. told me they had just dug him out. I had to carry Lt. Stratford to the Pill box. I was going out when they called me back. Take him out the Doctors said, and throw him over there. Well, they were piled up like cord wood. Poor Stratford, he was a good Platoon Officer. When we had a good Platoon Officer he did not last long."

Ross was an acting sergeant who had been commended for doing "excellent work . . . organizing men and directing repair of trenches, supervising the evacuation of the wounded under the severest of shelling, and saving a number of lives by digging out men buried by shell explosions."

It took perhaps ten minutes to extricate the pair who had been buried. During the walk to the pillbox, Ross would have heard his platoon officer's shallow breathing as well as the sound of incoming shells. Face down over his shoulder and across his back, George's head would have been almost at Ross's waist. That's how it was with me, when I took the same walk with a friend over my shoulder. Only when actors search out the details of a character do they begin to appreciate their lives. My great-uncle George seemed like me in so many ways that, with the help of an obliging friend, I wanted to walk the final leg of his journey. A deadweight body is different than carrying the groceries.

The evening after Ross delivered him to the pillbox, George's friends removed his dead body from "the pile," wrapped it in his brown blanket that served as a coffin, and slipped him into a grave they'd dug two kilometres west on the road to Ieper. They hammered in a wooden cross. As the winter wore on, the little battle cemetery was disturbed by visitations of artillery shells, whereupon the crosses and other bits were scattered about. After the war, exhumation teams looking for lost bodies used long steel rods to probe the earth. Should they hit something, on removing the rod from the ground the exhumer smelled the end for putrefaction, which would indicate there was a body beneath to dig for.

To me, in his last letters George just sounds tired.

" . . . otherwise I don't know how I would manage at all."

The exhumers never found him, or if they *did* smell him on the end of a rod, when their shovels made contact, there wasn't enough left to know it was George. So he remains an "unknown." His name appears on the south wall of the Menin Gate among thousands of other Unknowns. The words on the monument state "Their name liveth for ever" and promise that "They shall receive a crown of glory that fadeth not away."

War epitaphs can (and should) also be probed. If your rod emerges from the phrase and smells like a romanticization of the destruction, you can dig for meaning but the putrefaction of the epitaph's sentimentality probably means there is not much there. Judge for yourself; read the introduction by Lieutenant-Colonel Beckles Willson to his 1920 book *Ypres: The Holy Ground of British Arms*:

> "There is not a single half-acre in Ypres that is not sacred.
> There is not a single stone which has not sheltered scores
> of loyal young hearts, whose one impulse and desire was
> to fight and, if need be, to die for England. Their blood has
> drenched its cloisters and its cellars, but if never a drop had
> been spilt, if never a life had been lost in defence of Ypres,
> still would Ypres have been hallowed, if only for the hopes
> and the courage it has inspired and the scenes of valour and
> sacrifice it has witnessed."

I believe that the contrast between the lieutenant-colonel's words and what the war did to George and millions more throttles independence of the mind. Willson's words are close to criminal. He also didn't want the town of Ypres (Ieper) rebuilt.

I am glad that generations of visitors to the Menin Gate have stood silent every evening at eight p.m. within the monument's enormous arch. Traffic is turned away as they gather in dozens, or even hundreds, on the wide road running through the Gate. The sense of occasion helps them grasp the enormity of the loss they are remembering. I also hope that, surrounded by thousands of carved names of men whose bones remain somewhere in the farmland around Ieper, they question the war that brought little peace.

The Gate's structure *is* certainly a catalyst for reflection. Its size impresses but the heroic messaging of its engraved epitaphs leads you away from the possible criminality of the war. It is yet another instance where the stories told "afterwards" seek to catch the historical memory in a particular point of view—in this case, the heroic and solemn sacrifices of 54,395 men. But rather than the grandiosity of the monument, I think it is the intentions of the visitors' gathering each evening at eight that gives power to the occasion. Strip away the Gate's location and historic association, and it's a clumsy memorial. Strip away the *truly* loyal Ieper Last Post Association, whose members sound their bugles every evening, strip away the pomp and overwrought phrases that are often laid like bright flags over soldiers' unnecessary coffins, and you will find Siegfried Sassoon's poem "On Passing the New Menin Gate." Both Lieutenant Sassoon and Lieutenant George Stratford had spent time fighting in the Ypres Salient.

> *Who will remember, passing through this Gate,*
> *the unheroic dead who fed the guns?*
> *Who shall absolve the foulness of their fate,*
> *Those doomed, conscripted, unvictorious ones?*
>
> *Crudely renewed, the Salient holds its own.*
> *Paid are its dim defenders by this pomp;*
> *Paid, with a pile of peace-complacent stone,*
> *The armies who endured that sullen swamp.*
> *Here was the world's worst wound. And here with pride*
>
> *'Their name liveth for ever,' the Gateway claims.*
> *Was ever an immolation so belied*
> *As these intolerably nameless names?*
> *Well might the Dead who struggled in the slime*
> *Rise and deride this sepulchre of crime.*

If I could, I would commission a sculpture depicting the remnants of arms, toes, eyes, ears, abdomens, knees, hands, brains and testicles of the soldiers. I would ask Ieper's permission to have it installed on the road that runs through the centre of the Menin Gate. From speakers hung high inside its cavernous vault would come the sound of the men's laughter, gathered from the moments when they were delighted to be alive.

'Aren't you coming?' and every time Geordie would stick his head forward and grin like Charlie Chaplin, then pull it back again quickly—you know the way, and OH! it was funny."

The laughter would fade into a chorus of exhalations of their final breaths, and then finally into silence.

If George had lived and married, his grandchildren would have been about my age, perhaps a little younger. I am descended from George's eldest sister, Helen. We could have gone together as a group to find his brother Joe's grave. But that was not to be.

Walking to the remains of the pillbox, I am beside Private Ross, each of us with our burden on our shoulders. The only sounds are our boots and breathing. In both our worlds, though ten decades stand between us, it is mid-November. Ross listens for George's breath, I for my friend's. The private's back is broader than mine and I am certain Ross has done this before.

Before the cascading earth closed over George and Sergeant Stanborough, who knows what internal hemorrhaging resulted from the concussion of the exploding shell. Ross knew the lieutenant *was* alive after he had been dug out, but his abdominal arteries were probably shredded or crushed. Sergeant Stanborough, who'd earlier refused Ross's request for rum, had also been buried, but he was dead when he was brought to the surface.

No heavy army stretchers were available, so Ross and I have only our backs. Drifting in and out of consciousness, perhaps George tries to make sense of the upside-down landscape of shell holes, Ross's legs, weeds and barbed wire through which the private is trudging. Perhaps he thinks of his nightingale . . . *it didn't appreciate the value of wings or it wouldn't have been where it was.* Enough mud has been cleaned from Geordie's face and mouth to know that he is breathing, but the relentless Belgian dirt remains on his cheeks and in his hair. There are moans from the pain as his helmetless inverted head bobbles along.

I walk beside Ross as a witness.

Occasionally I hear him speak to the young lieutenant . . . *you'll soon be there now . . . no more war for you, my hearty . . .* and always on the lookout, he mutters . . . *careful, there's some dead Jerries.* Sliding into the slime of a shell hole while balancing a man on your back wouldn't be helpful. George's bleeding is probably internal, so there isn't much blood on show, yet the perpetual smell of human decomposition surrounds them that even the November wind couldn't clear away. *Lord almighty, what a stench. MO's got a bit of something to stop that blasted pain.*

As I trudge along beside Ross and George with my friend on my shoulder, I feel others joining us . . . *bit of trench here . . .* warns Ross to us all. They are George's grandsons and granddaughters who were never to be. Several of the great-grandchildren are being carried in their mothers' arms . . . *easy does it, mind that bit of wire . . .* And then I sense another pair of feet, those of the woman whom my tall great-uncle wanted most to be with us. Mary Elizabeth, his mother. Our group, both flesh and ghost, picks its way through the aftermath of battle, trudging quietly towards the pillbox. Accompanying George to his end was the least we could do. I remembered Wilfred Owen's words from "I Saw His Round Mouth's Crimson" on dying.

And in his eyes
The cold stars lighting, very old and bleak,
In different skies.

By the time we reached the dressing station, George had slipped away. The pillbox, a former machine-gun emplacement, had been abandoned by the Germans perhaps a week before. We all ached. It had been a long carry but *I* had made it. While Ross was in the dressing station, I set my real friend back on his feet. The rest of the family had silently disappeared just after the moment of George's passing.

Because I'd borne my obliging friend, he and I shared a laugh, and I thanked him for helping me remember my great-uncle's journey. Apart from that, I didn't know what to say. It's often in the silence that meaning can be found. After the doctor declared that the lieutenant was already dead, Ross had emerged from the pillbox with George's body and laid him among the growing stack of silent human cordwood. Then, too, Ross was nowhere to be seen.

To catch my breath, I sat with my back against the remains of the unforgiving concrete and thought of Margaret Osbourne in Bournemouth, packing up George's things to post them to Canada. And then of the nineteen-year-old sitting down to compose a letter of condolence to George's mother, describing one of her cousin's Charlie Chaplin moments. In the collision in my imagination between the pockmarked German gun position and her smooth, clean writing paper, nothing new had appeared, except for George's smile and Margaret's laughter.

"Mother kept turning around every six steps and saying 'Aren't you coming?' and every time Geordie would stick his head forward and grin like Charlie Chaplin, then pull it back again quickly—you know the way, and OH! it was funny! And he used to do it when we played rum, and now I can't help thinking of him every time we play.

One morning in the studio I sewed all the buttons on his tunic for him, it was a new one and too tight around his tummy, so I had to let it out, and we were so afraid that the marks of where the buttons were at first would show, but they didn't! and then we went and sat in the car and cleaned them. He could eat more for dinner that day! I never, never will forget how dear he was . . . I just miss him so."

In the Belgian town of Arlon there is a statue to King Leopold II. A few years ago someone from Black Lives Matter threw red paint at it. The metaphorical blood flowed across the monarch's chest and down his bronze pants. The monument looked messy but, to my mind, it was now complete. To clean up that nasty bit of colonial history, the town had the paint hosed off and then turned down those who petitioned to remove the statue altogether.

Should I travel to Arlon and find the statue still standing, I might amend its historical memory with a saw, by cutting off one of its hands and hanging it around its neck. Not wanting to get caught, I would perform this act in the middle of the night, just as I performed my vigil with the sword in Talbot House in Poperinge. Regarding my proposal for reimagining the Menin Gate, I am not confident that Ieper would accept a sculpture that depicted soldiers' body parts to be installed in its midst. We may have to find another way to augment its memory. If we are to achieve peace, it must be done in the bright light of the complete memories of all the wars that have ever been fought.

CHAPTER 17

NOT ABOUT HEROES

*This book is not about heroes. English poetry is not yet fit to speak
of them. Nor is it about deeds, or lands, nor anything about glory,
honour, might, majesty, dominion, or power, except War.
Above all I am not concerned with Poetry. My subject is War,
and the pity of War. The Poetry is in the pity.*
—unpublished preface by Wilfred Owen, killed November 5, 1918,
for a future publication of his collected poems

the wounded at the Queen's Canadian Military Hospital in 1917

In Ontario we have a Highway of Heroes along which bridges are
dedicated to members of our armed forces who lost their lives.
The highway memorial began while Canadians were fighting in
Afghanistan. When the Hercules aircraft landed at Canadian Forces
Base Trenton after the flight from Kandahar with the remains of the
dead servicemen or women, the coffins would be offloaded and cere-
monially driven down Highway 401 to Toronto. Were those in them
heroes? To many in Canada they are. They had certainly displayed
bravery by risking their lives while deployed in a war zone, but what
does someone have to do to earn the title?

Films and plays tell stories of heroes and antiheroes. I've performed as both, playing the antihero in *The Jail Diary of Albie Sachs*, about an imprisoned anti-apartheid South African lawyer, and the heroic Mark Antony in *The Tragedy of Julius Caesar*. That Shakespearean play, set in ancient Rome, concerns a political insurrection and assassination of the dictator Caesar. In the chaos of the coup, Cinna the poet is ruthlessly torn to pieces by a mob. Portraying Mark Antony was a challenge but I was young, entranced by heroes, and wanted to thrill the crowd at the Stratford Festival with my eulogy "Friends, Romans, countrymen, lend me your ears," delivered over the body of the freshly assassinated emperor. "O! pardon me, thou bleeding piece of earth, / That I am meek and gentle with these butchers," I had said to the corpse before vowing to take revenge. I was full of ideas about inflaming the mob by hoisting up the corpse of the slain Caesar in my arms, but I did not yet have the leather lungs needed to effortlessly fill an almost two-thousand-seat theatre. And a word of advice: if *you* ever stage this tragedy, never use retractable daggers to kill the dictator.

I say this because in our final preview performance, one of the conspirators *actually* stabbed Caesar. We had been rehearsing during the buildup to the 1982 Falklands War, and our director, who was British, was adamant that *his* production would have lifelike violence, meaning it would be frenzied and unpredictable. The historical record shows that Julius Caesar was stabbed twenty-three times, so our actor was to be stabbed twenty-three times. As the British Navy's armada sailed down the Atlantic to reclaim the islands Argentinians called the Islas Malvinas, the director became even *more* adamant that our violence be bloody. The Stratford Festival's special effects department prepared quantities of red syrup for us to smear ourselves with between our appearances in various battle scenes.

The Falklands War was fuelled by inflated affronts to the sovereignty of both Britain and Argentina. Both governments—one democratic and one military—were unpopular at the time and wanted to shore up their support at home by pointing daggers at dangers abroad. Prime Minister Margaret Thatcher was down in the polls, so dispatching an invasion fleet to replant the Union Jack in an insignificant colony eight thousand miles away was a good political move, as well as a last flourish of Empire.

In our onstage Rome, the lead conspirator, Gaius Cassius, was played by the fine actor Nicholas Pennell. He was in on the killing but, frenzy not being Nicholas's forte, I doubt that his dagger did the deed. For onstage stabbings, *please* rely on the actor's blade skills rather than the reliability of retractable daggers. Turning aside the tip of a dulled dagger in a stab's last second is simple, undetectable, and no one gets hurt. That was *not* how it played out in our production. Around thrust number nine of the assassins' frenzy, someone's retractable dagger malfunctioned and enough of the blade slipped by Caesar's concealed body armour and down he went—for real. The confused assassins were unaware that an injury had occurred. Twenty-three plastic blood bags had been sewn inside Caesar's costume to be burst by the twenty-three incoming daggers forcefully striking the hidden body armour beneath. When Caesar immediately crumpled to the stage after stab nine, the bewildered conspirators picked him back up and continued their work.

I was backstage preparing for the "Friends, Romans, country-men" speech when Jack, the wounded actor, was brought off covered in fake blood. Despite his pain and premature collapse, Jack had performed well at playing dead. "Only a bruise, R. H.," he said when I suggested that he should not come on as the corpse. "Only a bruise, of course, of course I can come on." He winced as I loaded him onto the funeral bier, so I told him I would cut the business where I grabbed the dead Caesar's armpits and hoisted him up to incite the crowd. "No, no, let's do it, I'll be fine." Actors are simply the best. The show must go on, even though no one knew that the blade that had not completely retracted, in bypassing the armour, had cracked one of Jack's ribs beneath his toga. And out we went onto one of the most famous and fabulous stages in the world.

Playing heroes cloaked in moral strength and standing clearly on the side of good and against evil makes you seem invincible. You have licence to inflict violence because you are on the side of right. You are bringing justice to the world. How often do we get to pretend we are exemplary human beings? I enjoyed the power of Mark Antony's messianic manipulation of the mob. Through almost seventy performances of *Julius Caesar*, Nicky Pennell watched me struggling to improve. And I did. My lungs grew stronger and I became more and more audible for those in the back row of that enormous and wonderful theatre.

In that fateful preview, the dead Caesar unexpectedly became *very* audible. As I pulled the corpse from the coffin to dangle it dramatically before the crowd, Jack visibly grimaced and then expressed something along the lines of "*AgghhHHHHHHHHHHAAAAAAAaa!*," which was probably the moment when his cracked rib punctured his lung. As the audience noted, the Emperor may have been dead but Jack was not.

These are surreal moments for actors. The brain hyperventilates on the problem while the lips continue mouthing the lines. The fish has been clubbed but the gills keep moving. Not grasping the real reason for Jack's outburst, I eulogized as if nothing had happened and got him offstage as quickly as possible. Jack was sent to the hospital and the understudy played Caesar for the rest of the run.

In one of our backstage conversations during that long season, Nicholas handed me the script of the play *Not About Heroes*. His interest was in the First World War poet Siegfried Sassoon and he was looking for someone to play Wilfred Owen, the other war poet in Stephen MacDonald's play. I never thanked him enough for his believing in me, I never performed it with him and I sincerely and deeply wish that I had.

Not About Heroes asks the same questions that I have about heroes. It describes the friendship of the poets Owen and Sassoon, both of whom served in the World War I British Army, both of whom were wounded, received medals for bravery and wrote poems that pulled the war apart. Siegfried Sassoon survived to write his savage thoughts about the Menin Gate: "Well might the Dead who struggled in the slime / Rise and deride this sepulchre of crime."

Wilfred Owen was treated for shell shock—a term that somehow doesn't convey having your nerves shredded and your emotional coping systems dismembered—in a hospital in Scotland in 1917. He returned to active service in 1918 and was killed in the fighting just six days before the war's end. He'd been a brilliant poet.

Nicholas's suggestion that I play Owen came early in my career, when I was bewitched by heroes of action or deed. Villains also enticed me, since truly bad people seem more interesting to portray than good ones. But I did not yet appreciate internal courage like that of Lieutenant Owen, whose poetry explores the collision between warfare and humanity. I loved the external rough and tumble of stage combat and the sensuality of swordplay. Épées and sabres cover my study walls. My well-worn rapier from a production of *Cyrano de Bergerac* hangs there beside my great-uncle Joe's cavalry sword. There are few of my costumes that I haven't sewn padding into to absorb blows. Who wouldn't want to dazzle audiences with physical daring?

But when I began to appreciate the perils of our inner journeys, the thrill of playing heroes and villains faded. External dangers can certainly seize young imaginations. Yet in Shakespeare's *Hamlet*, the prince's battle with the pirates doesn't even merit a scene, while his wrestling with questions of self-worth and self-slaughter is central to the story. David Young's intriguing play *Glenn*, about Glenn Gould, is solely the internal journey of a musician at the moment of his stroke. The final conscious seconds of an extraordinary artist's life fill the entire drama as Gould wrestles with everything his life has ever been. It makes uplifting and insightful theatre. The challenges and perils of the *inner* journey are formidable mountains to navigate. From their slopes one can see that much of the destruction wrought in the external world below is fuelled by the tormented beings within ourselves.

Consider again the courage of the child who composed "Shoes of the Dead" while at the Majdanek concentration camp in Poland.

Her job was to sort the footwear of her executed fellow prisoners. Her courage lay not so much in defying her captors as in defying the despair within herself. Her decision at twelve years old to conceive a poem while living amid the fumes of the Nazi mind shames those movie moguls who often spend $200 million on a story about a two-dimensional action hero. This nameless girl's brief life ended in a place of utter bleakness, and yet she found a few breaths of clear air before her impending murder. Her poem survived in the memories of those who heard it and could never forget it. Her questions spun threads for humanity's tapestry that the Holocaust had been determined to cut.

They are sorted by nervous, trembling hands,
The piles grow, piles like giants,
Becoming pyramids,
Rising above themselves,
Thrust into the sky like columns
Shouting: Why, why, why

Film performers who earn fortunes portraying pop-culture heroes are, for the most part, perpetuating the lie that others, not ourselves, are primarily the ones who create the perils of the world. The question is, are there consequences from such narratives? In his novel *The Famished Road*, the Nigerian-British poet and novelist Ben Okri writes:

"Nations and peoples are largely the stories they feed themselves. If they tell themselves stories that are lies, they will suffer the future consequences of those lies. If they tell themselves stories that face their own truths, they will free their histories for future flowerings."

Words matter. Stories matter. *Not About Heroes* is about warrior-poets advocating for the human spirit in the battle for our imaginations. Wilfred Owen describes the mental wounding from shell shock this way: "Foreheads of men have bled where no wounds were." In his poem "Futility" he writes about the winter morning when he came upon a dead soldier and arrived at the same question the girl would ask in the extermination camp:

> *Move him into the sun—*
> *Gently its touch awoke him once,*
> *At home, whispering of fields unsown.*
> *Always it woke him, even in France,*
> *Until this morning and this snow.*
> *If anything might rouse him now*
> *The kind old sun will know.*
>
> *Think how it wakes the seeds—*
> *Woke once the clays of a cold star.*
> *Are limbs so dear-achieved, are sides*
> *Full nerved,—still warm,—too hard to stir?*
> *Was it for this the clay grew tall?*
> *—O what made fatuous sunbeams toil*
> *To break earth's sleep at all?*

Were my great-uncles heroes? Judging from their letters, it doesn't seem that they thought they were. Yet hundreds of thousands of soldiers in the First World War performed extraordinarily courageous acts. Heroism was rampant, but that is not to be equated with authorities handing out medals. Officially bestowing the *title* of hero on a soldier becomes a verbal medal in recognition of their bravery, while it also serves to maintain respect for the army's brand and polishes up the rationalization for going to war in the first place. No medals are ever awarded for *opposing* a war.

Being named a hero supports the narrative of those who do the naming. I suggest it is linguistic statuary, sometimes as ill-conceived as the eighteenth and nineteenth centuries' "great man" statues that are now being questioned or toppled. The international club of pedestal men, heroes of past wars and nation-building exercises, were meant to be role models and instructors of patriotism. But often the history they stand for is at worst myopic and at best incomplete. Lord Nelson atop his column in Trafalgar Square is a member of that celebratory club of action and empire into which dictators, genocidal leaders and slave traders have been admitted. Consider King Leopold II's statue in Belgium, or Edward Cornwallis's in Nova Scotia. Cornwallis was a British officer who founded Halifax in 1749 and offered a ten-guinea reward for each captured or killed member of the Mi'kmaq Nation—an offer often referred to as the "Scalping Proclamation." Lethal racist attitudes such as Cornwallis's towards local peoples has meant their statutes have since been removed—save for the one of Leopold II in Arlon. Saddam Hussein's statues lasted only until American soldiers pulled them down after the Iraq War in 2003. The supporters of this mainly male community of stone and bronze gave little thought that their heroes might eventually become so burdened by their personal histories that many would tumble under the weight of them.

It takes a journey beyond simple physical deeds to be a heroine or hero. It requires an odyssey of body, mind *and* spirit that assumes risk, an odyssey for the benefit of others. Heroes return (hopefully) with insights that broaden humanity's horizons. Nelson Mandela emerged without hatred from twenty-seven years of political imprisonment by his apartheid oppressors. He went on to become president of the new South Africa, reminding us of the transformational potential in all our lives and the resilience of restorative justice.

Malala Yousafzai's resolve to survive both her physical and mental assaults is likewise inspiring. The fifteen-year-old's comeback from the execution attempt by fanatics who detested the education of Islamic girls contrasts with the thin soup offered by the superpower heroes of our popular culture. One of the would-be killers' bullets entered Malala's forehead, travelled down her neck and lodged in her shoulder. Surgeons removed parts of her skull, the blood clots and the projectile. Her infections were beaten back, her face and skull stitched together and, amazingly, she recovered and resumed championing girls' education, despite the Taliban's continuing threats. Malala has no extra powers, just remarkable courage, resolve and a vision of women's rights. She was awarded the Nobel Prize and recently completed her university degree. *She* is a heroine.

Owen's and Sassoon's poems addressed the contradiction of waging an inhuman war *and* respecting the humanity of the individuals who fought it. On becoming a soldier, recruits must set aside the part of their humanity that prevents them from killing fellow humans. For that they are accordingly awarded our respect, as well as our gratitude for being prepared to lose their own lives. Yet, should they not relinquish their human face while in uniform, not only are they afforded less respect—"not man enough" is one of the phrases that comes to mind—but they also become a liability for the army's system of defeating enemies. That was part of Wilfred Owen's reasoning. He felt that only if he excelled as a warrior would he be more widely accepted as a war poet. And he did excel. He was awarded the Military Cross (MC) for "leadership and conspicuous gallantry"— but he had been killed by the time the honour was announced. Yet his tenacity and courage served its purpose by saying *read what a heroic battlefield officer has seen.*

Armies, understandably, have little tolerance for human frailty. In the First World War, both British and French armies executed their own men, ostensibly for cowardice and desertion, when in fact it was the army's fear of weakness that bound the condemned soldiers to their execution posts—most of whom were probably bleeding from mental wounds, as Lieutenant Owen, MC, described it. The old men who commanded the armies neither accepted nor understood the mental condition of most of those tied to the posts. It was into the moral fault line between the humanity and imposed inhumanity of a soldier's life that poets such as Owen drove their poetry.

Parable of the Old Man and the Young
So Abram rose, and clave the wood, and went,
And took the fire with him, and a knife.

And as they sojourned both of them together,
Isaac the first-born spake and said, My Father,
Behold the preparations, fire and iron,
But where the lamb for this burnt-offering?
Then Abram bound the youth with belts and straps,
And builded parapets and trenches there,
And stretchèd forth the knife to slay his son.
When lo! an angel called him out of heaven,
Saying, Lay not thy hand upon the lad,
Neither do anything to him. Behold,
A ram, caught in a thicket by its horns;
Offer the Ram of Pride instead of him.

But the old man would not so, but slew his son,
And half the seed of Europe, one by one.

I have wondered if my father shared any of Owen's and Sassoon's anger. His red-pencilled comments in James Lamb's *The Corvette Navy* were sometimes directed at the onshore naval officers who sailed only desks into battle, while the corvette crews, battered and attacked on their ocean crossings, were seldom rewarded with more gold braid for their sleeves. Perhaps Woodburn's search for heroes was behind his desire to identify the aircrews who had flown out from Iceland to take on the U-boats that were using their acoustic homing torpedoes against ships such as HMCS *Sackville*.

What has changed that we have allowed the title of hero to be so generously awarded? Is it that we worry about appearing unfair, or are we reverting to the nineteenth century's heroic view of militarism? The romance between nationalism and the military in the leadup to 1914 helped assemble the ingredients for the global conflict. Or is it that today we are tired of appreciating complex individuals and yearn instead for a primary-coloured world of heroes without contradictions or nuances? Is it that we just want simpler messaging?

Whatever you think of Wilfred Owen or the nameless girl, neither they nor their poems are easy reads.

Our appetite for naming more and more heroes and consuming the film world's superheroes has coincided with the erosion of the public's confidence that "ordinary" people are capable of solving our looming global challenges. This has happened at the same time as our popular culture has been promoting the ascendancy of the individual over the collective. The title of hero is awarded mainly to individuals, not groups. Unfortunately, a robust democracy needs an electorate that *believes* in collective action, while robust authoritarian regimes and meritocracies do not. Perhaps it is not a coincidence that we are also witnessing the erosion of public confidence in our democratic institutions.

There still are individuals who fight *for* the collective, but they are rarely without controversy. Edward Snowden, a US government security analyst, risked his life and freedom to reveal the illegal mass surveillance of the American people being conducted by the (unelected) National Security Agency. Now living in exile in Russia, Snowden remains, to many, a traitor. His actions were heroic, but does that make him a hero? Then there is Greta Thunberg's youth crusade against the climate inaction of corporations and governments that will deliver her generation to the catastrophe of an altered climate. Her determination and drive are heroic, but is she a heroine?

At the time of writing, at least forty-six health-care workers in Canada—mainly women—have died after contracting COVID-19. During the pandemic, refreshingly, our definition of hero broadened to include the medical professionals who, in the months before vaccines were developed, exposed themselves daily to the deadly virus in order to treat the sick. At the height of the crisis, courageous compassion became almost as newsworthy as courageous action. Yet the heroines who faced down the virus were still not awarded the heroic narrative status of those who faced physical violence. If forty-six police officers had lost their lives in the line of duty, our press and police associations would have hailed them, while their memorializing would have been public events. Not so for the nurses and personal service workers who lost their lives while serving us. No flags were lowered to half-staff in their honour. No highway bridges have been dedicated to them. No superhero movies will be made of nurses soaring through the air while zapping viral villains.

⁓

Wilfred Owen thought that courageous action on the battlefield was important for his acceptance as a war poet. I think he was mistaken. But for those who object to Owen's views in his poems, his having been awarded the Military Cross diminishes their ability to dismiss him. For me, his Military Cross is part and parcel of his poetry's eloquence and anger. It is as if he wrapped his poems around his medal and hurled them at us through time.

There are other soldiers who've questioned wars and have actually thrown away their medals. In April 1971, Vietnam Veterans Against the War protested in Washington, publicly challenging what their government had sent them to do. The veterans called their march on the capital "a limited incursion into the country of Congress" and were met with barricades and court injunctions. Accompanying them were some Gold Star Mothers who, earlier in the protest, had been denied entry to Arlington National Cemetery, home to the graves of their soldier sons who'd died in Vietnam. On their final approach to the Capitol Building the veterans were stopped by a wall hastily erected to block them. In an emotional "divestiture" ceremony, one by one, the eight hundred addressed the crowd from the steps in front of the Capitol Building, and then threw their discharge papers, ribbons, medals, commendations and even their canes over the wall, at the government. The whole thing was captured on video:

"My name is Peter Branigan and I got a Purple Heart here, and I hope I get another one fighting these motherfuckers."

Throw.

"Bob Steed died for these medals. Lieutenant Paverol died for what he got these medals for . . . Sergeant Dobbs died for what he got with these medals . . . got a Silver Star, Purple Heart, Army Compensation Medal, eight Air Medals, National Defense and the rest of this garbage. It doesn't mean a thing."

Throw.

"Robert James, New York. I symbolically return all Vietnam medals, and other service medals given me . . . given me . . . by the hollow structure that has genocidal policies against the non-white peoples of the world."

Throw.

In 2015 Ben Griffin, a British Iraq War veteran, went further. To address the injustices that the army had ordered him to do while serving in Iraq, Griffin and two other veterans, Kieran Devlin and John Boulton, discarded their oaths of allegiance, military berets and medals onto to the pavement outside the British prime minister's residence at 10 Downing Street, London. Griffin had served in the British Army's Special Air Service (SAS) counterinsurgency operations in Baghdad. The SAS is a tough unit to be in and to face.

"I used to wear this hat as a soldier, it used to have great significance to me. I no longer want to keep hold of this symbol of militarism."

Discards beret.

"I was given these medals for service on operations with the British Army. This particular medal here was given me for my part in the occupation of Iraq. Whilst I was over there, I attacked civilians in their homes and took away their men, off to be tortured in prison. I no longer want these despicable things."

After Ben Griffin threw down his medals, he joined Devlin and Boulton and the three of them walked off down the street. Later, in a media interview, he spoke about the narratives contained in his medals and beret:

"These are things we once treasured, so it's a difficult thing to give away but we think it's really important that we do that—both in protest against this war but also because we want to get rid of the mythology around these things. Lots of young kids are looking at these medals thinking 'oh wow, I'd want some of those' and we want to show 'look, this is what we think of them; we earned them and this is what we think of them now.'"

It might be wise to be wary when soldiers are called heroes. Tocarra Mallard, an American writer in New York who describes herself as having grown up as a military brat, puts it this way: "Be careful if they call you a hero, because that means they don't care if you die."

I believe in heroism, but rarely in heroes.

CHAPTER 18

WHEN YOU LOOK FOR THEIR NAMES

HMCS Sackville *at sea*

November 11 parades and prayers were seldom to my father's liking. The Battle of the Atlantic, which governed his life for three years, bore little relation to the remembrance politics that came after the war. In his seventies he tried unsuccessfully to find the names of the Liberator aircrews who had flown the thousand miles out from Iceland on September 20, 1943, to help rescue the convoy his corvette was escorting westward across the Atlantic. When he told me of his search, I thought it odd, since I didn't yet understand the power that comes from "naming" someone, or how speaking a name from a neglected past can both respect and somehow "create" a life. Yet my father's search affected me, since I would later make my own odyssey to find the names of the estimated nine and a half million dead from the First World War.

My father mentioned once that he had never expected to survive the war. It was a moment of hesitant intimacy in a snippet of conversation. I was taken aback and had no idea how to respond, since I have the same kind of emotional hesitancy. But I believe he and I were searching for ways to tell each other how much we meant to one another. My father *thought* he'd found the bomber squadron that came to join the battle and had 10 SQUAD embossed on his car's licence plates, but he could never discover the crew's names.

The four-day sea battle south of Greenland had been going badly when forty-nine men in six aircraft appeared out of the low-hanging clouds to attack the German submarines that were sinking warships like my father's. One after another, HMCS *Sackville* and the other escorts were being hunted down by a pack of twenty-one U-boats. Woodburn felt that the battle only turned in their favour after the arrival of the forty-nine young flyers. After the loss of nine ships, the combined convoys ON 202 and ONS 18 eventually survived and sailed on to Halifax and New York.

He had described seeing the trails in the ocean of the U-boats' T-5 acoustic homing torpedoes as they locked on to the vibrations from the corvette's propellors. The "smart" torpedoes were a new variation of an old weapon. My father told of the hard turns *Sackville* took to try to avoid being hit. The escorts were having their sterns blown off because the German navy's revised strategy was to first eliminate the escorts and then turn their guns on the merchant ships. By the time the Liberators appeared, a British destroyer and a Canadian corvette had been sunk and others had been hit and were limping home. On the fourth day of the battle a frigate was sunk but HMCS *Sackville* was spared—and with it perhaps my father's life. He wanted to know the names of the aircrews.

History's headlines make no space for the details wherein lie the humanity of the events being reported. But our lives are only specifics and details. Grieving and graves are specifics. How do we reconcile the tension between needing to know the broad strokes of history, which help us navigate the road ahead, and knowing the *details* about how the road may have been lethal to humans in the past? A broad-stroke account is that six VLR (very long range) Liberators loaded with depth charges appeared out of the clouds on the third day of the battle south of Greenland. Does that mean the names of the men inside those fuselages aren't important? Does that mean that the thousand miles the crews had flown over the ocean, just to join the battle, are of no interest? Of course, to understand significant events in history we prioritize the information we are told, but the inhumanity appears when the details are dismissed. Perhaps there are just too many of them. Perhaps the details are not strategically important. Or in this case perhaps, like the Liberator aircraft's parts, the aircrews and their lives were also considered replaceable.

A number of years ago I decided to take up my father's search at the British Public Records Office outside London. He had assumed that it was an American squadron, since the Liberator was a US aircraft. But, digging through the Royal Air Force's 1943 records for Iceland, I saw no Americans and wondered if instead the young men were part of a British weather and patrol squadron that was flying an assortment of aircraft, including the VLR Liberator IIIs. Then, in a flurry of ineptitude in the Records Office, I found the names.

Having only a vague idea of how to research who exactly had flown out to ON 202 and ONS 18, I had resorted to speed-scrolling through aircrews' debriefing notes from September 1943, which were stored on what seemed like kilometres of microfilm. The notes were from *every* aircraft in *every* squadron that had flown from Reykjavik at that time. Squadron by squadron I loaded box after box of microfilm into the viewing machine and spooled through entry after entry. Nothing about a battle. Next roll of microfilm. Nothing. Next squadron. Nothing. Next roll. Nothing. No battles and no actions. I knew there was nothing because the entries were short, three sentences at most, because crews were only reporting on their weather and reconnaissance patrols.

```
Airbourne Reykjavik 08.07.A. S/c for the Denmark
Straits. 10.38. Met Ice Edge, and plotted it.
14.35. Recco complete 17.16.A. Landed Reykjavik.

Airbourne Reykjavik 10.00.A. S/c for area.
12.40. On Patrol. 16.50. Off Patrol. Owing
to poor weather to East. Scattered Icebergs
and what was thought to be ice edge sighted.
18.35.A. Landed Reykjavik.

Airbourne Reykjavik 07.33.A. S/c for area.
09.06. On patrol 2 Trawlers sighted in area.
19.11. Off Patrol. 22.12.A. Landed Reykjavik.
```

The references to ice made me wonder about the frigid ocean and the survivors of those sea battles, floundering in the water while waiting for a rescue boat that perhaps would never come.

With microfilm boxes and despair piling up beside me, I heard the Public Records Office give its final notice for visitors to pack up and leave, since they were closing for the day. With few hard facts on which to focus my search, I might have been looking for phantoms. "*This office closes in fifteen minutes. All documents must be immediately returned to the main desk in your area. Please return tomorrow,*" said the public address system. But I couldn't return, since my flight home to Canada left that evening.

And then, there before me on the screen was a long entry. At first I didn't believe it, since I am a last-minute Larry whose disbelief usually trumps my belief, but it was *long.* If S/c meant set course, C/v meant convoy, D/d meant destroyer, R.T. meant radio transmission, A.A. was anti-aircraft, M.G. was machine gun and D.C. meant depth charge, then I was reading the battle, as described from the air, that Woodburn had seen from the sea. And *there* were the Liberators, and *there* were names of the aircrews who had looked down on the convoy, the attackers, my father and the cold of September's North Atlantic Ocean. And there in the typed debriefing notes was a reference to

Sackville, just as my father had told me, being "homed" so he could sail back to help rescue survivors:

```
Sighted town class D/d. Down by stern, and homed
rescue ships
```

I'd moved closer to my father and his life. It was Flight Officer Kerrigan on Liberator R/120 who had seen HMCS *St. Croix* from his cockpit "down by stern," having been hit by two torpedoes and about to be finished off with a third. Kerrigan ordered his radio operator to signal *Sackville* and the other escorts the coordinates of where the *St. Croix* was sinking. At just past nine p.m., my father, standing on his corvette's bridge, might have made out the R/120 painted on the side of Kerrigan's Liberator. As *Sackville* set course in the growing darkness for the rescue, did he consider the fate of the *Polyanthus,* the corvette that had exploded after being hit several hours before? That sinking had left only one survivor. The fires onboard *Polyanthus* that night might still have been visible before being extinguished by the ocean closing over them. Of the nineteen escorts, two had been sunk or were sinking and two more were so damaged they had left the convoy for base. I know that those dying in battle are details and that military training keeps soldiers and seamen from dwelling on them. I know Woodburn was well trained, since during the four-day battle the situation was critical, sleep was scarce and clear thinking was needed. But I also know that he wanted the names of those who had helped his crew survive.

```
DATE: 20th | AIRCRAFT TYPE & NUMBER: LIBERATOR
III-R/120 | DUTY: Escort to ON.18 Met

TIME UP: 10.30/20 REY | TIME DOWN: 02.55/21 REY

CREW:
F/O. Kerrigan. Capt.
Sgt. Weiner. Co-Pil.
```

```
P/O. Rackham. Nav.
F/O. Hartrick. Engr.
F/Sgt. Foy. 1.W.Op.
Sgt. Chapman. 2.W.Op.
Sgt. Hunt. 3.W.Op.
Sgt.Grassam. 4.W.Op.
Sgt.Levinsky. 5.W.Op.

DETAILS OF SORTIE OR FLIGHT:
Airborne Reykjavik 10.20.A. S/c for C/v. 13.30.
Began Homing Procedure B - Unsuccessful. 14.36.
ONS.18. Carried out escort on request from SNO.
Searched for, and located C/V ON.202. Both
C/v.s. joined at 18.00 hours. 20.10. Witnessed
attack on U-Boat by N of 120. 21.04. Sighted
town class D/d. Down by stern, and homed res-
cue ships D/d. 22.33. Left C/v. 02.55.A./21.
Landed Reykjavik.
```

This was a remembrance I could live with. The debriefing notes of the forty-nine men were the best gift I was able to get for my father—to give him my understanding, much like the warmth shared when, having completed a long night drive home with the family, my six-year-old self tumbled sleepily from the car and felt his hands tuck me into bed, both son and father glad to have arrived. His determination to find Flying Officer Kerrigan, Co-Pilot Green, Sergeant Weiner and the others was what later led me to search for the millions from the First World War. Naming *is* at the heart of remembering. The war, the war deaths of his friends and those of his uncles in 1917 and 1918 had stayed with him, yet he rarely attended a November 11th ceremony. Like father, like son. Remembrance through abstract nouns was also not for me—or as Wilfred Owen stated it best in the unpublished preface to his war poems: "nor anything about glory, honour, might, majesty, dominion, or power."

DATE: 20th | AIRCRAFT TYPE & NUMBER: LIBERATOR
III-X/120 | DUTY: Escort to ON.202Met4 U-boats
sighted. U-Boat attacked twice

TIME UP: 05.07 REY | TIME DOWN: 19.48 REY

CREW:

F/Lt. Thompson. Capt.
F/O. Green. Co-Pil.
Sgt. Davies. Nav.
F/Lt. Lewis.
Sgt. Lesier. Engr.
Sgt. Bacon. 1.W.Op.
Sgt. Lund 2.W.Op.
Sgt. Dowling. 3.W.Op.
Sgt. Richardson. 4.W.Op.

DETAILS OF SORTIE OR FLIGHT:

Airbourne Reykjavik 05.07.A.S/c for C/v. 07.02.
Began Homing Procedure B - successful. 10.25.
Sighted fully surfaced 500.ton U-Boat. 2 miles
distance. Dived to attack, but bomb doors did
not open in time. Sighted D/d approaching, and
commenced homing D/d to U-Boat by R/T. U-Boat
opened A.A. Fire. 11.03. U-Boat sighted D/d
and submerged. 11.04. A/C attacked U-Boat. in
swirl position. 57.49.N 28.26.W. with 3 x 250.
lbs. D.Cs. 11.05. Attacked U-Boat with 2 x 600
D.C.s. D/d then arrived and carried out D.C.
attack for ¾ hour, then lost contact. 12.39.
A/C. set course for C/v. 12.55. Met C/v. ON.202.
Commenced Cobra Patrol. 15.05. Sighted two fully
surfaced U-boats in position 57.45.N. 30.26.W.
1 to Port and 1 to Starboard of A/c. U-boats
altered course immediately. A/c. informed C/v,
and suggested alteration of course. U-Boat on
Starboard was last seen at full-speed with D/
ds. in persuit, U-Boat on Port was attacked
with M/G. A.A. Fire returned by U-Boat. D/d was
homed to U-Boat and opened fire at five miles
range. A/c left U-Boat with D/d in close persuit. Attempted to home relieving Liberator

to C/v. Unsuccessful. 16.13. S/c Base. 17.07.
Sighted fully surfaced U-Boat five miles distance in position 59.45.N. 28.12.W. U-Boat
submerged immediately. C/v informed. 19.48.A.
Landed Reykjavik.

59°45' N and 28°12' W are the coordinates where Flight Lieutenant
Thompson in Liberator XIII–X/120 had made his final contact
with the submarines attacking the convoy southeast of the coast of
Greenland. It is also where Lieutenant Woodburn Thomson stood
on the bridge of HMCS *Sackville*. Flight Lieutenant Thompson, having informed the convoy that the U-boat "immediately" submerged,
then set course for the long flight back to Reykjavik to ensure that he
and his crew could land before their aircraft ran out of fuel.

I left the Public Records Office, still in disbelief and with little
time to make my flight from Heathrow that evening—last-minute
Larry once again.

On westbound flights the sunset lingers for hours. In the spec-
tacular twilight, gazing down at the ocean sliding by beneath me, I
could just make out the foaming crests of the ocean swells ten kilometres below. My thoughts were with my father, who was thirty-
three when he watched the propeller trails of T-5 torpedoes come at
him. After the aircraft appeared from Iceland he'd become hopeful.
From that convoy run he'd described men in the water, head and
shoulders in the flames from the burning oil of their sinking ship that
had spread over the surface, legs kicking in the frigid waters below.
He had spoken of the helplessness of *Sackville* being unable to stop
and rescue the burning men, for they'd dared not slow the corvette
and present an even easier target for the U-boats. The responsibilities
of the men in those ships, most in their twenties and thirties, and the
choices they faced are incomprehensible to me. The size of the ocean
and the rigours of the war are incomprehensible as well.

All this was before 9/11, and on the trip home the cockpit door
was left open as the flight attendants went in and out. I had *never*

visited a flight deck, so I asked an attendant if I could. "Certainly," she said and took me in. The pilots and flight engineer greeted me and motioned to the small spare seat. After a few moments of conversation, I began relating the battle southeast of Greenland and my father's account of the long-range Liberators appearing from Reykjavik. They listened as I rambled on about the events of September 20, 1943, and the aircrew names that had appeared on the microfilm *that* afternoon. The flight engineer asked if I knew roughly where the convoy had encountered the U-boats, and I remembered 59°45' N and 28°12' W. He glanced at his instruments and paused. He then asked if I wanted to know where we were flying over at that moment.

We were all silent. They were aircrew and I was the son of the man who had sailed. We were there. Our silence was disturbed only by the sound of the engines taking us over the "details"' that had been on the ocean far beneath our feet.

The aircrews

First Liberator: J. H. Frewen, H. J. Bennett, B. McKeague, B. J. Bennett, J. Duckworth, D. Auld, F. B. Pincott, J. Andrews.

Second Liberator: Thompson, Green, Davies, Lesier, Bacon, Lund, Dowling, Richardson.

Third Liberator: J. K. Moffat, Good, L. W. Lenz, V. C. S. Wilson, R. W. Barrett, F. H. Fitzjohn, J. P. Halton, J. A. Earp.

Fourth Liberator: Keill, Crank, Fraser, Hooker, Heseltine, Baxter, Laud, Mylchrest.

Fifth Liberator: Kerrigan, Weiner, Rackham, Hartrick, Foy, Chapman, Hunt, Grassam, Levinsky.

Sixth Liberator: G. L. Hatherly, B. Threlfall, E. A. Day, Britton, J. McGregor, Bartley, Bailey, Dyck

CHAPTER 19

THE KING'S SHILLING: A FAINTLY FEUDAL PAY

The King he has ordered new troops onto the continent,
To strike a last blow at the enemy.
And if you would be a soldier,
All in a scarlet uniform,
Take the King's shilling for Wellington and me.
—traditional soldier's song

the Stratford sons

The middle five boys in the picture above joined the army. They are my great-uncles from Brantford. The photo was taken in 1898 and the youngest five are standing on boxes to create a perfect rising row. First is Dave in his white christening dress, then Art, George, Joe, Jack, Harold, and Graham, the eldest. All of them would probably object to what my twenty-first-century head thinks about the net worth of soldiers. Apart from the royal family providing candy at Christmas, what *was* the pay scale of the middle five brothers in the First World War? Or the seventy-seven sailors on *Polyanthus*, which burned and sank in September 1943 off Greenland? What were they paid for working the guns and dropping depth-charge patterns from their corvette?

In the eighteenth century, "taking the King's shilling" referred to recruiting officers giving prospective soldiers an "earnest" (down payment) of a shilling. Once recruited, the new soldier would "attest" to serve the King and, on returning the shilling, would receive his soldier's pay. After the army had made deductions for his food and uniform, little was usually left. In the mid-nineteenth century, in the name of social progress, limits were put on the deductions so that each man was actually paid at least a penny a day.

Traditional assumptions still influence soldier's pay scales today. We may call them heroes but I don't think we pay members of the Canadian Forces enough for their readiness to lose limbs, lives or long-term health. How *do* we compensate those who do battle on our behalf? My short answer is "not well," and my long question is "What are our assumptions that we *expect* members of our armed forces to risk so much for so little pay?" Doesn't feudalism belong to the distant past?

We make our professional sports players—the entertainment warriors—wealthy but we relegate our actual soldiers to working-class income brackets. George Stratford's pay as a World War I corporal was $1.10 a day, which was almost doubled after his promotion to lieutenant six months before he was killed. It's difficult to determine what its value would be today, but it was certainly below or barely reached what a blue-collar worker would have made in 1914.

Warriors' lives on the cheap is an old practice. Wars can be somewhat less expensive when the men and women fighting them are prepared to subsidize them with their lives. If nations had to pay full freight for the armies they risk, the economics of war might change. But that would mean re-evaluating the worth of a soldier.

Shouldn't their lives be our most expensive pieces of military equipment? Should lives even be *owed* to a nation? Well, I suppose they have to be, or few would go to battle.

The 1914–1918 conflict shook some nations from their reverie that allowed generals to lose an enormous number of troops, provided replacements could be found. Yet much of the language that sustained that reverie circulates today. Here are some familiar examples, that are from the 1919 memorial publication by the Canadian Bank of Commerce: "following the path of duty"; "the ultimate sacrifice"; "patriotic duty"; "in the cause of justice and freedom."

In the war that my great-uncles fought, losing large numbers of soldiers was a legitimate military practice, which was referred to as "wearing down the enemy." But the staggering losses shocked enough people that afterwards Canada and other nations *did* try to reduce the human wastage, which was good for everyone. Militaries had learned that the faster a wounded man received treatment, the more likely he would be to survive. Tactics were adjusted to try to avoid battles in which soldiers would be mere cannon fodder. But even so, the butcher's bill for the Second World War reached roughly 27 million soldiers, pilots and sailors—but thankfully not my father.

So how do we put a price on a military life? I will walk carefully here, since I have no wish to offend those who served in Canada's wars, including my great-uncles and the rest of the family who I feel are *all* watching from the wings. How much should we pay for the extraordinary things we ask the members of our fighting forces to do? We support them symbolically by dedicating bridges to them, and gala dinners are eaten to raise money for disabled veterans, yet our serving soldiers remain poorly paid for the lives they lead and are sometimes *expected* to lose. There is something faintly feudal about this since it seems that the state has replaced the liege lord, duke, king or baron whom the soldier is expected to serve.

Since we live in a market economy, why not let the market decide by outsourcing compensation levels for members of our armed forces to the private sector? For argument's sake, let's take the year 2016 to compare some top pay brackets. The Toronto-Dominion Bank's CEO was paid more than $10 million, while Canada's chief of defence staff, our top soldier, made about thirty-five times *less* at $300,000. Our chief of defence staff commanded slightly more than 100,000 soldiers and reservists, while the bank CEO's employees numbered perhaps 85,000. There is no point is comparing the physical risks the two men had to manage.

Perhaps the CEO was paid more since he manages risks to the bank's assets (property) and the accounts of its customers. That seems reasonable, *if* we assume that safeguarding risks to property should be more generously rewarded than safeguarding lives. For the record, the chief of defence staff deals with risks to *both* lives and property— except that it's public property. The chasm between the two leaders' pay packages might lead one to conclude that we place a higher value on private property than on lives. Isn't that a value from feudal times? And, probably the private sector's compensation template *isn't* a good guide after all, since no government is going to pay its top soldier ten million a year.

Like any cheap labour pool, low-cost soldiers provide a market advantage in battlefield economies. Almost any war will do, but let's take the example of the fighting in Vietnam in the late 1960s and early 1970s. Yes, it was fifty years ago, but that means we have a fuller spectrum of accounts of the fighting. More than one million North Vietnamese and Viet Cong soldiers died, compared to the loss of more than 58,000 American lives. Yet the United States and its South Vietnamese allies, despite their technological superiority, were *still* unable to win since the North Vietnamese put a very low price point on their warriors' lives. If the wage differential between opposing armies gets too steep, then well-paid fighters are at a disadvantage—unless the nation paying the higher salaries goes nuclear, which is what American general William C. Westmoreland wanted the option of doing in Vietnam. Only after President Johnson heard of the secret plan, code-named "Fracture Jaw," which would transport nuclear weapons to the general's army in Vietnam, was the shipment stopped. It is worth reminding ourselves that the US was in no danger of being invaded by the North Vietnamese, which leads me to think that America's expenditure of blood and treasure was primarily to ensure that capitalism prevailed over communism—a system that threatened the *idea* of private property and challenged the power bestowed on those who own large amounts of it.

In our centuries-long climb away from believing that property has more value than lives, we have clambered past the point where slaves (people) and soldiers were property. Yet still our military struggles with racism and its treatment of women. It is disquieting when members of our armed forces—whom we assume to be the embodiment of obedience—have to agitate to gain respect as individuals. In the Great War, soldiers from many nations, including Canada, France, Germany and Russia, went on strike or rioted against their armies' feudal reflexes and the leadership that it produced. At the heart of the riots and disturbances lay the soldiers' objections that those in charge were using them as if they were not people but property. By and large, soldiers don't rebel, but when they do, as when the Vietnam Veterans Against the War threw their medals at the US Congress in 1971, the confrontation with those in power can be memorable.

Which brings me to George, who was not a rebellious man. He had the vote, possessed a university degree and probably assumed that any feudal treatment of foot soldiers in the Canadian Expeditionary Force was a thing of the past. In the centuries before George's enlistment, dukes and barons had recruited commoners who were paid little, fought when told, dismissed when not needed and forgotten when dead. The landed gentry regarded their land as theirs to do with as they pleased, as well as the lives of most of those who lived on it. It seems that some of those traditions still existed when my Charlie Chaplin–imitating great-uncle joined up in June 1915. He kept his vote but lost the rest of his rights.

George basically became the property of King George V. He was awakened by a bugle at 5:30 a.m. and the lights were turned out when the bugle sounded again at 10:15 p.m.

"I, George Stacey Stratford, do make Oath, that I will be faithful and bear true Allegiance to His Majesty King George the Fifth, His Heirs and Successors, and that I will as in duty bound honestly and faithfully defend His Majesty, His Heirs and Successors, in Person, Crown and Dignity, against all enemies, and will observe and obey all orders of His Majesty, His Heirs and Successors, and of all of the Generals and Officers set over me. So help me God."

—George's oath on attesting

A century later our recruits still take an oath of allegiance to His Majesty King Charles the Third, King of Canada, and our armed forces still hold the *right* to the lives of the men and women who serve in them. "Oh," we might say, "but they volunteered," which is certainly true if they did volunteer, but it's not true when military service is by draft or conscription. And yes, in the First World War compulsory service was (contentiously) introduced in 1917, and a more limited conscription was enacted near the end of the Second World War. But still we maintain that a nation has a right to the lives of its soldiers—which I will call "*le droit du pays*." We might consider extinguishing that right and paying full market value for each life, but that is probably as unrealistic as the 1928 treaty that wanted to outlaw war. Referred to as the Kellogg-Briand Pact, it was signed by almost fifty nations, but since the agreement was so unrealistic and had no enforcement mechanism, it is no wonder that no one remembers it.[5]

I can see now that Great-Great-Aunt Isabel is on her feet and glaring at me from the wings. She is angry at my suggestion that the soldier's duty to serve and sometimes die is evidence of lingering feudalism rather than a citizen's proud patriotic duty.

A Canadian corporal in 2005 who lost a leg from an IED (improvised explosive device) while travelling in a light armoured vehicle in

---

5   The Kellogg-Briand Pact was made in Paris on August 27, 1928. It was a multi-nation treaty in which the signatories renounced war as a policy instrument and sought to solve disputes through peaceful means.

Afghanistan made about *one hundred* times less than Gwyn Morgan, the then president and CEO of Encana. This was even after the soldier had received the army's monetary top-up of thousands of dollars for being an "in-theatre assaulter." In contrast, on Mr. Morgan's way to work his vehicle didn't take him within ten thousand kilometres of an IED, yet he got $6.4 million (and change).[6] But Encana's business was getting oil and gas out of the ground, which again is a matter of property.

If you think that a CEO deserves higher compensation because their job has greater responsibilities, then you haven't escaped the mindset in which soldiers are not only subordinate to business executives but also that their lives have less value. If you think that a CEO merits more pay because their company helps generate the wealth with which Canada pays its soldiers, then you *still* have not freed yourself from that way of thinking. If you believe (and I hope you do) that the life of a CEO and the life of a soldier are of *equal* value, then you must explain why the soldier is so poorly paid.

In 2019 a private in Canada's Joint Task Force at pay level PI3 made about $53,000 a year, which increased by $22,000 to $25,000 if he or she was "in theatre" as an "assaulter." The CEO of Restaurant Brands International Inc. (RBI), a holding company for fast-food chains—which have been challenged on the nutritional value of their products—was given compensation of about $8 million in 2016, according to the Canadian Centre for Policy Alternatives. The RBI man made at least one hundred times more than the soldier who was prepared to lose their life in combat.

I suggest that the assumption that top executives must make millions because large pay packages are necessary to attract the talent needed to run large corporations is a conclusion arrived at while standing in a hall of mirrors. That assumption reflects the values only of the men and women who endorse it. Or, to put it another way, the

---

6   Encana was renamed Ovintiv in 2019 and its head office was moved from Calgary to
    Denver.

conclusion is credible only if you live in the closed-circuit world of assumptions about executive's pay.

Louis XIV of France lived in such a closed circuit, which was why he was able to regard himself as the Sun King. He began to construct his Hall of Mirrors in the Palace of Versailles in 1678. Making large mirrors in the seventeenth century was an expensive and specialized craft. As a show of extravagance, more than three hundred of them were mounted in the seventeen arches opposite the windows of the hall at Versailles. As he walked by them, Louis XIV's majesty was reflected back both to himself and to his court followers. Even today if you visit the palace, you can sense how the Hall of Mirrors was an opulent echo chamber for privilege and power.

The extravagance of the CEOs' pay reflects to themselves and their courts the importance of their position. Of course great executives have great talent, but the reality remains that any executive is entirely capable of performing their work for less opulent compensation—just as our soldiers do when they assume so much risk when they go into battle. In their hall of mirrors, executives see their wealth reflecting back their importance to themselves and to the world, whereas the man or woman in the military seems to require no such flattery to do their job. These signs of what we value, as evidenced by discrepancies of pay, imply that there *are* feudal reflexes that still linger. The pay scale of our warriors, whom we ask to risk their lives, still belongs to the lineage of the King's shilling.

A few of my family are now close to revolt, having never agreed to be associated with this kind of thinking. Joe, who was awarded the Military Cross, seems especially upset. Yet no matter how much I question the institutions they embraced, I mean them no disrespect.

At times our double standard towards soldiering is brutal, the US war in Iraq being a stark example. We saw the market model for combat soldiers' pay in Iraq in the use of private security contractors—companies that provide *private*-sector soldiers (i.e., mercenaries) for "protective services" to governments and corporations. Blackwater Security Consulting (now part of Triple Canopy, in the

Constellis Group) was hired by the CIA for its operations in Iraq and Afghanistan. Blackwater was an American company that became infamous because some of its employees were killing Iraqi civilians, the worst incident being in Baghdad in 2007 in Nisour Square.[7] Blackwater's subsequent infamy and the lawsuits filed against it led to the company's rebranding itself, first as Xe Services and then as Academi, which merged with Triple Canopy.

The US-led invasion of Iraq in 2003 gave us a market comparison, since American taxpayers were paying to have *both* public and private soldiers working on their behalf. The private mercenaries were, of course, paid more than the public soldiers. But Blackwater's killing of innocent civilians meant that the US public paid even more (for its legal costs) to settle the lawsuits brought by families of the victims of the Nisour Square massacre. Private soldiers in Iraq could be paid more than $600 a day. The *Washington Post* reported on it in an article called "U.S. Pays Steep Price for Private Security in Iraq" in 2007:

"An unmarried sergeant given Iraq pay and relief from U.S. taxes makes about $83 to $85 a day, given time in service. A married sergeant with children makes about double that, $170 a day. Army Gen. David H. Petraeus, the top U.S. commander in Baghdad overseeing more than 160,000 U.S. troops, makes roughly $180,000 a year, or about $493 a day. That comes out to less than half the fee charged by Blackwater for its senior manager of a 34-man security team."

By 2010, more than 260,000 security contractor employees were working in support of the US military and governmental operations in Iraq and Afghanistan. According to James Glanz of the *New York Times,* they outnumbered the deployed US military forces.

---

7   In the Nisour Square massacre, employees of Blackwater Security killed seventeen Iraqis. An investigation by the FBI determined that fourteen had been shot without cause and the US State Department reported that innocent lives were taken. Four Blackwater employees were convicted, one for murder and three for manslaughter. They were subsequently pardoned by President Donald Trump in 2020.

"Responding to the Congressional research report, Frederick D. Barton, a senior adviser to the Center for Strategic and International Studies in Washington, said it was highly questionable whether contractors brought the same commitment and willingness to take risks as the men and women of the military or the diplomatic services. He also questioned whether using contractors was cost effective, saying that no one really knew whether having a force made up mainly of contractors whose salaries were often triple or quadruple those of a corresponding soldier or Marine was cheaper or more expensive for the American taxpayer. . . . Congress appropriated at least $106 billion for Pentagon contractors in Iraq and Afghanistan from 2003 through the first half of the 2008 fiscal year, the report says."

Besides the pay discrepancy, not only were the *public* soldiers paid less but they actually engaged in combat. The private mercenaries were forbidden from combat unless they were in personal danger. The armed employees of Blackwater and other private security companies in Iraq were usually ex-soldiers who could be assigned only to protective duties. So why were American presidents and lawmakers prepared to generously reward private-market mercenaries while paying their nation's sons and daughters who go into combat so little? Well, because the nation had assumed the role of the feudal baron. I believe that *le droit du pays* is as outmoded as the monarchs who admired themselves in mirrored rooms in palaces. As with the shutting down of so many royal houses after the First World War, it is time to move beyond this feudal way of thinking.

A glance into the wings reveals that a ruckus has broken out. Isabel, outraged by my references to Americans, whom she considers "cowards and poltroons" has left the theatre. Cuthbert is waving his cane at me, regretting that he'd sent me on that battlefield tour of Europe. Wildy and Warren are adamant that I cannot impose ideas from my time onto theirs. Jack, Harold and Fred protest that I have been taking liberties with family memories and am upsetting the women. Even George, with whom I feel closest after my walk to his grave, is surprised: *My dear great-nephew Robert, our past is not yours to imagine. How can you ever know why we went and what we felt?* Art is circumspect. Of all the great-uncles, he was the wariest about how the war was waged. *Think what you like, Bob, but we joined up to stop the Kaiser.* But Joe remains vehement: *You are not a soldier. You have never been. And if you were, I would have you brought before one of my court martials. Stick to your plays and please take my sword down from your wall.*

I feel my godmother Margaret is somewhat understanding, since she had seen so many broken bodies on the beds in front of her, yet . . . *I may not be able to forgive you for unsettling my aunt Mary Elizabeth. You know that she suffered a stroke soon after the war, don't you?*

Have I gone too far? Soldiering *was* a patriotic duty for them. The monarchy was sacrosanct and receiving gifts from the royal family at Christmas was an honour. I care most about my father's opinion. Does he approve that I have aired the subject of what warriors are worth? And my great-grandmother Mary Elizabeth has not said a word. After sensing her footsteps beside me on my walk with George to the pillbox, hers is the heart that I worry about most. But I would like to feel that my great-grandmother is pleased that I am so interested in her children.

CHAPTER 20

TRAGEDY BY CANOE
AS WE STAND ON THE WHARF

A story covered by more than 150 years of dust lay at the bottom of my family's memory suitcase. It was an account of a deeply offensive act. A friend with whom I share an interest in delving into history's corners sent me an essay by Greg Lange in which a member of my family appears. Recognizing the extremism of the incident, which previously I'd known nothing about, shook my regard for what my family history means to me.

Racism was ubiquitous in the 1860s and episodes of virulent prejudice didn't carry a lot of special meaning—at least for the white culture. But some of what happened was evil. During the years of the *The World Remembers* odyssey, I sat down with reasonable people from World War I and World War II nations who had been our foes and knew of foul deeds in *their* family's and country's conduct of wars. Then, on reading Lange's essay, I wondered about *my* own family's past.

"I heard about this—what happened . . . before my time—what they called smallpox . . . They couldn't tell how many people had died. Some women lay down dead, and the little baby was still sucking their tits, and they'd be dead."

That account, the essay notes, was passed down to a member of the Heiltsuk Nation in Bella Bella, British Columbia, in the late 1980s. Smallpox arrived at the settlement of Victoria in March 1862, threatening both the white and Indigenous inhabitants. Members of my family on my mother's side, the Pembertons, had emigrated there from Ireland in the 1850s. At that time the Vancouver Island town had a population of eight to ten thousand, of which at least half were either local First Nations or from bands farther up British Columbia's coast. Among those who had come to trade, work and socialize were Heiltsuk, Tsimshian, Haida, Tlingit and people from the Fort Rupert area on the northern tip of Vancouver Island.

The smallpox contagion is a virulent airborne disease, carried on the breath of its sufferers. The violence done in Victoria by some of the white newcomers, such as my family, in the name of self-preservation was brutal. People with power used a form of biological warfare against the powerless. It was intended as genocide.

"Great alarm exists at the village, and it is thought that nearly the whole tribe will be swept away."

—*Daily British Colonist,* April 26, 1862

My family stories usually provided comfort, inspiration and values by which I could live. This one did not. I'd assumed that Canadians had *always* fought on the side of justice, and that moral darkness resided only in our enemies. My great-uncles in the Great War and my father in World War II all fought to preserve the freedom and fairness that comes with democracy. Wouldn't my family have remembered its own cruelty? Hadn't Canadians always had a sense of justice towards others, or was that just my wishful thinking in cheerful primary colours? *The World Remembers* had appealed to many nations, at least in part, because it was proposed by a nation whose history appeared to have generated relatively little malice.

"Were it likely that the disease would spread only among the Indians, there might be those among us like our authorities who would rest undisturbed, content that the small-pox is a fit successor to the moral ulcer that has festered at our doors . . . [But] chances are that the pestilence will spread among our white population [because] . . . [t]he Indians have free access to the town day and night; and are even employed as servants in our dwellings, and in the culinary departments of our restaurants and hotels."

—*Daily British Colonist*, April 28, 1862

My belief in the inherent goodness of my family's stories crumpled when I found that, five years before Confederation, my great-great-great-great-uncle had knowingly spread smallpox to British Columbia's West Coast Indigenous nations. The disease had arrived with an infected passenger onboard the ship *Brother Jonathan*, on its way from San Francisco to the gold mines along the Salmon River. The vessel had stopped in Victoria's harbour in March 1862 and several days after the ship's departure, fevers, vomiting and skin rashes began to appear and spread in the town. Decades earlier a vaccination for the disease *had* been discovered, and Victoria's public health authorities advised people to get inoculated. Whites were more likely to receive the crude vaccine, while Indigenous people were not.

Since the late eighteenth century, outbreaks of smallpox had been appearing in areas on the BC West Coast. And along with the white population, Indigenous communities were also vaccinated if the supply held out. In fact, the Hudson's Bay Company had a policy of vaccinations for *all*, both Indigenous and newcomers, because it was just good for trade. Fifty years before the outbreak in Victoria, tragic numbers of deaths had already been suffered by Indigenous communities. However, in 1862, Victoria's attitude towards the outbreak was different.

As people fell sick and the dying began, the white citizens wanted the Indigenous bands to leave the Victoria area for fear that they would help spread smallpox. Their concern focused primarily on the "northerners," members of nations farther up the coast of Vancouver Island, and as far as Haida Gwaii, who had come south and set up camps on the outskirts of the city. The people of Victoria called for their shelters to be burnt. Some northerners left and some did not. The police commissioner, my great-great-great-great-uncle Augustus Pemberton, with the assistance of a British Navy gunboat, ordered the remaining Indigenous people to leave. More left. Then, almost two weeks later, according to Greg Lange's essay:

"Pemberton went further than just demanding that the Indians leave. On June 11, 1862, the Police Commissioner and a group of policemen forced about 300 men, women, and children camped near Victoria to return to their northern homeland. The gunboat *Forward* (Captain Lascelles), took a 15-day trip to Fort Rupert towing 26 canoes full of natives. Included were 20 canoes of Hydahs [Haida], five canoes of other Indians from the Queen Charlotte Islands, and one canoe of Stickeen [Tlingit] Indians."

By towing canoes carrying contagious people to their homelands up the Pacific coast, the authorities of Victoria were deliberately spreading a disease they knew could be fatal.

But hadn't Canada's stories spoken of the fairness that we extended to the First Nations? Our "Indian" policies differed from those of the United States, a country that had used the tools of conquering and killing. Extermination was the American way, while assimilation was ours. However assertive our policies were, weren't ours more peaceful? As a child, I had proudly learned that the Lakota chief Thatȟáŋka Íyotake, commonly known as Sitting Bull, had left the turmoil of the United States and the Sioux wars of the 1870s and brought his people north to the safety of Canada. In 1877, as the story went, he was met peacefully at the border by just one inspector from the North-West Mounted Police.

That much is true. What I was *not* told was that four years later, Canada in effect forced the chief and his people back to the United States by refusing to provide land or food. Hunger was a weapon that helped clear Canada's western lands of Indigenous people for settlement by European farmers. Moral darkness was what Canadians had fought *against* in two world wars, yet a century before we had been conducting a slow-motion war against the First Nations—and the actions of my relative Augustus Pemberton lay in the darkest part of that fighting.

The slow war against Canada's Indigenous peoples was a multi-century, step-by-step affair, fought skirmish by skirmish, broken treaty by broken treaty, battle by battle, trial by trial and residential school by residential school. Our aim was simple: to take the land. And let us not excuse ourselves by engaging in "presentism"— the argument proposing that we can't fairly judge the past if we use the standards of the present—because subjugation is subjugation and genocide is genocide.

Augustus, an upright man in his fifties, did not accompany the three hundred with their "loathsome disease" on the fifteen-day trip up Vancouver Island. But he probably stood on the wharf in his frock coat and watched them depart, satisfied that he was helping keep the colonists of Victoria safe. Ten days later, he likely read an editorial that appeared in the *Daily British Colonist*:

"How the mighty have fallen! Four short years ago, numbering their braves by thousands, [the Indigenous men of the Pacific northwest] were the scourge and terror of the coast; today, broken-spirited and effeminate, with scarce a corporal's guard of warriors remaining alive, they are proceeding northward, bearing with them the seeds of a loathsome disease that will take root and bring forth a plentiful crop of ruin and destruction to the friends who have remained at home.

At the present rate of mortality, not many months can elapse 'ere the Northern Indians of this coast will exist only in story."

—June 21, 1862

It is the children that particularly haunt me, loaded as they were by Victoria's blue-uniformed police into the twenty-six canoes with their parents, uncles and aunts. Perhaps it took an entire morning to round up the three hundred, then coerce them into the cedar vessels tethered behind HMS *Forward*. Steam as well as sail powered the gunboat that stood as a symbol of civilization. So, no doubt, smoke billowed from *Forward*'s funnel as the ship's boilers built a head of steam that would begin to pull the three hundred north from Victoria on their miserable two-week journey. Probably even the children knew that vomiting would mean the sickness had begun and the smallpox lesions that followed could completely cover the skin. Eighty percent of infected children died from the disease. The twenty-six canoes were a perverse Pied Piper procession.

At least on the voyage north the children had the company of their families. But on arriving at their homes, according to eyewitness H. Spencer Palmer's account from 1863, children who fell ill were taken from the band's lodges, led away from the village, and tied to a tree to prevent them running back into the arms of their loved ones.

"Numbers were dying each day; sick men and women were taken out into the woods and left with a blanket and two or three salmon to die by themselves and rot unburied; sick children were tied to trees, and naked, grey-haired medicine men, hideously painted, howled and gesticulated night and day in front of the lodges in mad efforts to stay the progress of the disease."

According to Robert Boyd's estimates in *The Coming of the Spirit of Pestilence*, fourteen thousand Indigenous people who lived along the Pacific from Victoria to Alaska died—roughly half of the remaining coastal peoples.

Augustus had children. From which part of his self came that cruelty? In my family's stories the Pembertons are remembered with warmth and affection. They were early settlers, and Augustus's great-niece Philippa was my favourite grandmother. I've spoken of her time in Versailles in 1919, her empathy for the horrors brought by World War I, and her nightmares about her brother's pain-filled death after his Royal Flying Corps accident. There were no cruel bones in my grandmother's body. To what part of my own history do I assign Augustus's malice? Although I must acknowledge that the decision to expel the three hundred may have been made by Victoria's ruling council. Yet even if it was, Augustus acted on the order. I'd never even heard of his actions until I read the Greg Lange essay that had been sent to me.

The term *genocide* was coined in 1944 to mean race-based mass killing, but it had long been a tool of the race wars. Victoria's authorities likely justified their actions by saying the "heathen savages" had put the "civilized" white population in danger. Yet however they tried to define themselves free from the responsibility for the act, they wanted it done so that colonists could have the land and rid themselves of what they assumed was an inferior race. Because, throughout the nineteenth century, Indigenous populations had been shrinking, First Nations people were presumed to be fated to eventually disappear altogether. This is one reason why much of British Columbia was not subjected to treaty agreements. Why bother treaty-making with peoples who were dying in such numbers that soon, as the *Daily British Colonist* stated, ". . . the Northern Indians of this coast will exist only in story." Today, because many BC First Nations never ceded their lands through treaties, their legal claims have an almost unassailable validity. Try running a pipeline through those courts.

⁓

With his white wing collars and black silk tie, did Augustus understand that there is no civilized way to kill fellow human beings?

The Pembertons were Anglo-Irish, the descendants of English settlers in Ireland from centuries before who subsequently became major landowners. Augustus knew of Ireland's Great Hunger of the 1840s. Before emigrating from Dublin to Victoria, he knew of the potato famine: the hunger brought on by a blight on the potato crop that created food shortages, resulting in the starvation of perhaps a million of Ireland's poor. Despite the famine, merchants continued to export food from the island to England.

If civilization means the rule of law, respect for life and justice for all, then we are not civilized. If it means complex, technologically advanced societies with tools such as steam engines, communication satellites and social media, then we remain barbarians in frock coats on Facebook. In the name of protecting Victoria's settlers, my great-great-great-great-uncle set in motion a mass murder. We prefer to think of ourselves as civilized—one of our greatest achievements has been the Universal Declaration of Human Rights, created by the United Nations in 1948—yet it seems that we might not be.

"At the present rate of mortality, not many months can elapse 'ere the Northern Indians of this coast will exist only in story."

Daily British Colonist, May 27, 1862

I understand that I do not carry guilt for Augustus's actions, but I do carry the burden. There has always been this unimaginable weight in the family suitcase, but now I realize that it must be carried. As for suggesting that we might *not* be civilized, have I gone too far? Consider this: at our moment in history we are in the process of loading *one million* species into canoes for a miserable journey to extinction. As a result of loss of habitat, pollution, pesticides, herbicides and climate change, a 2019 Intergovernmental Science-Policy Platform on Biodiversity and Ecosystem Services (IPBES) report estimates that one million animal and plant species may be only objects of curiosity one hundred years from now.

We stand with Augustus Pemberton on the wharf and watch the canoes being assembled. We have the power to shut down the gunboat's engines, untether the canoes and address the situation, yet we have not acted because we worry about *our* survival and are accustomed to having *others* die to ensure it. The Anthropocene is the geological epoch that includes Earth's sixth mass extinction. The prefix *anthro-* means that the epoch is being driven by our inaction on the wharf. Some say the Anthropocene began in 1945 when, while still at war with Japan, we detonated Trinity, the first nuclear bomb, to ensure our survival. I leave that for you to ponder.

We have assumed that the story of humanity's evolution is that we have *always* been advancing. I believed we had evolved to be more resourceful, more aware, more knowledgeable in ways that helped us have better lives and live longer. Our remarkable progress in fighting diseases with vaccines, in understanding even a fraction of our universe in ways previously unimaginable, in building enlightened, inclusive and democratic civilizations, gave me standards by which I could live. I'd assumed that moral darkness resided mainly in the past, and that generally the human race stood on the side of progress towards universal rights.

But what was done to the people in the canoes, we will do to any living thing that gets in our way. The Canada that now lives in my head is darker. Pain-filled episodes of prejudice and malice crowd out the brighter colours of my childhood imaginings of my country. My family has certainly endured sorrows, but some, like Augustus, also inflicted them. My belief in inevitable historical optimism has gone. The hill ahead is now steeper. But climb it we must, and climb it we will.

CHAPTER 21

THE SILENCE OF THE MOTHERS: LISTENING FOR THEIR LANGUAGE

Aapiji bgan miiniwaa znagad wii-nsastamaa
we besha e-yaa'aanh enji miigaadiig
—words from Mary Elizabeth's 1917 letter home to Canada,
spoken in Odawa in 2017
It is very quiet and hard to realize that I am any nearer to them.
—that sentence in English

my great-grandmother Mary Elizabeth Stratford

Several decades after the tragic events in Victoria, on the other side of the country, Mary Elizabeth was raising her family in Brantford, Ontario. The Stratfords also had a farm on Oxbow Road beside the Grand River which flows through the land of the Six Nations. Each spring the river usually floods the fields along its banks. The lands have been lived on and travelled through for millennia by the peoples of the Haudenosaunee Confederacy—the Mohawk, Oneida, Onondaga, Cayuga, Seneca and Tuscarora, among others. When the floodwater recedes, the mud can offer up remnants of their old settlements: pottery fragments, amulets, arrowheads. As a teenager I found a flint amulet, threaded it with a leather bootlace and hung it around my neck. I presumed it had had significance for someone, yet wore the amulet with little thought for those who had carried it before me.

I had sixteen great-great-great-grandmothers and thirty-two great-great-great-great-grandmothers. Too many to know much about. There are faded photos of a few but I am not sure about their names. The family seems to have pulled shadows over two of these women, pushing them even further into the past, so that it's difficult to see if they are even still there in the darkened wings of my imaginary theatre.

The town of Brantford was named after the Mohawk leader Thayendanegea, or Joseph Brant, who had fought with the British against the American revolutionaries in the late 1770s. In return for his service, the governor of the Province of Quebec granted the Six Nations Confederacy the lands six miles on either side of the Grand River, reaching from its headwaters north of Brantford south to the shores of Lake Erie. The land also became home to the Haudenosaunee who had left their territories south of Lakes Erie and Ontario that had become part of the newly independent American republic. Through property sales and chicanery, the Six Nations lands are now only a fraction of their original size. Some of what was sold in the nineteenth century became the fields of the Stratford farm on Oxbow Road. As I picked through the earth searching for arrowheads or pieces of Mohawk pots, I wondered how much my great-grandmother had known about the history of the land, and whether the spring floods had come and gone forever.

Our planet is restless with geological activity that is constantly erasing the fingerprints of our history. Mimicking perhaps our Earth's indifference, we have tried to erase peoples unlike ourselves, wearing them down to insignificance through imperialism, slavery, prejudice or butchery. We have decimated rival nations and tribes in wars as well as emptying the land and seas of many living things. Is indifference the default of our solar system? The shards of pottery and fragments of flint in the fields by the Grand River are the fingerprints of Indigenous peoples that are being washed away not only by spring floods but also by unaware teenagers picking through them looking for curiosities.

Mothers in both Brantford and the Six Nations had seen their sons set off for the Great War. I can tell you about my great-grandmother Mary Elizabeth and the loss of her children, but I am unable to tell you of the Seneca or Onondaga women who saw their sons depart. More than four thousand men from all the Indigenous nations volunteered for the war. Their relationship with Canada was as troubled as the Irish soldiers' relationship with Britain, since both served countries that were not particularly mindful about serving them.

In previous conflicts such as the American Revolution, Indigenous warriors, especially from the Six Nations, had fought on the side of the British Crown. Therefore, when joining the 1914–1918 Canadian Expeditionary Force, they considered themselves members of nations that were *partners* with the British. They believed they were in a nation-to-nation relationship. In addition, since the eighteenth century, many Indigenous nations had assumed that the agreements they had made with the Crown meant that they were in "kinship." Some nations regarded the treaties they'd signed as kinship ties. In those cases, *brother* meant more than being good buddies. It implied a bond, as in a family bond. That was definitely *not* how the Canadian government saw the situation.

In Ireland, veterans returning home from the Great War were sometimes denounced by their own people, since they were Irishmen who had fought in the British Army at the same time as the British were using military force to deny Ireland its independence. Some veterans hid their war record in shame, and others chose never to set foot in Ireland again. Indigenous veterans returned to an ungrateful Canada that would show them little respect. It seems to be a tradition that rulers usually neglect the common folk who serve in their armies. I suspect that many First World War veterans were shabbily treated, but I know that Indigenous veterans received the worst treatment of all.

How my great-grandmother lived with the loss of her four sons is a mystery to me. But what of the women of the Six Nations just a few kilometres away, who saw their children return to such indignity? After enlisting, a Mohawk man would be given (through the Military Voters Act) what had been previously denied him: the right to vote. But the moment he left the army, that right was taken from him. Canada welcomed Indigenous warriors when they offered their lives, but those who survived the war could *keep* their voting rights *only* if they extinguished their treaty status. Only in 1960, after First Nations soldiers had served Canada in World War I, World War II and Korea, were they granted full voting rights. It was sorry treatment by a nation that was flexing its *internal* imperialism to assimilate peoples by having them step away from their indigeneity. I cannot speak for the Mohawk, Oneida, Cayuga, Seneca, Onondaga and Tuscarora mothers of the Six Nations, but their pain was surely twofold: first, for their children killed or wounded in the war, and second, for the indignities their surviving warrior sons were subjected to on returning home to a bigoted nation.

Like most Euro-Canadians in 1918, Mary Elizabeth probably didn't have much time for "Indians." I have no way of knowing how she felt, but her sons' wartime letters didn't embrace minorities and sometimes reverted to the casual racism common to the time. Imagine then what might have been my great-grandmother's surprise when, a century later at a national concert in Ottawa marking the centenary of the First World War, First Nations artist Waasikogammising-ikwe honoured Mary Elizabeth's sorrow by voicing in Odawa what she had written about her fears of the war.

In 1917, to be closer to her five fighting sons, my great-grandmother had taken a passenger ship to England to spend nine months with her firebrand sister Isabel in Bournemouth. Her letters home rarely reveal her concerns about having children in a war that had already killed millions and was gearing up to consume more. More than once she apologizes for writing "very uninteresting letters," but what she wrote shortly after her arrival in Britain gave me pause.

"It is very quiet and hard to realize that I am any nearer the war. The nurses here say that word has been sent to have one million beds ready for the big push in the spring, doesn't it seem awful? How little we can see into the future. They say they are sending every available man over very soon. Everyone seems to think there will be an awful fight. It makes me shudder to think what a terrible slaughter it means."

"The Song of the Mothers" is part of a choral-cycle that *The World Remembers* co-commissioned with the National Arts Centre Orchestra. The music is set to extracts that I had selected from the letters and journals of three women who had lost sons in the conflict. You have already met Käthe Kollwitz from Germany; the second was Mme. Mialaret, who'd been a second mother to Joe Stratford and also had a son in France's army, and Mary Elizabeth was the third. The text was arranged as if the three were speaking with each other. Music navigates through our emotions by means that we still do not fully understand.

Before the inaugural performance I spoke briefly to the audience about the three mothers before retreating to a chair in the corner of the Southam Hall concert stage. Then Waasikogammising-ikwe—also known by her English name, Barbara Assiginaak—performed a lullaby she'd composed to commemorate missing and deceased children. She then addressed the packed hall in Odawa:

Aapiji bgan miiniwaa znagad wii-nsastamaa we besha
e-yaa'aanh enji miigaadiig
Mashkikii-ninii-kweg kidoog, kidiwen gii-niindaadim,
wii-teg ooshime mdaaswaak nbaaganan wii-zhiitaamigak
awi sa nji wii-gchi-gaanjiwebinangaadeg mnookimig.

Barbara was just a few metres away and, glancing at my program, I was taken aback when I realized that she was speaking my
great-grandmother's words. I am uncertain what exactly came over
me, but by expressing the white mother's words in Odawa, Barbara's
compassion had embraced the pain of all other mothers. I was rooted
to my seat. She then closed with a question in four languages for all
of us in the hall:

Where are my children?
Wo sind meine Kinder?
Ou sont mes enfants?
Aaniindi dash ayaawaag niniijaansag?

This was from an artist whose family and land had been col-
onized for centuries. As an Odawa poet, composer and musician,
Barbara was well acquainted with Canada's inquiry into the thousands of missing and murdered Indigenous women and girls. How
many of her grandparents, parents and great-grandparents might
have been taken from their homes as children and sent to Canada's
residential schools to be stripped of their language and culture?
Compassion for mothers *from* colonizing cultures was a reconciling
act within her performance. Hearing Mary Elizabeth's fears about
war expressed in Odawa began to shift the shadows that had lain
over some of the great-great-great-great-grandmothers on my mother's side of the family.

Among the fingerprints most easily erased from the Earth are
languages. Meteor prints take millennia to weather away, but languages can disappear in a cosmological nanosecond. An impact crater
leaves a ring of the meteor's rare metals, melted upon impact but
soon refrozen into an inventory of the celestial traveller's life history.
Odawa, like all languages, is an inventory of a people's history. That
it is spoken today makes us all richer, and that the language can help
to reconcile makes us wealthier still.

When the shadow shifted, it seemed as if one of my great-great-great-great-grandmothers had stirred. I know almost nothing about her, yet that has not stopped me looking for signs. My mother's family tree refers to a "Jane French, *possibly* a Coughnawaga Mohawk," but apart from that she remains unknown. If Jane *were* Mohawk, I'd like to at least know her Indigenous name and imagine a glimpse of how she might have appeared. Just as the Mars rover *Perseverance* surprised us by recording the faint sounds of the red planet's remaining winds, so histories can be revealed in unexpected ways. My surprise would be glimpsing what I thought was a likeness of the forgotten Indigenous women in the family in my mother's face.

She had died from complications after a fall at the cottage. As her children, we wanted to see her to the grave with care. Fifteen years earlier we had bought an off-the-shelf casket for our father's body. The wood had looked plastic, the padded velvet interior was inappropriate, and the pressed-metal handles were nothing my fingers wanted to grip when carrying a parent for the final time. My sister said to me, "Why don't you make our mother's coffin?"

It was a bold idea, risky because of my limited carpentry skills, and I wasn't sure if do-it-yourself coffins were permitted at funerals. Years before, again at my sister's request, I *had* built a cradle for her baby daughter. Woodworking has always calmed me, whether running my hand along a piece of clean pine or taking in the perfume of fresh-cut hemlock. The music of the trees as wind moves among their needles or leaves also balances me—provided it's not the dark symphony of a malevolent gale.

It was not an easy time for the family after my mother's death. Her fall had begun a cascade of medical complications, and eventually she decided to refuse further treatment. She was dead in less than a day. Cicely had been her usual sharp mental self, but late one night she asked the nurses to call the local minister to her hospital bedside. In the very small hours of the morning a vicar was summoned from his slumbers and jotted down her final wishes. Then, soon after sunrise, we were woken by the call that she was gone. My mother had always been a determined woman.

"All right," I said. "I'll build it."

The cradle had been built with materials from a lumberyard and plans from a magazine, but the coffin had to be constructed from a design in my head. For decades the cradle has been passed around our family and has rocked multiple newborns to sleep, including my two sons. The coffin would hold but a single soul since my mother had wanted to leave in a storm of flames. Cradles embrace while coffins carry, but both are intended to bring comfort and peace.

I wanted my mother's coffin to be truly hers, made only with materials she had known. The boards for the box, the rope for handles and the fasteners for the lid all had to be from *her* world. I chose the wood from trees she knew. The maple planks had been cut several years before from cottage trees toppled by a violent storm. A cedar from outside her bedroom window provided the edge trim, and the white pine could be found everywhere on our land by the lake. Constructing it was a solace.

The funeral home in Richmond Hill had already collected the body from the hospital, but I had questions. Were do-it-yourself caskets acceptable? What about the regulations? Do bodies leak? They said not to worry, as long as what I constructed would fit onto their *trolley*—my term for the draped cart on which caskets are rolled into churches. The family had decided that *we* would carry the coffin rather than have it wheeled in by professionals. But would it hold together as we walked it up the aisle? No one wanted a Monty Python moment.

Once finished, my mother's casket travelled from the cottage to the funeral home on our roof rack—an odd object to lash to a small car on a large highway. Being the ultimate amateur, I saw no need to rent a truck. I was reassured about my carpentry when everything arrived at the funeral home intact. The home's director declared my work acceptable and asked, "Shall you and I place your mother in it?" He took the head and upper body while I lifted her hips and legs, a light bundle that had given life to three children. The last time I'd wrapped my arms around my mother's hips was probably when I ran to embrace her as a child.

Her body fit the coffin perfectly. And then to my surprise, a likening of our forgotten family began to appear.

In addition to Jane French, our family tree, cobbled together by generations of relatives, identifies a second Indigenous ancestor, Elizabeth Chouinard, who was Métis. She had married Jane French's son Peter Dease, a trader with the Hudson's Bay Company. So Cicely's great-great-great-grandmother had been Métis. We know more about Elizabeth Chouinard, the fur trader's wife, since when she and her husband retired with their five children to a farm near Montreal, an HBC factor James Keith commented that Mr. Dease was governed "by his Old Squaw & Sons. She holding the Purse strings & they spending the Contents *par la porte et par les fenêtres*." If Elizabeth did indeed hold the purse strings, she was just one of a line of strong women in the family. When you are looking into your parent's coffin, you sometimes see the parts of your life that were determined for you. But I also felt I was glimpsing two women from the shadows of my family. And unwittingly, my brother, sister and I had contributed some of the signs.

Regardless of its appearance (I thought it handsome), the coffin pleased me. I had chosen its elements with the same care as my mother had when dressing me as a child. The pine and maple were from the forest that she'd enjoyed with my father. Her headrest was a block of cedar I'd saddled with a chisel so her head wouldn't roll. She was *ours* and the coffin was *hers*. No velvet padding was needed, as if it were a container whose contents might shift during shipping. The white pine sides hugged her shoulders when we lowered her in.

My mother was from Vancouver Island and my brother, who still lives there, arrived with a large section of bark from a Douglas fir. The aroma from its resin was of Cicely's summers as a child.

We fixed it to the lid of the coffin as though it were her coat of arms. I'd chosen four brass screws to secure the lid, and proposed that each of us drive one in. They were from the *At Last*, the dinghy that my father had built and my mother had sailed on—*Woody, you're going to dump us!* The boat's remains had been with us for years and its screws were brass, a nautical must to avoid rust. My father had secured them into his homebuilt boat and now his sons and grandsons would secure them into his wife's homebuilt casket. Rope from another retired sailboat provided handles when looped through holes in the coffin's sides. The aged hemp had already been repurposed once, since I'd run it along the side of the dock for my mother to grasp when entering the lake to swim in her elderly years.

In the funeral home's work area we felt free to talk or improvise with whatever impulse came to us. My mother was in a plain blue dress that my sister had chosen, with her hair brushed back from her forehead. Past rigor, her limbs were loose. After settling her in, her head cradled by the cedar saddle, the funeral director and I crossed her hands on her chest. My brother had also brought sweetgrass from Vancouver Island, and before securing the lid we arranged the braid of grasses—a symbol of spirituality and peace for many peoples—between her fingers.

And *there* in her face was my mother's Indigenous family—her great-great-great-grandmother Elizabeth Chouinard and her "possibly" Mohawk great-great-great-great-grandmother Jane French. I was unprepared for the appearance of a part of her I'd never known. In the parlance of her BC family's British-biased identity, she had "the look"—a trope inside which nestled the prejudice that had placed the shadow over that part of Cicely's past. Lying there, my mother couldn't help but be everything she was. The sweetgrass rested easily in her hands.

A silence was speaking. Passing a brass screw to each of my sons and my brother, I felt as if the missing women in my family had come into view—my distant, distant mothers, and my sons' distant mothers as well.

Where are my children?
Wo sind meine Kinder?
Ou sont mes enfants?
Aaniindi dash ayaawaag niniijaansag?

Sitting at the side of the Southam Hall stage in Ottawa and taking in Barbara's translation from "The Song of the Mothers," I knew the words were from my great-grandmother on my *father's* side of the tree, but that seemed immaterial, since the song was about *all* the mothers. Barbara knew little of my family's history, yet nevertheless her language reached out to me. What might Elizabeth Chouinard have thought, knowing that her memory was stirring in her great-great-great-great-grandson on a concert stage in Ottawa?

The last words in "The Song of the Mothers" are "The pain has vanished, I am glad to be alive." Meiro Stamn's elegant composition and the talent of the singers and musicians who performed it had evoked the joy, longing, despair and apprehension of the women. Soon after the First World War, my great-grandmother Mary Elizabeth had disappeared into the eternal silence of a stroke. The final note of the song sustained and then faded. The hall broke into applause.

The mothers had been heard.

EPILOGUE—THE FUTURE

when I was six

Stories can be magic places. They create worlds that we visit and sometimes live in. The tales of victories, wars and enemies that I heard as a boy became the foundation timbers of my imagination and, despite a lifetime of learning and listening, they still retain their power. Do they influence the man? I don't think so. Yet how could they not, burrowed as they are deep in my mind? Rooting them out would be essentially tearing down the house I grew up in. Again, I agree with Thomas King when he proposes that, in ways, we are nothing but story.

I think that is why, after each performance of *The Lost Boys*, friends and strangers would tell me their stories. I *know* that you have ones important to your family, that I hope *you* are passing on to your children. What I heard from so many in my dressing room is one of the reasons I created *The World Remembers*. There is no story that is not important in some way to someone. To date, more than twenty Great War nations have agreed to participate in our remembrance project, and four and a half million names have been assembled, each of which will be displayed. And still the search continues for more. At least four and a half million stories, from friend and foe, are attached to those names. Almost 900,000 of the dead are from Germany's Great War army, thus their stories are German. And in my memory suitcase, they somehow *remain* the enemy. My adult self says, "*No, of course they're not*," but the six-year-old boy says, "*Yes, they are*." Therefore it is fitting that this epilogue takes place in Berlin and includes an account about a German teenager and a French necklace.

It may take many more years to achieve the goal of *The World Remembers*, which is to name every lost soldier from every World War I nation. It will be a remembrance not just of famous dead generals but of *everyone*. We have the technology to ensure that the names of those nine and a half million men and women can stand together, whether we project them on walls or display them in virtual places such as websites or electronic kiosks. Virtual versions of Nelson's Column in Trafalgar Square will mean that instead of a single person at the top, millions will be there. Whatever form our commemoration takes, physical or virtual, it must be an *inclusive* memory to which *every* family can come should they wish to search for their relative's name. Our real-world display can now be seen at the Canadian War Museum in Ottawa, where each November the names are projected onto a wall in the entrance hall. The virtual version, through either our website (theworldremembers.org) or the interactive kiosk installed at the museum (and hopefully soon at other locations), gives people the opportunity to look for family members lost in the Great War—whether they were Italian, Canadian, German, Slovenian, British, Belgian, Hungarian, French, Algerian, Austrian, American, South African, Slovakian, Czech, Ukrainian, Polish, Croatian, Indian, Pakistani, Turkish, Australian, New Zealander, Romanian or Chinese.

This commemoration is my response to a thousand years of neglect of the soldiers who died in battles. It is my revenge for those killed on the Plains of Abraham, forgotten for two centuries until Quebec City did watermain work. It is my vengeance on the fertilizer merchants who profited after the Battle of Waterloo from grinding up and selling dead soldiers' bones. It is my reply to one hundred years of Remembrance Days in which we have considered *only* our own. I have yet to untangle the politics of bringing onboard the remaining First World War nations and accessing their records (if they have them) of the missing names. So the odyssey continues, and again Germany is one of the nations that remains key for my success.

I resist stories that employ external threats to gain narrative power. I disagree with those who preach the danger posed by others in order to marshal their own followers. Inhaling the ideology of *Our enemies are only from elsewhere* creates a mental fortress inside which we can bestow innocence on ourselves and villainy on others. So secured, we often grant ourselves licence to use violence with impunity.

Germany is a nation that, following its defeat in the Second World War, recognized itself as having been the enemy—a rare example of assuming that responsibility. I was meeting again with the German Foreign Office in Berlin to ask them to encourage their war graves organization, VDK, to recommit its support of *The World Remembers* so that we could build our ongoing physical display for the museum in Ottawa. Not far from the Foreign Office's headquarters is the almost two-hectare site of the Memorial to the Murdered Jews of Europe, dedicated to the millions killed by the generation of grandfathers of those who live in Germany today.

My conversation with Irmgard Maria Fellner, Director of Cultural Relations Policy for Foreign Affairs, had broadened into a discussion about reconciling after wars. How do we redirect the rivers of carcinogenic nationalisms and hatreds that nourish the cycles of violence and retribution? It was a late, overcast March afternoon and in my mind my great-uncle Jack and the four *Feldgrau* soldiers whom he had "persuaded" to surrender their belt buckles were also there. As Jack had written to his brother, "the 'perswasion' stuff . . . comes from the ammunitions dumps every day." Sitting together in the German Foreign Office headquarters, the five seemed comfortable in each other's company.

Both the director and I admired the artist Käthe Kollwitz, so I explained how in selecting the text for a choral composition called "The Song of the Mothers," to be performed by musicians in their teens or early twenties from the National Youth Orchestras of Germany and Canada, I had used extracts from Kollwitz's journals, as well as from the letters of French and Canadian mothers who had sons in the First World War.

"She lost a son in World War I, didn't she?" asked Irmgard. "Yes," I said. "Her son Peter was killed two months after the war began. Also, her grandson was killed on the Russian front near the end of World War II." "That is incredible. There is an enlarged version of Kollwitz's *Pietà*-style statue called *Mother with Her Dead Son*, you must see it. It's just around the corner from here," said the director, pointing out the window behind her. "Just walk a little beside the canal there and then turn left on Unter den Linden Boulevard and you will soon see a Greek temple–style building—it's called the Neue Wache. It's in there." I said that I would.

Our conversation became personal and, while touching a necklace that she wore, the director began telling me about the French pen pal she'd been twinned with when she was a teenager. In the 1960s France and Germany had signed a student exchange treaty so that in the turmoil after the Second World War, young people could be paired as pen pals and spend summers with their counterpart's family.

The young Irmgard was aware that her nation had brutalized and murdered millions. Nevertheless, she and her pen pal's French family had bonded—except for the grandmother. The entire family welcomed Irmgard, but the French grandmother, who had lost two brothers in the Great War and had later lived under the Nazis in World War II, refused to meet the German girl. She either avoided Irmgard or would not come out of her room. After years of such shunning, the French pen pal wrote: "Come with us this year to our picnic in the country because my grandmother will be there, and she won't be able to lock herself away, so she must meet you now."

Finally the grandmother approached Irmgard and said to the young woman, "It is not you that is the problem, it is something within myself." Born in 1898, her hatred of Germans, who had killed her brothers when she was a teenager, had never left her.

"And after that I always called her Grand-mère Jeanne. I now have a French family as well as my own German family," said Irmgard, still touching the small necklace. The old French woman died aged 102. Irmgard hadn't been able to attend the funeral but her pen pal's family had sent the director the necklace, which Grand-mère Jeanne had left to the German girl in her will.

As our meeting went on I took notes, but without referring to them I can't recall anything of substance. But I do remember almost everything about Irmgard's story as if she were still telling it. Information can escape through our fingers but the personal is rarely forgotten. And that was what her grand-mère Jeanne had to forget.

When I spoke with Irmgard Fellner in Berlin in 2018, *The World Remembers* had sixteen participating nations and our displays included just over three million names. Through appeals to schools, embassies and universities, our commemoration exhibits had been shown in Riga, Rome, London, Dresden, Winchester, Berlin, Brussels, Kansas City, Ottawa, Yellowknife, Ieper, Vancouver, Geneva, Toronto, Winnipeg and many more cities. The names of Käthe Kollwitz's son

Peter and Grand-mère Jeanne's two brothers had appeared in all those places. But the total military deaths in the Great War were well over *nine* million, so the odyssey continues today. Each year a few more nations are persuaded to participate, some because they wish their country's story of the war to be heard and others because they feel the dead must be named.

"Names and naming are essential in the sacred view of the world. Repeating the name of a lost one keeps their memory alive. The act of naming creates life. Your project has deep roots in that direction. Thanks for creating this important moment and encouraging people to reflect."

—Celia Rabinovitch, artist, writer, historian of religions

In 1917, fearing reprisals, the Ontario town of Berlin changed its name to Kitchener. The *very* British King George V, who sent nice notes to my great-grandmother Mary Elizabeth after the deaths of George and Joe, really *wasn't* British. George V's family was German, being of the House of Saxe-Coburg-Gotha. Fearing an anti-German backlash against the monarchy, in 1917 George V renounced the name Saxe-Coburg-Gotha and the Royal House of Windsor came into being. Just recall that the London *Sunday Times* wrote skeptically about *The World Remembers* because a century after the First World War, the Red Baron's German name might appear, among millions of others, on a wall close to Britain's Cenotaph.

No wonder, then, that the new Germany is so politically careful. Friction between extreme views generates violence. They remember the street battles that plagued Berlin and the rest of Germany in the 1920s and 1930s. Facing off against each other were fascists, communists, anarchists and socialists. In 1933 the violent disorder created the opportunity for Germany's National Socialist Party (the fascists) to seize power and begin shutting down Germany's democracy and rule of law. For the next twelve years the Nazis took their playbook to Europe and other parts of the world. Even in 1945, as the Third Reich was collapsing and the Russian army was fighting its way into Berlin, far-right German groups were hunting down and killing their political foes, while the Nazis set about executing their political prisoners before Berlin's final surrender. And lest we forget, amidst the collapse and disorder, there were countless thousands of rapes.

It is a wonder then that so many nations are now throwing political caution to the wind, resurrecting the invective, intolerance, hate-mongering, sloganeering, xenophobia and extreme partisanship that feed fear and turn people against each other. The politics of the hard right has resurfaced in the mainstream discourse of the United States, France, Belgium, Brazil, Italy, Germany, Turkey, Canada and too many other nations.

Yet reconciliation through remembrance has made progress. The story of Grand-mère Jeanne's necklace is one example. Another is France and Germany's joint remembrances that began in 1994 when President Mitterrand and Chancellor Kohl held hands at the memorial in Verdun. Belgium's In Flanders Fields Museum recognizes *all* World War I soldiers who died on their land, and *The World Remembers* has been successful in recruiting more and more countries.

But what about the Second World War? Could its commemoration ever include the names from both sides? How much uncalled-for pain might that inflict? I have been asked if *The World Remembers* might expand to include the 1939–1945 war. Would the names of German and Japanese soldiers appear alongside Canadian, British, Russian and American ones? It is time to consider that question. Certainly when World War II's last direct participants have died, the path to an answer might be more straightforward.

But ask yourself this: In "remembering" the current war in Ukraine, could there ever be a presentation of the names of both the Ukrainian *and* Russian dead, side by side? The immediate (and understandable) response is that it would be offensive, inappropriate and inconsiderate of those who have suffered so horribly. But if we are ever to stop the recycling of wars and hatreds then eventually it must be done. Is that realistic? No. Is it needed? Yes.

I had said I would visit the Käthe Kollwitz sculpture, and I did. The bronze mother holding her son's body is almost life-sized. The Neue Wache was first built as a nineteenth-century guardhouse and later played a prominent role in Nazi Germany's annual Heroes Memorial Day celebrations. Today it is the Central Memorial of the Federal Republic of Germany for the Victims of War and Dictatorship. Its only occupant is the seated woman cradling her dead son. Buried beneath the stones at her feet are the bodies of an unknown soldier and an unknown Nazi concentration camp victim. They are isolated on every side by empty space.

The only illumination is from an oculus almost ten metres above the grieving mother's head. Through this large circular roof opening enters light from the sky above, as well as the rain or snow that falls on the figures below. The space with its solitary pair is utterly still, yet ever so slightly changing in the shifting light from the sky. It was almost six p.m. when I arrived and the mother and son were in the early evening gloom. The austerity of the memorial provided little comfort to her or to me, but it is magnificently personal. I wondered if my great-grandmother Mary Elizabeth had ever wished to envelope her dead sons that way. The Neue Wache is essentially a stone cell in which the imprisoned woman sits. Given the history of the German people, in her arms are millions of sons.

I am disturbed that so many lost in wars have so easily drifted from our minds.

The stories from my early years now exist in an ever-widening perspective. The wings of the stage are now crowded, since so many of my family have been watching. It is the largest cast I have ever been part of. They came because I summoned them. Photos show them costumed for party skits and local theatricals as sailors, pirates, chorus girls, French counts and grand ladies. So perhaps they came because they wanted to have a look at the descendant who made a profession of it.

Mother with her Dead Son *under a cover*
of light snow. Neue Wache, Berlin

I believe Jack was taken aback that I imagined him with me at the meeting in Berlin, but I wanted him and the four *Feldgraus* to hear the story of the French grandmother's necklace passed down to the German girl. However, Great-Aunt Isabel has been incandescent over my cautions about externalizing the enemy. Most everyone, including Joe, Harold, George, Art, Wildy, Cuthbert, Florence, Helen, Margaret, Mayden, Warren and Fred, were caught off guard by my lack of reverence for royal dynasties and the best-ness of all things British. Well, perhaps not Art, who I suspect was an iconoclast and internationalist like me. By the time Art with his Zulu warrior's shield and stabbing assegai took the streetcar up Spadina Avenue to surprise his sister on his return from war, he had learned some of the language of each nation in which he had fought: Arabic, French and Chinyanja. He might understand why Canada is at last working to find an equitable relationship with Indigenous nations. Yet, after more than six post–World War II decades of progress towards peace, our world is again polarizing into extremes.

Walking back to my hotel from the Neue Wache, I encountered a street demonstration. I AM NOT OVARY ACTING and FRAUEN VERTRAUEN § 219a, were some of the messages inked on placards and flags. I was struck by the carefulness of the protest. The proposed changes to Germany's federal laws on abortion, specifically paragraph 219a, had restarted the culture wars over abortion rights. A giant papier-mâché coat hanger was being marched along. When I spoke to a Spanish student who was also watching the protest, she replied, "Here they are very careful politically. Germans are careful." Even the police scattered throughout the area seemed subdued.

With so many dark clouds over the country's history, it was no wonder that even the litter in Berlin seemed careful. Every so often a marcher would spring out of the parade and deposit their coffee cup or snack wrapper in the receptacle beside me before rejoining the demonstration. Drummers and slogan-chanters approached and then passed. A bleaker moment arrived when a fast-moving man slapped a sticker on a pole before disappearing back into the crowd. It was small, the size of a palm print, and showed two men in black face masks under the slogan SMASH FASCISM. I thought of Marshall McLuhan's observation that "all forms of violence are quests for identity."

The march concluded in a park, with final speeches rallying those who had stayed to the end. I heard an activist from Iran urging the crowd (in English) to support women trapped in the patriarchal cultures of Iran and Saudi Arabia. The recent surge of migrants into the EU from Syria and Africa had been polarizing Germany's careful people.

In the growing darkness I was aware of more police, albeit sitting quietly in their vans.

Then in a different part of the park I saw another group, well, I *heard* them first, since demonstrative male voices have force even at a distance. They were animated, as if they'd been drinking. These were protest predators who I assumed were from the far right, whom the police had prepared for in case they confronted the final moments of the International Women's Day demonstration. By the time I left at about 9:15 p.m., the police were still in their vehicles. Nothing untoward had taken place and there were no media reports of clashes the next day. Yet it had been an eerie walk through a city of the new Germany where so much old violence had taken place.

In Romania's semi-mountainous area east of its border, a region that in 1918 was still part of Austria-Hungary, arguments broke out in 2019 over whether certain First World War soldiers' bones were Hungarian or Romanian. In the graveyard surrounding the Úzvölgye memorial, competing national flags and shouted histories confronted each other. Because of *The World Remembers*, I had begun to explore the mountainous terrain of Eastern European history, in which the jagged peak of the Treaty of Trianon looms large. Its signing one hundred years ago at the Paris Peace Conference formally ended the Great War, but the treaty also transferred more than two-thirds of Hungary's territory to Romania, Czechoslovakia and the Kingdom of the Serbs, Croats and Slovenes. Many Hungarians regarded it as a national death sentence and even today the loss of land generates dissent. The present-day political cult protesting Trianon has taken many forms, one of which is a monument in the form of a guillotine whose blade hovers above a map of Hungary. At the Úzvölgye cemetery, after defiant words were exchanged over the nationalities of old skeletons, committees were struck and political solutions explored to resolve the issue.

Nationalisms are often not content to leave the dead in peace. But at least Hungarian and Romanian mothers had got a cemetery in which to weep over their soldier sons, and perhaps even graves to stand by as their children were lowered into them. The graves that Mary Elizabeth and the mothers of Warren, Wildy and Fred wished to stand by were an ocean away.

More of the family have left the theatre over my trespassing on their lives. They are bound by their stories, as I am by mine. His grandson's ruminations on war and its death-on-demand economy got Cuthbert's cane swinging and he muttered his way past the stage manager's office and through the stage door soon after Isabel stormed out. I suspect my grandfather never liked theatrical performances anyway. Philippa has lingered, not wishing to abandon me completely. She enjoyed watching me in stage plays in Victoria as much as seeing me perform here. We cherish our grandmother-grandson bond, and I would have liked to talk more with her about ghosts, Versailles and the war, but sadly that is no longer possible.

Regrettably Mary Elizabeth has slipped away too. I may have exhausted her by exhuming too many family memories. After George's death she received a condolence letter with phrases that repulse me: "In the loss of so many of our best and bravest . . . my own faith is that these brave lads are promoted for higher service." Perhaps great-grandsons shouldn't challenge the dulling of pain with religious sentiment and patriotism. Margaret Killmaster and Mayden helped her on the way out, past all the backstage paraphernalia of props and my opinions, much as they had cared for Mary Elizabeth after she retreated into the years of silence following her stroke.

My eight great-uncles on whose war I trod the most are divided about their appearances here. Their afterlives have long flickered in my imagination and I am proud to have named them in *The World Remembers* commemorations in so many nations. Perhaps it was their surprise that their names actually appeared in displays in Britain and Germany, as well as Canada, that kept them watching from the wings.

Great-Uncle Jack, the Steyr semi-automatic pistol man, has been observing me closely. As the one who did the most fighting, it is his approval that I seek the most—which is why I wanted him to speak so extensively through his letters. Jack's postwar years in the sanitorium in Gravenhurst gave him time to think, before he eventually drowned in his own fluids because of what the war had done to his lungs. Joe, his younger cavalry-officer brother, though still angered by my dragging his military and his mother through these chapters, has been intrigued by my endeavouring to complete *The World Remembers* and get its display of names presented beyond Canada's borders. So are all his brothers.

Wildy and Fred were perhaps taken aback at the idea of such an inclusive commemoration. Their revisiting of Warren's death from burns is always hard. I want them to know that my memories of Warren are held in the two-and-a-half-metre wooden propellor splintered by his aircraft's crash landing, which has found its way to my home and is propped up in a corner of the living room.

Walking through these thoughts, I cross the stage a last time. The photons cast by the ghost light pace my shadow along the darkened walls. Those remaining are animated by the shifting of light and shadow, much like the paintings of animals in the Chauvet Cave. They are there, watching me now. Once I leave and close the theatre door behind me, will they again go still and return to the past? The light must remain on, or they might disappear forever. Brick-and-mortar theatres rarely go to complete black, so neither will I do that with my imaginary one.

I still hear my father's music as if it were coming from a dressing room far above in the wings—Bach's Prelude and Fugue no. 1 and the Don Cossack chorus. He's probably doing what we both liked to do while listening to records, moving his arms as if conducting the music. Another wind on which we both loved to sail. Wind *is* the music of the world. Speeding through the interstellar winds, *Voyager 2* is still carrying Bach's Prelude and Fugue no. 1 on its journey to the Andromeda galaxy. But as a boy it was the cries of the Cossacks that made me first ponder the pain and sorrow that wars can bring. Now it is the ache of missing him.

Ghosts are part of the wonder of theatres. After each performance a play's characters never entirely vanish, since they live on in the memories of all who saw them. Actors also leave something of themselves behind, like faint renditions of the handprints the painter with the crooked finger left on the cave wall. We step out of our characters and remove our costumes, but the echoes of our voices never entirely leave the building. I have stood on empty stages and felt the presence of those who performed there before me—which is why theatres always seem somehow inhabited and the ghost light is left on.

In time I will take my own place among the relatives, the characters and the animals forever waiting to be reanimated. Should ever a son or niece of mine, or *you*, wish to revisit by walking this stage with all its memory machinery, these lives might be heard again. Should you look closely, you will see that your family might be here as well. After all, the stories that many of you told me helped build this theatre in the first place. We have only to find someone to pace the stage again, remember, and then listen.

ACKNOWLEDGEMENTS

Know lies at the centre of ac*know*ledge. There are many who helped me on this journey, and it is a pleasure to both know and acknowledge them. The entire adventure was suggested by my (then soon-to-be) editor Scott Sellers and publisher Martha Kanya-Forstner, who after reading my play *The Lost Boys* proposed a book based on the losses in my family in the First World War. Being in awe of great writers of fiction, nonfiction, plays and screenplays, I was reluctant yet interested. Having assisted in the creation of new works for theatre, I knew that good writing can sing a story forward and poor writing can render plays into concrete blocks that actors have to drag uphill each night. So, to all those wonderful writers, I envy you and salute you.

And then there is my family, both nuclear and extended. Thank you to Laurie, my wife, who with heroic patience endured my daily drag up the stairs to the place of solitude from which words might hopefully come. To my supportive and tolerant sons, MacIntosh and Andrew; to my brother John and sister Janet; to cousins such as Rosemary Cureton-Lane and my sister-in-law Carmel Thomson, all of whom had family memories or photos to share. My niece Jean Thomas, a published writer herself, was always understanding of the struggle, and her husband, Nicolas Lamp, was helpful for some of the German aspects of the book, since he is himself German. To Dr. Graham Stratford, my grandmother's cousin, who because of his impressive accumulation of years was able to share memories from the 1930s of my warrior great-uncles and produce photographs that I'd never seen before.

And then there is former publisher Doug Gibson (later turned writer himself), who early on offered guidance. Like a parent holding on to the life jacket of a panicking child, who knows the water is over their head, time and again Doug kept me dog-paddling forward until my feet finally reached the shore.

There are also those who helped with *The World Remembers* First World War commemoration odyssey, as believers, donors, inspirers, political connectors, board members or advisors. Without them I would never have travelled to so many capital cities to hear how storytelling about wars sits in other nations' cultures. Here are a few of them: Michael Blondeau, Michael MacMillan, Jim Wright, Jacques Fauteux, Jonathan R. Vance, Clifford Goldfarb, Cathy Burrows, David Brady, Keith Durrant, Charles Anderson, Luce Veilleux, Margaret MacMillan, Adrienne Clarkson, Major-General Lewis MacKenzie, General Richard Rohmer, Sir Hew Strachan, Hilary Weston, Tim Cook, Jim Fleck, John Cleghorn, Mark O'Neill, Fred Eaton, David Bajurny, Don Lenz, Robert Richards, Richard Wernham, Bill and Meredith Saunderson, Blake Goldring, Duncan Jackman, Red Wilson, Graeme Thomson, Richard Rooney, Robert Kierns, James and Sandra Pitblado, Don Cranston, James Estey, Ian Giffen, the Burns family, the Fountain family, Stuart Coxe, the Right Honourable Paul Martin, Pauline Couture, and of course my friend Martin Conboy, a designer of vision with light and an early collaborator.

And then there are the ambassadors and staffs of Canadian missions abroad who facilitated my conversations with archivists, military historians and foreign affairs officers in many countries. Little of the early progress of *The World Remembers* would have been achieved without their personal and professional interest. At home, the Departments of Veterans Affairs, Global Affairs and Canadian Heritage, individual MPs, a few cabinet ministers and the occasional senator, such as Hugh Segal, helped me navigate the political corridors along which the success of the project lay. They became an ad hoc shadow team for the attempted creation of the first inclusive commemoration of a war. They are numerous and they are *gratefully* acknowledged.

And then there were the officials and directors at museums who listened, advised and installed *The World Remembers* commemoration display: the Canadian War Museum in Ottawa, the In Flanders Fields Museum in Belgium, the Bundeswehr Museum of Military History in Germany, and the National World War I Museum and Memorial in the United States. At each of those museums I was gifted with conversations that influenced my thinking about how wars are recalled and for what purpose they are remembered.

Others from Penguin Random House Canada and Knopf Canada must also be mentioned, since *their* interest is why these words are before you now. They are Kristin Cochrane, Susan Burns, Kelly Hill, Emma Lockhart, and Owen Torrey.

I also want to acknowledge everyone who shared their memories and stories with me. One of my great-uncles who survived the First World War still carried, in the small of his back near his spine, the bullet that had hit him in 1915. One of the wonders of my childhood was trying to feel for it through his shirt at Christmas parties. Despite his urging me on by describing it as "a hole the size of an eighth-inch drill," I never succeeded. Memories can be as elusive as Art's sniper's bullet, yet indelibly real.

Finally, I acknowledge *all* the lives of the estimated nine and a half million military personnel lost in the Great War, as well as the millions of civilians who also died. The fact that their names were so easily rolled into the forgotten zone of history is the reason I embarked on the journey of this book and *The World Remembers*. Many did speak for themselves through their poetry, letters, and journals before they lost their lives, but most did not. Therefore, some of us should surely speak for them.

Dramatis Personae

THE STRATFORD FAMILY
on the author's father's side

Mary Elizabeth Stratford . . . . mother of thirteen children, and the author's great-grandmother

Helen "Susie" Stratford. . . . . eldest of Mary Elizabeth's ten surviving children, and the author's grandmother who married Robert Thomson

Graham Stratford . . . . first son of Mary Elizabeth

Harold "Jum" Stratford . . . . second son of Mary Elizabeth, died in 1927 from lung damage as a result of the war

John "Jack" Stratford . . . . third son of Mary Elizabeth, married Florence Kelly in 1929 and died in 1931 from lung damage as a result of the war

Joseph "Joe" Stratford . . . . fourth son of Mary Elizabeth, killed in France in 1918

George "Geordie" Stratford . . . . fifth son of Mary Elizabeth, killed in Belgium in 1917

Arthur "Art" Stratford . . . . sixth son of Mary Elizabeth, survived the war

Reginald "Rick" Stratford. . . . . seventh son of Mary Elizabeth, too young to enlist

Mayden "Mayd" Stratford . . . . second daughter of Mary Elizabeth and the author's great-aunt

David "Dave" Stratford . . . . eighth son of Mary Elizabeth,
                                                      too young to enlist
Isobel, John, and Doris Stratford . . . . Mary Elizabeth's children
                                                      who died in infancy
Isabel Osbourne . . . . sister of Mary Elizabeth
                                                      Stratford and mother to
                                                      Margaret Osbourne
Margaret "Margie" Osbourne . . . . daughter of Isabel
Jack Osbourne . . . . the bow-tie-wearing son
                                                      of Isabel
Margaret Killmaster (MK) . . . . niece of Mary Elizabeth
                                                      Stratford, a First World
                                                      War nurse and the author's
                                                      godmother
Florence "Flossie" Stratford . . . . the Gravenhurst sanitarium
                                                      dietician who married
                                                      Jack Stratford in 1929
Madame Mialaret . . . . the Frenchwoman who wrote
                                                      to Mary Elizabeth after Joe's
                                                      death in 1918, requesting a
                                                      photograph of him

AND ASSORTED COUSINS AND SECOND COUSINS

TIME: *From 1914 to 1923*
SETTINGS:
✤ Various army rest camps, hospitals, battlefields and cemeteries in Belgium,
France and Portuguese East Africa (now Mozambique)
✤ Stratford family home in Brantford, Ontario, and their farm just south
of Brantford near The Six Nations Reserve
✤ The Queen's Canadian Military Hospital, situated in a former English
country house in the south of England close to the army camp at Shorncliffe
✤ Isabel Osbourne's home in Bournemouth on the south coast of England
✤ A rented cottage on Lake Joseph near Footes Bay, Ontario

THE HOLMES AND PEMBERTON FAMILIES
on the author's mother's side

Philippa Pemberton . . . . the author's grandmother
who married Cuthbert Holmes
in 1917

Henry Cuthbert Holmes . . . . the author's grandfather;
husband of Philippa

William "Wildy" Holmes . . . . younger brother of Cuthbert;
killed in 1916

Lona Holmes . . . . younger sister of Cuthbert
(twin of Wildy); committed
suicide in 1940

Frederick "Fred" Pemberton . . . . eldest brother of Philippa;
killed in 1917 when his aircraft
was shot down in France

Warren Pemberton . . . . older brother of Philippa, died
of burns from a Royal Flying
Corps accident in 1916

Armine Pemberton . . . . older sister of Philippa
(twin of Warren)

Mab Pemberton . . . . younger sister of Philippa

Suzie Pemberton . . . . aunt of Philippa

Sophie Pemberton . . . . aunt of Philippa

Augustus Pemberton . . . . great-great-uncle of Philippa;
and Commissioner of Police for
the colony of Vancouver Island,
1858–1862

TIME: *1862 to 1920*

SETTINGS:

✤ Victoria, British Columbia

✤ Paris Peace Conference, 1919 and 1920

✤ Various battlefields and cemeteries in Belgium and France

THE THOMSON FAMILY
on the author's father's side

Robert Thomson . . . . the author's grandfather; married Helen Stratford

Margaret Thomson . . . . older sister of Robert Thomson, never married; the author's great-aunt

Anne Thomson . . . . younger sister of Robert, never married; the author's great-aunt

Nell Thomson . . . . younger sister of Robert, never married; the author's great-aunt

Woodburn "Wood" Thomson . . . . son of Robert; the author's father

Cicely Thomson (née Holmes) . . . . eldest daughter of Philippa; the author's mother

MILITARY AND NAVAL TERMS

A.A.	anti-aircraft gun
A.B.	able-bodied seaman (usually merchant navy)
Battn.	battalion
B Co.	B Company
big boy	a large artillery shell
Blighty	"getting a Blighty"; a World War I reference to a wound serious enough to warrant being sent to a hospital in England
Boche	French slang for German soldiers, also used by the British
calso	a signal flare
Capt.	captain
Corps.	medical corpsman
CWGC	the Commonwealth War Graves Commission
C/V	convoy
D.C.	depth charge
D/d	destroyer
F/Of	light officer
F.G.H.	the Fort Garry Horse, Joe Stratford's regiment
Fritz	British slang for a German First World War soldier
gold braid	a two-inch strip of gold braid worn on the left uniform sleeve of those who had been wounded
H.E.	high-explosive artillery shell
HMCS	His Majesty's Canadian Ship

HMS	His Majesty's Ship (British Navy)
H.Q.	headquarters
Imperials	shorthand for a regiment of the British Army
jake	slang for "just fine"
landowner	World War I soldier's ironic term for being killed and buried in France or Belgium
marked out	after a stay in hospital, deemed fit to return to one's regiment
M.G.	machine gun
Minnie	shell fired from a German Minenwerfer trench mortar, World War I
M.O.	medical officer
O.C.	officer commanding
"old 10th boys"	combat-experienced soldiers of the 10th Battalion
O.T.C.	officer training course
pillbox	military term for low, concrete guardhouses with openings for defensive firing
poilu	World War I slang for a French soldier
PPCLI	Princess Patricia's Canadian Light Infantry (the "Princess Pats"), George Stratford's regiment
R.T.	radio transmission
S.C.	set course
Sister	short for nursing sister, a military nurse
SNO	senior naval officer
S.O.S.	the universal distress signal in Morse code
supports	support trenches located behind the front-line trenches
tin lizzie	a British soldier's steel helmet
Tommy	a British soldier
Town Class	WWII corvettes named after towns, such as HMCS *Sackville* and HMCS *Lunenburg*
V.A.D.	Voluntary Aid Detachment; civilian volunteer nurses in World War I

VDK	Volksbund Deutsche Kriegsgräberfürsorge (German War Graves Commission)
V.E. Day	Victory in Europe Day, World War II
"went over"	"over the top": climbing out of a defensive trench to engage the enemy
whizz-bang	World War I slang for an incoming German artillery shell
wounded teas	afternoon refreshments in private homes for wounded soldiers from local military hospitals

REFERENCES

Beckett, Samuel. *Waiting for Godot: A Tragicomedy in 2 Acts.* New York: Grove Press, 1954.

Borden, Mary. *The Forbidden Zone: A Nurse's Impressions of the First World War.* 1929. Reprint, London: Hesperus Press, 2008.

Boyd, Robert T. *The Coming of the Spirit of Pestilence: Introduced Infectious Diseases and Population Decline among NorthWest Coast Indians.* Seattle: University of Washington Press, 1999.

Brondizio, E. S., et al. *Global Assessment Report on Biodiversity and Ecosystem Services.* Bonn: IPBES, 2019.

Canada. "Joint Task Force 2," July 6, 2018. https://www.canada.ca/en/special-operations-forces-command/corporate/organizational-structure/joint-task-force-2.html [archived].

Canadian Bank of Commerce. *Letters from the Front.* Vol. 1. Toronto: Southam Press, 1920.

The Daily British Colonist. https://archive.org/details/dailycolonist.

Dathan, Matt. "Veterans Throw Away Their War Medals in Disgust at British Air Strikes in Syria." *Independent,* December 8, 2015.

Davies, Caroline. "Ypres, Where the Last Post Plays Every Single Day." *The Guardian,* November 9, 2008.

Dyer, Gwynne. *War: The New Edition.* Toronto: Random House Canada, 2004.

Encana. "Notice of Annual Meeting of Shareholders." Calgary, April 26, 2006.

Fisher, William. "The End of HMCS *St. Croix* and HMS *Itchen*." *Royal Canadian Monthly Review*, August 1944.

Gance, Abel, dir. *J'accuse!* Forester-Parant Productions, 1938. DVD, Chicago: Olive Films, 2016.

Giovannitti, Len, and Fred Freed. *The Decision to Drop the Bomb*. New York: Routledge, 1965.

Glanz, James. "Contractors Outnumber U.S Troop in Afghanistan." *New York Times*, September 1, 2009.

Hedges, Chris. *War Is a Force That Gives Us Meaning*. New York: PublicAffairs, 2002.

Hellen, Nicolas. "Cenotaph Tribute to German War Dead." *Sunday Times*, January 20, 2013.

Hitler, Adolf. *Mein Kampf*. Berlin: Franz Eher Nachfolger, 1925.

Hochschild, Adam. *King Leopold's Ghost*. Boston: Mariner Books, 1998.

IPBES. *Report From the 2019 Intergovernmental Science-Policy Platform on Biodiversity and Ecosystems Services* (IPBES).

Johnson, Mac. *Corvettes Canada*. Toronto: McGraw-Hill Ryerson, 1994.

Kollwitz, Hans, ed. *The Diary and Letters of Kaethe Kollwitz*. Translated by Richard and Clara Winston. Evanston, IL: Northwestern University Press, 1989.

Lamb, James. *The Corvette Navy: True Stories from Canada's Atlantic War*. Toronto: Stoddart, 2000.

Lange, Greg. "Smallpox Epidemic of 1862 among Northwest Coast and Puget Sound Indians." April 2, 2003. https://www.historylink.org/File/5171.

Le Queux, William. *German Atrocities: A Record of Shameless Deeds*. CreateSpace, 2016.

"The List of Names." In Flanders Fields Museum, Ieper, Belgium. https://www.inflandersfields.be/en/bezoek-e.

Macdonald, David. "Climbing Up and Kicking Down: Executive Pay in Canada." Ottawa: Canadian Centre for Policy Alternatives, January 2018.

Macdonald, Lyn. *The Roses of No Man's Land*. London: Penguin, 1993.

MacDonald, Stephen. *Not About Heroes*. London: Faber and Faber, 1983.

MacMillan, Margaret. *Paris 1919*. New York: Random House, 2001.

———. *The War That Ended Peace*. New York: Penguin Random House. 2014.

Magee, John Gillespie. "High Flight." Washington: Library of Congress, 1943.

Newman, Stephen K. *Ratcliffe W. H. Historical notes Regimental Museum Archives/With the Patricia's in Flanders 1914–1918 Then & Now*. BHP, 2000.

Okri, Ben. *The Famished Road*. London: Jonathan Cape, 1991.

Owen, Wilfred. *The Collected Poems of Wilfred Owen*. Edited by C. Day Lewis. London: Chatto & Windus, 1963.

———. *Poems by Wilfred Owen*. London: Chatto & Windus, 1920.

———. *The Poems of Wilfred Owen*. Edited by John Stallworthy. New York: W.W. Norton, 1986.

———. *The War Poems of Wilfred Owen*. London: Penguin, 2013.

Pincus, Walter. "U.S. Pays Steep Price for Private Security in Iraq." *Washington Post*, October 1, 2007.

Richards, Phil, and John J. Banigan. *How to Abandon Ship*. Centreville, MD: Cornell Maritime Press, 1943.

Sagan, Carl. *Cosmos*. Season 1, episode 1, "The Shores of the Cosmic Ocean." Aired September 28, 1980, on PBS.

Sassoon, Siegfried. "On Passing the New Menin Gate." In *Collected Poems, 1908–1956*. London: Faber & Faber, 1986.

Seton, Ernest Thompson. *Rolf in the Woods*. New York: Grosset & Dunlap, 1911.

"Shoes of the Dead," a poem reported to have been conceived and spoken by an unknown Jewish girl sometime between 1942 and 1944 in the Majdanek Concentration camp outside the city of Lubin, Poland. The text is on display at the Bundeswehr Museum of Military History in Dresden, Germany.

"Vets Throwing Medals at Washington." April 22, 1971. YouTube video, 2:11. Posted by tarot1984, October 29, 2008. https://www.youtube.com/watch?v=j7jhs-bGyFQ.

Weil, Simone. *The Iliad, or The Poem of Force.* Wallingford, PA: Pendle Hill Press, 1956.

Willson, Henry Beckles. *Ypres: The Holy Ground of British Arms.* 1920. Reprint, Uckfield, UK: Naval and Military Press, 2020.

Winter, Jay. "How the Great War Shaped the World." *The Atlantic,* September 29, 2014. https://www.theatlantic.com/magazine/archive/2014/08/how-the-great-war-shaped-the-world/373468/.

World Trade Organization. *The WTO Building: The Symbolic Artwork of the Centre William Rappard, Headquarters of the World Trade Organization.* Geneva: WTO, 2008.

Yeats, W. B. "The Second Coming." In *The Collected Poems of W. B. Yeats.* London: Macmillan, 2010.

PHOTO CREDITS

Chapter 1.   My father standing on a chair on the bridge of HMCS *Lunenburg*, 1945. From the collection of Leonard Hare. www.forposterityssake.ca.

Chapter 2.   Serbian hospital ship, transport of the dead. Provided by the Serbian Ministry of Defence to *The World Remembers*.

Chapter 3.   Stratford family at a rented cottage in Muskoka, 1919. By permission of the family.

Chapter 4.   George Stratford after his promotion to lieutenant, 1917. By permission of the family.

Chapter 5.   My father, Woodburn Thomson, at a rented cottage in Muskoka, 1919. By permission of the Stratford family.

Chapter 6.   Casualty records of the Izmailovsky Regiment from Russia's military archives, Moscow. Photo by Margaret Watts.

Chapter 7.   Isabel Blanche Osbourne, sister of the author's great-grandmother Mary Elizabeth Stratford. By permission of the Stratford family.

Chapter 8.   German artist Käthe Kollwitz, 1927. Portrait by Hugo Erfurth. Courtesy of Alamy Images.

"Mother with Dead Child," etching by Käthe Kollwitz, 1903. Library of Congress, Washington, DC.

Grieving Parents, sculpture by Käthe Kollwitz, 1933. Vladslo German War Cemetery, Belgium. Courtesy of Alamy Images.

Chapter 9.   Battlefield in Belgium, 1919. Photo by Philippa Holmes. Courtesy of Rosemary Cureton Lane.

Chapter 10. Portrait of Philippa Holmes, 1919 or 1920. By permission
             of the family.

Chapter 11. Wildy Holmes's grave, 1919. Photo by Philippa Holmes.
             Courtesy of Rosemary Cureton Lane.

Chapter 12. Joseph Stratford, 1915. By permission of the family.

Chapter 13. German naval officer with his sisters, 1935. Courtesy of the
             Bundeswehr Museum of Military History, Dresden, Germany.

Chapter 14. German trench mortar in front of McConaghy Public School,
             Richmond Hill, ON, 1954. Courtesy of Richmond Hill
             Public Library.

Chapter 15. Margaret Killmaster at the Queen's Canadian Military
             Hospital, Beachborough Park, England, 1917. From
             Margaret's photo album, owned by the author.

             The dining room, Queen's Canadian Military Hospital.
             Photo by Margaret Killmaster. From Margaret's photo album,
             owned by the author.

Chapter 16. George Stratford while on leave at his aunt Isabel's house
             in Bournemouth, England, 1917. Courtesy of Dr. Graham
             Stratford.

Chapter 17. Patients at the Queen's Canadian Military Hospital, 1917.
             Photo by Margaret Killmaster. From Margaret's photo album,
             owned by the author.

Chapter 18. View from the bridge of HMCS *Sackville*. From the collection
             of Leonard Hare, www.forposterityssake.ca.

Chapter 19. Seven of the Stratford sons, Brantford, ON, 1898. Courtesy
             of the author's family.

Chapter 20. The Pacific south coast of British Columbia. Courtesy of
             Hugh Oddie.

Chapter 21. Mary Elizabeth Stratford, 1914. By permission of the family.

Epilogue   The author at the age of six. Courtesy of the author's family.

             Käthe Kollwitz, *Mother with her Dead Son*, 1937 or 1938.
             Neue Wache, Berlin. Courtesy of Alamy Images.